RETURN OF
THE KING

Also by Brian Windhorst

The Franchise:
LeBron James and the Remaking of the
Cleveland Cavaliers

LeBron James: The Making of an MVP

RETURN OF THE KING

LeBron James, the Cleveland Cavaliers,
and the Greatest Comeback
in NBA History

**Brian Windhorst and
Dave McMenamin**

GRAND CENTRAL
PUBLISHING

NEW YORK   BOSTON

Grand Central Publishing
Hachette Book Group
1290 Avenue of the Americas, New York, NY 10104
grandcentralpublishing.com
twitter.com/grandcentralpub

First Edition: April 2017

Grand Central Publishing is a division of Hachette Book Group, Inc. The Grand
Central Publishing name and logo is a trademark of Hachette Book Group, Inc.

The publisher is not responsible for websites (or their content) that are not owned
by the publisher.

The Hachette Speakers Bureau provides a wide range of authors for speaking
events. To find out more, go to www.hachettespeakersbureau.com or call
(866) 376-6591.

Library of Congress Cataloging-in-Publication Data has been applied for.

ISBNs: 978-1-478-97168-9 (hardcover), 978-1-538-75968-4 (ebook)

Printed in the United States of America

LSC-C

10 9 8 7 6 5 4 3 2 1

To the NBA family and the league's fans, whose professionalism, support, and passion have enabled a dream job to come true.

—BW

To Mom, Dad, Melanie, Shawna, Brian, Jeff, Rob, Ollie, Conall, Magooch, and Dr. James Naismith. Thanks for all your support as I continue to follow the bouncing ball around the world. I love you.

—DM

CONTENTS

INTRODUCTION

As told by Richard Jefferson

This is a story that not many people know.

Sure, they know how the Cavaliers became the first team in fifty-two years to bring a major championship back home to Cleveland. They know how the Cavs became the first team to overcome a 3–1 deficit in the NBA Finals to come back and win. They know how we beat the first team ever to win 73 games during the regular season to do so. They know we became the first team since the Washington Bullets in 1978 to win a Game 7 of the Finals on the road and hoist the Larry O'Brien Trophy on the same floor that our opponents fought so hard to host the game on.

But they don't know what happened to the Larry O'Brien Trophy three days later when more than a million people descended upon downtown Cleveland for a championship parade the likes of which has never been seen before.

The story starts with me and Channing Frye.

We were supposed to be in our own individual cars to soak it all in during the parade route. Somehow, Channing ended up on a flatbed truck with his family. We both have little kids. I was like, "Yo, I'd rather jump in here with you guys than be stuck in a convertible." Because it was hot out. So me and my family, we jump in that car with the Fryes and we're just taking in the scene and it was mayhem.

People everywhere. Lined up fifteen–twenty deep wherever you looked. On rooftops. Climbing out of windows. Hanging on streetlamps. Everywhere. I realized the magnitude of what this day was. You could tell that the city had never planned a championship parade in, well, fifty years. They didn't know that they needed to have guardrails up. They didn't know what hit 'em.

Kind of like the Warriors, actually.

I remember about halfway through the parade, me and Channing look over and I see this guy running next to the car with a big towel covering up something in his arms. I was like, "That looks like the trophy."

And the guy, he's running—and he's not running fast because our cars aren't really moving—and he says to us, "Hey, do you guys want this?" And I'm like, "Yeah! We'll take it!" In my head, I'm thinking, "Oh, this is our turn. He's just taking the trophy from car to car and everyone gets some time with the trophy." So he gets on the truck with us and after a few minutes, after we've been raising the trophy, and after the crowd is going crazy every time we lift it up and the sun shimmers off its polished, sphered head, the guy was like, "You don't understand how happy I was to see you guys."

I mean, *everyone* was happy to see us that day. We just won a championship for Cleveland. But there was a different level of appreciation coming from this guy.

I was like, "What are you talking about? Didn't you just bring this over from another player? You've seen one Cavs player lift this thing up, you've seen 'em all, right?"

He was like, "Richard, the trophy was on the back of a truck that went the wrong way at the start of the parade route. So all of the sudden, it's me, the trophy, one million fans, and no security, no nothing."

Oh.

He was panicked. He unbolted the thing and started running around looking for a place to put it. He said, "Your car was the first one that we happened to see and we latched on like Rose to the floating door in *Titanic*."

So that's the story of how it came to be that the only people with video or pictures with the trophy during the parade are me and Channing—two lifelong friends ever since I helped recruit him to our alma mater, the University of Arizona—because some guy ended up stumbling upon our truck in the parade route. He didn't bother bringing it to anybody else—you know, like that LeBron James guy.

It kind of felt like all the things that had to happen for us to become champions. I know the city of Cleveland can relate. While Northeast Ohioans lived through The Shot, The Fumble, The Drive, and The Decision, I had my own downfalls on the biggest stage before I finally had my championship moment.

In the days leading up to Game 7, in my head I ran through all of them. I've come up just short so many times. I lost back-to-back Finals with the then New Jersey Nets. I've been top 10 in the league in scoring multiple years and didn't make an All-Star game. I've been on the U.S. Olympic team, but it was the team with Larry Brown and a bunch of misfits, and we had to fight just to win the bronze. So it was just like always so, so close. This was my entire life. This was my entire career. I'm not Tristan Thompson who is twenty-five years old. I'm not Kyrie Irving who has his whole career in front of him. This could be it for me.

When I was a kid, I'd imagine what I'd do if I was fortunate enough to win it all. Somehow it worked out just the way I pictured it. As soon as the buzzer sounded, everyone takes off, jumping and hugging and piling on top of one another, and I was the one guy on the bench that just kind of froze there and just put my head in my hands and started crying. I wouldn't say I was sobbing. I wouldn't say I was weeping. It was just more of, "Wow, man." Not only have I been through so much in fifteen years in the league, but to feel it for those ten days just slipping through your hands again after falling down 3–1 and to come this close, it was something. After the amount of stress that was in all that, the championship feeling was a feeling of relief. The initial feeling wasn't that of joy for me, it was of relief.

But as the night unfolded, that scene was everything I wanted it to be. Everything I dreamed it would be. Everything I imagined it ever would be. It was all of those things. And so what did I do? My big mouth started telling anyone who would listen in the locker room, as my feet splashed through puddles of champagne, that I was retiring.

When I initially said it, I really was done. I was so emotionally spent. It was a wrap for me. Like, you're talking about not sleeping for ten days. I took Tylenol PM at 6 a.m. one time to try to get some sleep. You're going East Coast to West Coast and you're running on fumes at that point and time.

Three days later, I was at the rally downtown after the parade, standing in front of hundreds of thousands of people and shouting into a microphone that I was coming back.

What changed?

I wouldn't say things calmed down, but you start to enjoy it. You start to think. Was I all the way out when I said I was retiring? No. But the same, I was thinking, "I don't know if I can go through this again," even being on the winning side of it. Even being on the winning side of it, I don't know if I could go through it again, just because it was that stressful.

And finally at the end I just thought about it and it was more about my family: They are enjoying it. My body: It felt great even in my midthirties after playing in 100-something games. And then the championship experience: It doesn't end at the parade.

Part of winning a championship is being there on opening night when they raise the banner. Part of winning a championship is getting your ring from Adam Silver before that first game. Part of winning a championship is going into every city and just feeling that respect and also trying to defend your crown. One of the reasons I always wanted to be a champion was so I could defend it. That was half of it. So the more I started thinking about it, the more I was just like, "Okay, I don't want to miss out on that experience." Because this is once in a lifetime.

And this team is once in a lifetime.

There's no way you could come back the way we did, from 3–1 down, unless you are tight, unless you are brothers.

It doesn't mean that you have to be best friends. It doesn't mean that all fifteen of you guys are out together at every dinner. We're all different personalities. Nobody could match my personality anyway, come on, let's be real.

The thing is, you have to be able to look each man in the eye and say, "Hey, I'm going to do my job. If you do your job, we're good. If you're struggling, I'll lift you up." And all year long there was always speculation about *this* dynamic and *that* dynamic and what *this* meant and what *that* meant. It was just like people would see LeBron and Kyrie or LeBron and Kevin get frustrated at each other, but they wouldn't see them at dinner the very next night cracking jokes.

We did get closer as the season went along. We did love taking part in social media and putting stuff on Snapchat for the fans to see how we really are. That did make us closer. I think for a while people saw us and thought, "How am I going to root for guys that hate each other?" They would rather believe that guys are awesome and hang out, because they want to believe that. And I think once we kind of showed that to the fans and allowed them to see for themselves that, yo, LeBron, as much as he's special on the court, he's a big goofball. And, man, Kev doesn't take himself too seriously. That's cool.

It was just like everybody was going to have fun with this ride and it didn't matter if we won 10 straight to the start the playoffs, if we had lost two in a row in the conference finals, if we were down 0–2 in the Finals, if we were down 3–1 and on the brink of elimination. We stayed pretty consistent throughout this whole thing.

And so did Cleveland. They got behind us like no fan base has ever gotten behind a team I've played for before. It was like, even if you weren't a basketball fan, if you weren't from Cleveland, the fact that you knew that the so-called story of the town was that there hadn't been a championship in fifty years, you were rooting.

For my son, Little Richard, there's now a connection to him and Cleveland. Little Rich learned how to walk in Cleveland. These guys, my brothers on the Cavs, they've watched him go from being carried, to taking his first steps, to running around, and now all of the sudden he's in the locker room and he *loves* basketball. I'd like to think we gave him a pretty good first taste of what the game is supposed to look like at its best.

Say what you want about LeBron, but not many people in a team sport can say, "Hey, I'm going to come back to my hometown, to a city that's never won a championship in half a century and a team that's never experienced a championship run, period, and I'm going to go and we're going to win one."

Actually, forget I said not many people say that. *No one says that.* No one in the history of a team sport has ever said that.

This is all LeBron has ever known. This is all he's ever known: basketball and being the best. That's all he's ever known since he was probably about fifteen years old. That will mess with your psyche a little bit. You can lose touch. Hell, maybe you need to have a messed-up psyche to do what he did and leave Miami to come back to the Cavs.

But I will say this about LeBron: At his core, all he wants to do is win. And he does it by wanting to be a good teammate and by wanting everyone to be successful. That's just who he is.

Oh, one more thing.

My wife is pregnant again. Our daughter is going to be born in Cleveland. Which I think is awesome. She'll come into this world in the city of champions.

RETURN OF
THE KING

Chapter 1

ALL NOT FOR Z

The lights were shut off, and for a moment, the crowd of 20,000 roared with the sudden excitement of anticipation. Just as quickly they fell silent. A million-dollar 3-D video projection system, leased and installed in the ceiling for this moment, lit the arena with a mixture of visual tricks that made it seem like the hardwood floor was as liquid as water, followed by an incredible display of video highlights, graphics, colors, and audio clips that took programmers weeks to design.

Watching from the darkness at the edge of the room were dozens of men in suits, all flown in at great expense by the Cleveland Cavaliers franchise, to be tangential parts of the most elaborate jersey retirement ceremony the NBA had ever seen. Not even Michael Jordan had gotten the sort of treatment Zydrunas Ilgauskas was getting on this night.

It was March 8, 2014, a carefully selected date that was months in the planning and years in the plotting.

After speeches and congratulations from numerous former teammates, coaches, team executives, trainers, and friends—and after his father, who'd come from Lithuania, symbolically kissed the center-court logo—Ilgauskas's two sons punched a button that sent his No. 11 jersey to the rafters as smoke machines billowed to make it more dramatic.

Fans recorded it with their cell phones, many wearing giveaway T-shirts in the team's wine and gold color scheme that read "#AllforZ." This was charming, but it also wasn't totally true. It wasn't all for

Z, Ilgauskas's nickname. A lot of it was for someone else, one of the men in the sea of suits.

This was also for LeBron James.

The Cavs' thinly veiled strategy to recruit James back four years after his departure clicked into public action with this expensive investment. Retire Ilgauskas's number, yes, but also show James he could come home again and he would be loved again just like his peer.

In 2010, just three days after James announced he was signing with the Miami Heat on a national television broadcast and while Cavs fans and owner Dan Gilbert were still in a hot rage, Ilgauskas announced his intention to follow James to Miami as a free agent. After twelve years as a Cav, making two All-Star teams and setting a slate of franchise records, this move was seen as adding insult to injury.

Ilgauskas soon got in on the blowback James had gotten for his choice. There was plenty of vitriol from the Cleveland area to go around. James's departure, announced on an hourlong television show on ESPN, *The Decision*, had deeply scarred the region. It was devastating to the team, but James was also a local leaving for the glamour of Miami. That hit a lot of people where they lived. In an economic downturn that had lasted for decades, many children of Northeast Ohio had left home looking for success outside the rust belt. Ohio is home to numerous well-respected universities, both large state institutions and small liberal arts colleges. For years it had raised and educated young stars only to see them take their talents elsewhere because of limited opportunities at home. It was a compound problem. Now James, one of the state's most treasured citizens, was doing it too.

Targeting James for the way he announced his decision was a convenient excuse for amplifying the symbols of hatred. Many would've hated James for leaving no matter how he'd done it. Ilgauskas was proof of that. After deciding to leave, Ilgauskas bought a full-page ad in the *Cleveland Plain Dealer* thanking the fan base for taking him in when he arrived from Lithuania and supporting him so it would become his home. If it dimmed any of the negativity, it was hard for him to notice.

It was hurtful to Ilgauskas, who had actually been traded away from the Cavs the previous season, only to get a buyout from his new team, the Washington Wizards, before ever playing a game so he could immediately re-sign in Cleveland. Having already been traded and after losing his starting job when the Cavs acquired Shaquille O'Neal the previous year, Ilgauskas felt he'd been given a pretty good indication the team was moving on from him as a core player.

Perhaps the worst was when it started to affect his wife, Jennifer, who owns successful healthcare-related businesses in the Cleveland area. Her business started suffering when standard referrals began drying up, which Ilgauskas believed was a kind of retribution. He was also booed mercilessly when he returned with the Heat.

But after his retirement in 2011, Ilgauskas proved how he felt about the city when he moved back. He later went to work for the team's front office. This was a minor miracle, because Ilgauskas was also offended by an infamous letter to fans Gilbert released the night James announced he was leaving, calling James's move a "shocking act of disloyalty" and a "cowardly betrayal." Ilgauskas felt like some of those accusations now essentially included him as well.

Ilgauskas and Gilbert had never been very close. In 2005, four months after Gilbert bought the Cavs for $375 million, Ilgauskas thought he'd have to find a new home. He was a free agent and got the impression Gilbert wasn't interested in retaining him. In early July of that year he was about to leave on a planned trip to Asia, figuring he might be on another team by the time he got back.

Danny Ferry, a former Ilgauskas teammate who'd just been hired to be the team's general manager, convinced Gilbert to re-sign Ilgauskas. Ferry was concerned about the owner-player relationship, so he asked Gilbert to close the deal personally. This led to a fascinating little chase as Gilbert and newly hired coach Mike Brown left the Cavs' Summer League team in Las Vegas on Gilbert's plane to fly to Los Angeles to catch Ilgauskas during a layover before he left for Hong Kong.

When they landed at LAX's private terminal, Gilbert ran into Howard Schultz, the founder of Starbucks and later the owner of the Seattle SuperSonics. Gilbert blanched, knowing the Sonics were a team rumored to be interested in Ilgauskas as well. He wondered if he was being beaten to the punch. Out of a movie script, Gilbert ordered his driver to follow Schultz's car to see where he might be headed. But Schultz got on the freeway; Gilbert and Brown breathed a sigh of relief and went to the international terminal, where they bought tickets on Ilgauskas's flight so they could get through security. Nervous they had nothing to present, they bought cheap flowers and balloons at an airport gift shop to bring to the meeting. When it was over, Ilgauskas had agreed to a five-year, $50 million deal.

That ended up being the high point of the relationship, especially after Gilbert's behavior when Ilgauskas and James left. Yet not only was Ilgauskas back working for the team, here he was being adored by fans at a ceremony.

That was the understated but serious message to James. The two had commiserated in Miami about how they'd been treated for their business decisions. They'd cursed Gilbert and the shortsightedness of fans who'd once claimed to love them. They'd basked in the winter sun and wondered how they'd lived through so many snowstorms.

But Ilgauskas was back in the cold North and happy to be raising his family there. And here he was being honored, the fans already having forgotten his foray to Miami. That is what those in the Cavs organization wanted James to see personally—that when it really mattered, Cleveland had the ability to move past what happened in 2010. It was to show that James too could come back and be happy raising his family at home and be embraced again by his home fans.

The display was funded by Gilbert but was the brainchild of Chris Grant, the Cavs' general manager, who had replaced Ferry in 2010. During James's second season in Miami, he took the surprising step of indicating publicly that he could see himself returning to play in Cleveland sometime in the future. In what would turn out to be a crucial moment, he opened the door and extended an olive branch on a snowy day in February 2012.

"I think it would be great, it would be fun to play in front of these fans again. I had a lot fun times in my seven years here. You can't predict the future, and hopefully I continue to stay healthy. I'm here as a Miami Heat player, and I'm happy where I am now, but I don't rule out returning in no sense. And if I decide to come back, hopefully the fans will accept me."

James said this after a Heat practice inside Quicken Loans Arena in Cleveland on an off day. Within seconds, the words had reached Grant's ears ten miles away at the team's training facility. The concept of a James return had been whispered about, especially after he admitted he struggled with the transition to Miami. But here he was saying it, that he'd consider coming back. Though some dismissed it as James attempting to reduce the vitriol in Northeast Ohio, where he still lived in the offseason, some took it quite seriously. Especially Grant, who was perhaps the first, and for a while the only, Cavs employee who truly believed the franchise could get him back.

The following summer, a content James went even further. After winning his first championship in five games over the Oklahoma City Thunder and shedding the burden of never having won a ring, he was in London and on the verge of winning a second gold medal with the Olympic team. It was the most triumphant few months of his career. Getting wistful in an interview with the Associated Press, he again referred to missing Cleveland. "I wish I could have won one there. I could only imagine how the parade would have been down East 9th Street. Of course I thought about it because Cleveland helped me get to that point. The days that I spent there helped me get to the point where I was able to finally win one. It's just unfortunate I wasn't able to do it there."

This was seen as salt in the wounds to some in Cleveland, which lamented seeing James win elsewhere. And Cleveland indeed saw it. Ratings reports from the 2012 Finals showed the strongest local ratings outside the South Florida and Oklahoma City markets were in Cleveland. But others, including those daring to dream inside the Cavs offices, saw it as another gesture.

Gilbert responded with his own coded message. The next time James visited Cleveland for a game, in the 2012–13 season, Gilbert put out a message to fans on his social media: "Cleveland Cavaliers' young talent makes our future very bright. Clearly, LeBron's is as well. Time for everyone to focus on the road ahead."

Even with all the time that had passed, the polite tone from the man who essentially championed an anti-James movement was revealing. Gilbert had been fined $100,000 by NBA commissioner David Stern for sending out the letter in 2010, but had said in subsequent interviews he had no regrets. After James left, Gilbert hired Jones Day, one of the largest law firms in the nation, to investigate whether the Heat had been engaged in long-term recruiting of James, which would've been a violation of NBA rules. In 1995, the Heat essentially admitted they were guilty of this sort of tampering when negotiating to bring Pat Riley in to run the franchise while he was coaching the New York Knicks. The Heat ultimately agreed to send the Knicks $1 million and a first-round draft pick to settle the matter, which might've been the best deal Miami owner Micky Arison has ever made considering Riley's positive influence on the franchise.

Gilbert eventually decided not to file formal charges against the Heat. The burden of proof for such things is quite high and the gray area teams operate in is quite wide. Grant was also against it, wanting to move on and not extend the issue. It wasn't bringing James back at that point anyway. Plus the Cavs had held firm in working on a sign-and-trade deal with the Heat for James, getting two first-round picks and two second-round picks as a return for helping the Heat construct their superteam that included Chris Bosh and Dwyane Wade. Not only was that a haul greater than the Cavs probably would've gotten had they been able to prove a tampering charge, but the Cavs agreeing to trade James to Miami undercut any potential argument.

Gilbert had continued to stew, though, and in meetings he refused for several years to say James's name. So his sending out a message encouraging the fans to move on from the James hate was relevant. It also worked. For the first time that night, some fans at the arena applauded when James was introduced. It was far from the majority, but it sure was a departure from previous visits. During the game, a young fan named James Blair wandered onto the court in the middle of the game and approached James. He wore a T-shirt that read "We Miss You" on the front and "Come Back 2014" on the back. The 2014 reference was the first year James could be a free agent, more than a year away.

Security swarmed Blair, but before they could take him off the floor, James disarmed the situation and went over to embrace him. It was a symbolic moment—there was a thaw happening on both sides. Blair was banned by the Cavs from attending future games, but the moment quickly became famous. The Heat, who can be masters at public relations, soon invited Blair to a game in Miami and gave him Heat gear in an effort to swing the situation. But it only revealed that the Heat had started paying attention to the James-Cleveland developments.

The following summer, James made another significant move when he left his agent at Creative Artists Agency, Leon Rose, and hired his longtime friend Rich Paul as his basketball agent. CAA had played a significant role in helping James go to Miami two years earlier, as it also represented Wade and Bosh and negotiated all of their contracts in concert. From its inception as a Hollywood talent agency, CAA had always been about "packaging" clients on films and shows to maximize commissions. This was what they did with their three biggest basketball clients, wrapping them up in a bundle. Business was business, but this left some level of animosity between the Cavs and CAA.

Paul worked for CAA at the time as a junior agent, but he'd managed to stay on good terms with the Cavs. The first game the Cavs played in the post-James era, a home game in October 2010 against Boston, Paul attended in his role as a CAA agent. He lived in Cleveland and represented one of the Cavs' 2011 first-round draft picks, Tristan Thompson, which meant he was around the team frequently. It was Paul who called the team to inform them that James would be going to Miami, a move that was professional. Grant believed Paul operated in good faith and felt he could work with him.

When Paul established his new agency, Klutch Sports, he partnered with Mark Termini, an experienced Cleveland-based attorney and agent who'd dealt with the Cavs dating to the 1980s when he represented star Ron Harper. As it would turn out, James's new representatives had both history and respect from the team.

So as James headed into the final year of his Heat contract at the start of the 2013–14 season, Grant started to put plans into action. The Heat had now won back-to-back titles and James had won two Most Valuable Player awards and two Finals MVP awards. He looked not only to be thriving in Miami but entrenched there, the concept of his leaving seemed far-fetched. But Grant wasn't deterred, especially once the Heat released Mike Miller, who was one of James's closest friends, to reduce luxury tax payments the following season.

When James signed in Miami, CAA worked with Heat president Pat Riley to reduce the stars' salaries from the max level down to make room on the payroll for a couple of role players. One was Udonis Haslem, a CAA client, and the other was Miller. Ultimately James, Wade, and Bosh were in agreement to take less money, but James was not deeply involved in the process. The Heat were eventually able to work complex sign-and-trade deals to make all the math work.

As time passed, the way it unfolded ended up upsetting James and contributed to his decision to leave CAA. Shortly after doing so, he signed with William Morris Endeavor, CAA's Hollywood enemy, to represent him in film and television work. So he was also displeased when the Heat released Miller, a move that saved the team $17 million in luxury taxes, because he was still receiving a smaller paycheck to pay Miller's salary.

The Heat's roster was aging—they'd traded so many draft picks to acquire James and Bosh that they'd been unable to bring in many young players—and their heavy spending had made their luxury tax bills start to pile up and challenge their ability to keep the team together.

Grant had a multifaceted plan. He wanted to sign a few veteran players to add to what was a promising young core, namely former Rookie of the Year Kyrie Irving, to help the Cavs make the playoffs. The Cavs had a sweet spot coming in the summer of 2014 when James was a free agent, where their young players hadn't yet graduated to big-money contracts so there would be salary-cap space available to sign James. He also rehired Mike Brown, who coached James between 2005-10 before being fired, as coach. Grant believed Brown's past success would help the team into the playoffs. Despite reports James hadn't approved of Brown in the past, Grant had vetted the idea and felt confident Brown would be an asset in a possible James chase.

Then there was the Ilgauskas jersey retirement, perhaps the most intriguing maneuver of them all. Since Ilgauskas was an employee of the team, a Cleveland resident, and a lock to have his jersey retired, the Cavs could've done the ceremony at any time. They could've done it the next game, or they could've waited a year. There's no standard for such matters. But Grant wanted to use James's closeness to Ilgauskas to the franchise's advantage. He wanted to open a window to bring James to Cleveland alone, without the Heat, for the event.

So in the fall of 2013, the Cavs' and Heat's schedules were placed side by side and studied. A date was found in March that was amenable to Ilgauskas as well. The Cavs were playing at home on a Saturday night against the Knicks. It was later in the season, where the team would, in theory, be making a run toward the playoffs. The Heat had an off night in nearby Chicago. They were coming to Cleveland for a game ten days later when James would've been there, and Ilgauskas's jersey could've been retired then. But Grant didn't want that—they wanted him to come as a guest, not as an opponent. And they had cover to anyone who might ask that this was a weekend when it would be easier to bring friends and family in and it wouldn't have the baggage that Heat-Cavs games carried.

Would James be willing to come to town for it? The concept was presented to his representation. James did not commit, but it was made clear he would come if things worked out. It was a silent victory. In October 2013, the Cavs announced the date with the hope James would be there. And as they made their plans, which got grander and grander, they did so with him in mind.

But then there were some hiccups, primarily in the team's play. The free agents the team signed, veterans Jarrett Jack, Andrew Bynum, and Earl Clark, failed to make the expected impact. Bynum, a high-risk, high-reward signing, was particularly an issue as he clashed with the coaching staff. He was traded at midseason for veteran Luol Deng. The team also didn't respond to Brown, known for his defensive coaching skills, and lagged in the standings, starting the season 10–21.

In February 2014, the Cavs lost an embarrassing home game to an injury-riddled Los Angeles Lakers team that finished the game with only four eligible players. The Cavs gave up 119 points and lost by 11. The team was roundly mocked for the result, which was a sixth straight loss to drop them to 17 games under .500. The plan to impress James had gone awry. Frustrated, Gilbert fired Grant the day after the Laker loss as the unofficial "get LeBron back" plans officially went off the track.

A month later, however, James announced he was chartering a private jet at his expense to fly from Chicago to Cleveland to see Ilgauskas's jersey retired. The Heat publicly endorsed the decision but privately weren't pleased, and not just because they had a game the next afternoon against the Bulls on national television. They sent team personnel and security with James, but he was courtside to watch the spectacle, smiling and embracing Ilgauskas as he left the floor. Fans screamed to him, not at him. There wasn't a boo to be heard.

The Cavs, of course, lost by 10 points to the Knicks that night in a new losing streak that was four games long as their playoff hopes were essentially crushed. The organization wondered if all the planning they'd poured into it had even been worth it.

The next day in Chicago, James played poorly, missing 15 of 23 shots as the Heat lost. But he was still smiling from the moment with Ilgauskas.

"It was a special, special time for Z," he said that day. "And I'm so happy I was able to be a part of it."

James had once fed on the hatred he felt in Quicken Loans Arena. When he made his first return there, in December 2010, he scored 38 points and led a 28-point drubbing despite a flood of negative energy. Fans used social media to coordinate mocking chants. His old jerseys that hadn't been destroyed were used in various ways to attack him, with new and inventive names replacing his on the back. Cavs fans were burned by his departure. In the rush to try to understand James's choice, theories rushed in to fill the information void. They ranged from salacious to bizarre. Some fans were convinced that James had constructed an elaborate protracted plan that included the previous season's playoffs when he suffered an ill-timed slump in a series loss to the Celtics.

James has said many times these claims were untrue. Dwyane Wade and Chris Bosh, the free agents who joined him in Miami, said they didn't get serious about plans to all go to Miami until after all of their previous seasons had ended. Not everyone believed them. James was suffering from a sore elbow that somewhat limited him in the

Celtics series. But Cleveland's relationship with the favored son had become radioactive; nuance and sworn statements did not matter.

With all that baggage in the recent past, here still was James coming back for a ceremony. No one, not even James himself, fully knew what any of it would ultimately mean. And no one could've guessed that the next time the Knicks visited Cleveland for a game, James would be there for that one too—in a Cavs uniform.

Chapter 2

TARGET ACQUISITION MODE

The Cavs ended the 2013–14 season losing four of their last six games to settle at 33–49, missing the playoffs by five games. It was the end of a disastrous six months.

The No. 1 overall pick from the previous year, Anthony Bennett, had a terrible rookie season, and his conditioning and work ethic were as much in question as his talents. Their free agent signings from the previous summer had all flopped to varying degrees. In desperation to make the playoffs, they made two midseason trades, one for forward Luol Deng and the other for center Spencer Hawes, and gave up five draft picks to do so. Both players were free agents at season's end and were showing little interest in re-signing, meaning they'd turned into failed rentals.

Their first-round pick from two years prior, Dion Waiters, had played alongside franchise player Kyrie Irving for two years, and their chemistry was so poor at times that they'd regularly had to deny there was a personal rift between them. Meanwhile, Irving had failed to establish a relationship with new coach Mike Brown, in part over Brown's desire for defense and Irving's lack of consistent interest on that end. That was a problem for two reasons. One was Irving was about to be asked to sign a contract extension, and the organization, attempting to encourage stability, had signed Brown to a five-year, $20 million contract.

The franchise was spinning its wheels and had a leadership void. David Griffin had become the team's acting general manager two months before the end of the season, following the firing of predecessor Chris Grant. Unsure of whether he'd even keep the job, Griffin held a bold press conference a week after the season ended in May 2014.

With limited power and unsure of his future at the time, Griffin announced the team was moving from "asset accumulation mode" into "target acquisition mode."

This was welcome news to many in the fan base who'd grown tired of Grant's slow rebuild the previous four years, which involved trading for six additional first-round picks, ten extra second-round picks, and a build-through-youth approach. Grant's covert campaign to lure James had become a forgotten measure while the team managed its various problems. The concept of the Cavs aggressively attempting to add talent to make a rapid improvement using their stash of draft picks, young players, and salary-cap space was a needed change, of course. But it remained unclear just how Griffin and the Cavs would realistically be able to go about it.

In a first step, Cavs ownership came to Griffin and offered him the formal general manager title. In a surprising move, he turned the job down and instead asked for some concessions. He'd turned down general manager jobs in the past. In 2010, he got into deep talks with the Denver Nuggets about their GM job and was even consulting on roster moves, starting the first stages of a Carmelo Anthony trade, before talks collapsed and he walked away.

Griffin had a bit of a different outlook than a typical NBA executive. He was not a former player, coach, or son of someone in the NBA, the three most popular routes to get into a front office. He was raised by a single mother in a rough neighborhood in West Phoenix. He worked his way through high school so his family could afford the tuition at Brophy Prep, an all-boys Jesuit school, then ground his way through Arizona State, eventually earning a degree in political science. His first job in the league was as an intern for the Suns when he was just twenty. He did odd jobs on the side, like keeping statistics for the local arena football league team. Slowly he worked his way up the ranks and became a member of the front office.

His life changed forever in 2006, when he was diagnosed with testicular cancer. He went through a grueling chemotherapy. As he and his wife, Meredith, celebrated the end of his successful treatment as they walked on the beach near Kona, Hawaii, he made a promise that many people who face life-threatening situations do. He wasn't going to sweat the small stuff, which is a difficult proposition when working in the high-pressure world of pro sports.

In 2011, a few months after Griffin came to Cleveland to join the Cavs front office, a doctor informed him his cancer had returned. The moment the doctor told him—to Griffin, it had felt like the physician said it in passing, almost like a waiter telling him the soup of the day—stuck with him for years. He won that battle too. Now he has a habit of knocking his fist against his head whenever he mentions any good fortune that comes his way, his method of "knocking on wood." He's a man keenly aware of enjoying what he has but who also knows how fragile it all is. It hasn't exactly left him with an endless desire to climb the NBA's executive ladder.

That's why he hesitated when he was offered the Cavs' top job when the team's owners offered to remove his interim label. After days of talks, though, Griffin and owners Dan Gilbert and Nate Forbes did find common ground and Griffin agreed to take the job.

Shortly after he got the interim job the previous February, Griffin's grandmother passed away. He wasn't able to get to Phoenix to see her because he had to stay in Cleveland to execute the trade deadline. The last time he'd talked to her was over Skype to tell her he'd made his first trade, for Hawes. He was gutted when he didn't make it back to say goodbye. The family waited for the funeral until he could get away from trying to handle the mess the Cavs' season had turned into. Griffin was a survivor in every sense.

All of that made it a little unfair that there was an absence of joy when Griffin accepted the job. Reaching a mountaintop in one's profession is a moment where there's usually at least a few celebratory days with friends and family. Griffin practically had to introduce himself, as owner Gilbert did not attend the press conference to announce the decision, which was unusual. The honeymoon period was nil, as Griffin's hiring came at the same time as Brown was fired, announced in the same press release. The Cavs would be looking for their third coach in three seasons, projecting an aimless organization. More challenging, as he started the coaching search Gilbert was looking to hire him a boss.

The Cavs' two previous coaches, Byron Scott and Brown, had been hired and fired several times. Gilbert wanted a new face and he wanted someone with a successful résumé. This naturally left him looking to the college ranks, especially in the wake of the early success of Brad Stevens, who'd left a successful program at Butler University and been winning positive reviews after his first season with the Boston Celtics.

When he had a coaching opening in 2010, Gilbert chased several high-profile college coaches and made a $7-million-per-year offer to Tom Izzo, the Michigan State legend, whom Gilbert had come to know and admire as an MSU graduate. Izzo, though, was unable to get an assurance about the future from James, then a free agent. After seriously considering Gilbert's offer and making a high-profile visit to Cleveland, Izzo passed.

Now, five years later, there'd been a shift in the coaching landscape. Doc Rivers had become the president and coach of the Los Angeles Clippers. Flip Saunders had taken on a similar role in Minnesota. Gregg Popovich had such a job in San Antonio. Two days after the Cavs fired Brown, Stan Van Gundy was given the coveted dual roles in Detroit.

As Gilbert sought another college coach, the stakes had been raised. Highly respected coaches and those secure in what were essentially lifetime jobs wouldn't just be looking for a huge paycheck but supreme power over the front office too. And with power they wanted assurances in the form of long contracts. Gilbert had parted ways with three GMs in nine years as owner and was paying two coaches he'd recently fired.

But there was also a sudden shift in the Cavs landscape. A week after Griffin was hired, he went to New York for the NBA's annual draft lottery. The Cavs had the ninth-best chance of winning, an uninspiring 1.7 percent. While in rebuilding phases between 2011 and 2013, Gilbert made the lottery a major event. He brought his son, Nick, to be the team's onstage representative and rejoiced when winning in 2011 and 2013. He brought a group of supporters in on his private plane in 2013, many of them wearing bow ties as was Nick Gilbert's tradition. When they won that year, with a 15.6 percent chance, the group exploded in celebration at the normally staid event and was criticized for it. That pick was Bennett, and his flop had significantly contributed to the Cavs being compelled to return to the NBA's convention of non-playoff teams again.

Because of those circumstances, the Cavs contingent arrived at the ABC studios on May, 20, 2014, like a lamb. There was no traveling party and no Nick or Dan Gilbert, who was not in the studio. As when Griffin was hired, he was thrust out to be on his own. As it came down to the final envelope, he rubbed a pin on his lapel, an angel with a tiny diamond that had been one of his grandmother's few valuable possessions. When the Cavs won the top pick the only clapping came from him.

The lottery was televised before Game 2 of the Eastern Conference finals between the Miami Heat and Indiana Pacers. There were two televisions in the visitors' locker room in Indianapolis that night. One showed film of the Heat's Game 1 loss two nights earlier. The other was on the lottery. As Griffin celebrated and tapped the pin over his heart, James watched as he was being stretched for the game.

The Cavs were already thinking big when it came to their coach. Gilbert was further emboldened to chase a famous name now that the job came with the chance to draft Andrew Wiggins or Jabari Parker, the two options at No. 1. Gilbert's first target was University of Kentucky coach John Calipari. But Calipari had some huge contract demands, starting with a ten-year deal. It was later reported that the stakes reached as high as $80 million. But Calipari had just agreed to a new seven-year, $53 million deal with Kentucky and had a loaded team coming for the following season, a team that eventually would take an undefeated record into the Final Four and see four of its players drafted in the top 14 picks of the 2015 NBA draft. The Cavs' prospects were unclear and James at that point wasn't a legitimate part of them. Calipari passed.

The big game hunting did not stop. Griffin called Mike Krzyzewski, Duke's legendary coach. He'd turned down much better NBA offers in the past than this one. Again, the Cavs had no James to offer. They'd continued to have dialogue with Paul, James's agent. Paul gave zero assurances other than to indicate Cleveland would be an option if James chose free agency. That was no small thing, but it was far from concrete and the Cavs couldn't sell it.

Griffin flew to Lawrence, Kansas, to do on-the-ground research with Bill Self, the Jayhawks' respected coach, who had two high draft pick choices, Wiggins and Joel Embiid. At a meeting with Self, Griffin offered him the coaching job out of the blue. Self was surprised, which was Griffin's intention, and offered to think about it. He did some research on the job over the next few days but, like Calipari, also passed.

Next was Florida coach Billy Donovan, who'd won two national titles and sent numerous high-profile players to the NBA. Donovan indicated he might be ready for the NBA, and soon he and the Cavs were talking. He eventually flew to Cleveland to formally interview. But as talks progressed, Donovan's contract demands caused the Cavs to hesitate, and the sides eventually moved on before the negotiations reached a serious stage.

Griffin attempted to recruit Steve Kerr, who had been his former boss in Phoenix and was ready to go into coaching. By the time Griffin got to him, however, Kerr had already been offered the New York Knicks and Golden State Warriors coaching jobs and was soon to choose the Warriors. Griffin talked to Kevin Ollie, who'd just won a championship with the University of Connecticut and was popular among NBA players, but Ollie signed an extension to stay.

As the process unfolded, Griffin ended up focusing on two other candidates with NBA experience, both of whom worked for the L.A. Clippers. Alvin Gentry had known Griffin for years and was once the head coach of the Suns while Griffin was there too. Tyronn Lue, a retired journeyman point guard, had become known for his ability to connect to players and had studied for several years under Rivers in Boston and Los Angeles.

Gentry's résumé, filled with a few failed head coaching jobs at previous spots, was similar to Scott's and Brown's, and that didn't impress Gilbert. Neither did Gentry's close relationship with Griffin. Brown was very close to Grant, and that mix hadn't created success for the recently fired pairing. Gilbert wanted to avoid a repeat.

Lue was intriguing, especially to Griffin, but light on experience, especially when entered into a field with names like Calipari, Self, and Donovan.

As the process played out, another development happened in the league. Kevin Love, the Minnesota Timberwolves All-Star, had been put on the trade market. In the wake of Saunders being hired to run the team, Love was approached about signing an extension as he was heading into the final year of his contract. He declined, saying that he planned to become a free agent in 2015. After years of Love's teetering on this delicate matter, the Wolves had finally decided to move on from him. They were looking for a high draft pick as the centerpiece of a trade.

After he'd taken the job, Griffin had lunch with Saunders and they had some discussions about doing a deal for Love. Saunders said he'd be interested if the Cavs ended up with a top three pick to offer. When the Cavs won the draft lottery, Griffin called Love's agent, Jeff Schwartz, who is one of the league's top power brokers. Griffin asked if Love would be interested in staying in Cleveland long-term, a prerequisite to trading a valuable asset for a player with just one year on his contract. Schwartz was frank with Griffin: No, Love was not interested in Cleveland. Griffin dropped the matter and returned to the coaching search.

Love and Schwartz didn't foresee James as part of the picture, and, just like during talks in the coaching search, neither did Griffin. As for Gilbert, his thoughts on the short-term outlook of his team revealed themselves in another subtle way.

As the Cavs were going through a disappointing winter and spring, Gilbert was active in helping Cleveland put together a bid to host the 2016 Republican National Convention. As controller of Quicken Loans Arena, Gilbert was an integral part of the process. The RNC was looking to host their convention as early as June, not August as in previous years, to more quickly access general election funding. That meant that the host venue would have to be available from mid- to late May, during the heart of the NBA playoffs. The other finalist for the convention was Dallas. But Mavericks owner Mark Cuban told the *Dallas Morning News* a June convention would be impossible because it would conflict with possible playoff games and he'd be unwilling to make his arena, the American Airlines Center, available in May. Gilbert, his team out of the playoffs for four consecutive years, was willing to promise his arena could be made free as early as May 2016. Cleveland, for various reasons, including arena availability, won the bid before James made his free agency decision.

With the coaching search extending, the team was pitched a different kind of candidate, one who was an out-of-the-box option like Gilbert was searching for. David Blatt, the American coach of Euro-League power Maccabi Tel Aviv, quietly hired an American agent and began looking for a chance in the NBA. He interviewed for several jobs over the phone while his season in Europe was still going on. He eventually had a Skype interview with Gilbert that went well. In mid-June, he announced he was resigning to pursue coaching opportunities in the NBA. Blatt—who had coached in Italy, Russia, Turkey, and Greece as well as Israel—had been on the radar for several years, especially after Ettore Messina, regarded as one of Europe's finest coaches, joined the Lakers as an assistant coach in 2011.

Blatt had just finished a most impressive season, leading underdog Maccabi to several unlikely victories in winning the EuroLeague title. His stock also was high after coaching the Russian national team to a bronze medal at the 2012 Olympics, a surprising result. While Russia's coach for the 2010 World Championships in Istanbul, he'd gotten into a war of words with Krzyzewski, the Team USA coach, over the 1972 Olympic gold medal game, which the Russians won controversially over the United States. Despite his American citizenship, Blatt backed his employer and said the Russians had won fairly. Krzyzewski was not amused.

Nonetheless, it displayed the type of guile Blatt had become famous for coaching in Europe, even if only far-flung NBA scouts got to see it. During the 2012 Olympics in London, he ejected two of his best players from the bench because they'd talked to each other while he was trying to go over a play in a huddle. There were many of these stories in his past, but this one played out on American television.

Within days of his resignation, Blatt came to the United States after his father passed away. Shortly after the funeral, he met with Kerr, who was filling out his coaching staff with the Warriors. Kerr, who spent much of his childhood in the Middle East, shared an agent and a sensibility with Blatt, who'd been in Israel for most of his adult life after graduating from Princeton. Kerr was prepared to make Blatt his lead assistant, and Blatt verbally accepted the job.

Then the Cavs, running out of options, called asking for Blatt to come for a two-day interview in Cleveland. Gilbert had just met with Lue, who'd become a finalist, and then met Blatt.

Gilbert was intrigued by Blatt because, like the college coaches he'd gone after previously, Blatt had a record of championships. He'd coached under adverse conditions everywhere from Saint Petersburg, Russia, to Treviso, Italy, to Thessaloniki, Greece. He'd won coaching defense-based teams. He'd won using the Princeton offense. He'd won using fast-breaking schemes. And he'd shown guts along the way. Shortly after the meeting ended, Gilbert got in the car for a ride from Cleveland back to Detroit, where he lived, and immediately started making calls, doing a personal vetting. He called coaches he knew, he investigated what the media's reaction might be to hiring essentially a foreign coach. The Cavs would later reach out to people at USA Basketball to get their impression. Blatt, unsure how'd he done, made plans to fly to San Francisco the next day and get ready to start work with Golden State.

"We talked to like 30 people in Europe. There wasn't a person who wouldn't rave about this guy," Gilbert said. "We talked to four or five American players who played for him over there. Rarely do you call a player and ask about an ex-coach and he is complimentary. But they were."

Despite the recommendations, there wasn't universal agreement on Blatt. It was a risk because he'd never coached in the NBA and had lived abroad for thirty years. But he'd performed well in the interview with his mix of confidence and experience. Some in the organization suggested that the adjustment from coaching in Europe to the NBA might be easier than the adjustment from coaching in college to the league might be. This had never been tried before; what if the team had unearthed a formula? He was American, but he was also exotic by NBA standards. He'd be a bit of a unicorn. Gilbert liked the idea that he might have been able to discover the next great NBA coach. And Blatt was Jewish, a factor that helped connect him to Gilbert as well.

Griffin, an NBA lifer who'd spent plenty of time scouting in Europe over the years, wasn't as sure. With Gentry out of the picture—he'd eventually take the top assistant job with the Warriors that Blatt ended up passing on—Griffin was interested in Lue. Lue had a vast network of allies and bonds with players and teams around the league. Everyone who played with him didn't just seem to like him, they seemed to admire him. Griffin thought this was perhaps rarer still than Blatt's résumé.

Gilbert, though, had reached his choice with Blatt. As they talked about the direction, ownership and Griffin discussed a compromise. Attempt to hire Lue as well. Try to get Lue to be the top assistant, getting both their choices. The experienced veteran would bring in fresh European sensibilities to lead, and he'd have an ultimate insider and former player as a lieutenant.

On its face, the concept was awkward. The runner-up would act as the winner's forced right-hand man. Many experienced NBA coaches, which Blatt was not, would have rejected such an idea. Griffin also wanted to keep another assistant, veteran Jim Boylan, meaning Blatt wouldn't have hiring power for much of his key staff.

But the compromises cascaded down the line. In hiring Blatt, Griffin would retain personnel power and still be the head of basketball operations, which wasn't a possibility with some candidates. Blatt was getting what he'd dreamed of, a head NBA job, and it would come with a three-year contract that guaranteed him more than $10 million and had an option and bonuses that could kick in millions more. That made it easier for him to accept Lue, who was lured away from the Clippers when Gilbert green-lighted the largest contract ever given to an assistant coach, four years and $6.5 million.

After it all came together, Gilbert raved about his new unicorn: "David Blatt is going to bring some of the most innovative approaches found in professional basketball anywhere on the globe. Time and time again, from Russia to Israel and several other prominent head coaching jobs in between, David has done one thing: win. He is not only an innovator, well-trained and focused on both sides of the court, but he is always learning and always teaching."

Blatt was excited and loose in his big moment as he was introduced as coach. Though he was coming onto the biggest stage of his career, he joked that he was more than ready for the scrutiny of being a head coach. "If you lost one game with Maccabi," he said, "there was a countrywide investigation."

The hiring became official just a little more than twenty-four hours before the draft. On the same day, James opted out of his contract with the Heat. The Cavs and the rest of the league certainly noticed, but it did not greatly change their focus.

Blatt and Lue weren't part of the evaluation process for the draft picks, which Griffin was conducting. The Cavs had favored Wiggins from the start, specifically because he'd shown a commitment to playing defense in his season at Kansas, and Parker, who was a massively talented offensive player, had not during his year at Duke. Then there was Parker's workout with the team, which was a buzzkill. The Cavs were astounded at what they perceived as a lack of intensity and energy during the visit from Parker, to the point they suspected he'd tanked the workout in an effort to get the Cavs not to draft him. The Milwaukee Bucks, who had the No. 2 pick, were closer to Parker's hometown of Chicago. Nonetheless, here was another top player who looked like he didn't want to be in Cleveland, not exactly a jolt of confidence for a team hoping to rebuild itself quickly. On draft night the pick was easy for the Cavs. They took Wiggins No. 1.

What Blatt and Lue were doing that week, however, was talking to Irving. After taking over as interim GM the previous winter, Griffin made creating a bond with Irving a priority. Irving's first three years in the league had been traumatic, as he'd gone through several coaches and several systems and had to watch the Cavs mishandle draft picks and slow play other improvements around him.

Irving's father, Drederick, was a huge influence in his life. Dred, as his friends called him, grew up in a housing project in the Bronx as part of a large single-parent family. He quickly became a basketball star in high school and later at Boston University. There he met Elizabeth, who was the daughter of a Lutheran minister, a trained classical pianist, and on the university's volleyball team. They later married. After college, Dred signed to play for a team in Melbourne,

Australia, where Kyrie was born. When Irving was four, Elizabeth passed away from an illness, a moment that shaped his life. Even as an adult, Irving has said filling out paperwork halts him when he has to leave his mother's information blank.

The family ended up settling in New Jersey. On September 11, 2001, Drederick was walking through the lobby of Tower One at the World Trade Center when the first plane hit the building. He'd worked there for years as a stockbroker for Cantor Fitzgerald, the firm that took a direct hit from the aircraft. He'd recently moved to a nearby building, but he wasn't sure his children knew and he couldn't reach them. He ended up walking to the Bronx that day to find a way to get home, his ten-year-old son wondering if he'd lost a second parent.

Irving became a teenage star like his father before him. The two poured in hours working on technique, with his father schooling him on how to practice awkward shots that would trick defenders. On weekends, Drederick would take his son back to the Mitchel projects in the Bronx, letting Irving learn to play on the blacktops as he did.

Irving loved practicing dribbling, working on moves for hours. He studied star Rod Strickland, a close friend of his father's, and his ability to use his dribble to score below the rim. He watched Allen Iverson highlights on YouTube. He loved Jason Williams, the slick point guard of the Sacramento Kings, who had the nickname "White Chocolate."

"I'd watch the highlights on YouTube and I'd go out on my driveway and try it. And then I'd watch more YouTube videos and I'd go back out and try it. It would be an all-night thing," Irving said. "It was not being afraid to try that move that your coach tells you not to do, like being on a fast break and doing double moves and your coach wants you to do a regular layup. I don't believe in that. I believe in having creativity in the game and bringing excitement to what everyone kind of is afraid to do."

Irving attended a private-school power, St. Patrick, where his highlights eventually became YouTube hits. One of his teammates, Michael Kidd-Gilchrist, later became the No. 2 overall pick in the draft. They were one of the best high school teams in the nation. Irving would become the No. 1 recruit in the nation and ended up at Duke.

Dred was by his son's side always. He was very present in Cleveland in Irving's first years there, and his displeasure over the direction of the franchise was not quiet. The Cavs got sufficiently concerned over Irving's willingness to sign an extension with the organization that they held internal conversations about trading him. Highlighting the disconnect, Brown was in favor of moving him despite his immense talent. The Cavs ultimately ruled it out, but there were fractures in the relationship.

From the moment Griffin took the job, he worked on managing the Irving relationship. During the coaching search they kept in regular contact. As soon as Blatt and Lue were hired, Griffin put them in touch with Irving. Griffin came from an offensive background in Phoenix, and he made it clear offense would be a part of the team's future, not as much as the defense-based team under Brown. As with much of the league, Kyrie and Dred had a positive opinion of Lue, a former point guard now in position to be a major part of the organization. All of these were seen as positive signs from Irving's perspective.

Even with their stated mission of improving the team quickly that summer, and despite having $20 million in cap space, the Cavs' first free agent move was to approach a player under contract. That was Irving, who was eligible to sign an extension that would kick in the following year. The Cavs had until October 31 to do such a deal, but they wanted to make Irving their number one priority.

So on June 30, Gilbert and minority owners Forbes and Jeff Cohen joined Griffin, Blatt, and Lue on a jet to New York City. There, at midnight on July 1, they had dinner in a private dining room in the basement of a Manhattan restaurant with the Irvings and Kyrie's agent, Jeff Wechsler. They formally presented a five-year, $90 million extension offer. While the promises and conversations in the room were important, the groundwork laid by Griffin, Blatt, and Lue prior to the meeting had already convinced Irving things would be different. The prospect of James joining the team was not a major topic of conversation, but other free agents the Cavs were going to chase were discussed. Around 1:30 a.m. the parties shook hands; the deal was done.

As the Irving deal was being closed, other members of the Cavs front office were calling free agents. They had several on their radar. They called Gordon Hayward, who'd had a promising start to his career in four years with the Utah Jazz. The Cavs envisioned Wiggins starting at shooting guard and Hayward, who was from nearby India-napolis, at small forward with the newly committed Irving running the point.

The Cavs also called Chandler Parsons, another young small for-ward who surprisingly became a free agent when the Houston Rockets didn't pick up an option in his contract. The Cavs were also interested in veterans like Trevor Ariza and Channing Frye.

At about 2 a.m., as Griffin headed back to his hotel, he called Paul and let him know the Cavs were interested in James too. Paul thanked him for the interest and told him they would be in touch. No prom-ises, no hints. The Cavs moved on with their business.

On July 2, the Cavs set up a visit with Hayward, who was a restricted free agent, for the next day. If the visit went well there was an understanding that the Cavs might be ready to offer him a four-year maximum-level contract that started at $15 million for the next season, the bulk of the Cavs' available cap space. Gilbert's jet flew to Indianapolis and picked Hayward up.

But on that day, July 3, something happened. Even as the Cavs pre-pared to show Hayward around their practice facility and have him meet with Blatt, Griffin's phone rang. It was Paul. He told Griffin he'd be meeting with teams regarding James's free agency over the next few days at his office in downtown Cleveland.

James was not a lock to return to the Heat. He was indeed on the market. Was this the moment the Cavs had been dreaming of? They weren't sure. But they had to call Hayward's agent. There would be no contract offer right then. The Cavs had just slammed on the brakes.

On everything.

Chapter 3

MIDNIGHT IN MIAMI

There was exhaustion. There was relief. There may have even been a little joy. It was certainly unlike most Finals-losing locker rooms in NBA history. This was June 2014, the fourth year in a row the Miami Heat had made it to the championship round, and it was the first time they'd been outclassed, losing in five games to the San Antonio Spurs. The reality and finality of it left the room devoid of the type of pain usually reserved for the end of a long journey. The duration and the circumstances had stripped it all away.

The Finals had been frustrating. After he scored a basket to make it a two-point game with four minutes left in Game 1 in San Antonio, LeBron James's legs cramped so badly that he had to leave the game, and the Spurs instantly pulled away for the victory. The air-conditioning had failed inside the AT&T Center and temperatures on the court surpassed 90 degrees. Some suspected it was a ploy by the Spurs akin to those of Boston Celtics coaching great Red Auerbach, who was accused of manipulating temperatures inside Boston Garden for years.

James had previously experienced cramping issues in warm arenas, especially in later playoff rounds as summer arrived and heated the exterior air. He acknowledged that playoff games caused him more stress and he was more prone to becoming dehydrated. Several times he needed IVs following playoff games, and he began a routine where he'd carry a jug of water around with him to constantly drink during the playoffs. He explained that "playoff sweat is different than regular-season sweat."

During the 2012 Finals, James cramped during Game 4 in Miami and was ultimately unable to finish. The Heat won that night, but in subsequent years the engineering department at AmericanAirlines Arena in Miami cranked the air-conditioning on playoff game days to the point where it was almost uncomfortably cold.

The AT&T Center had a bit of a reputation across the league for bizarre events. Bats were known to fly through the building on occasion, and once Spurs star Manu Ginobili captured one during a game, thereafter needing days of rabies injections. Just a few weeks before the air-conditioning failed, the Portland Trail Blazers found a snake in the visitors' locker room before a playoff game. The air-conditioning failure instantly became part of lore and fodder for conspiracy theorists, who noted all fans were given noisemakers that night that could be used as hand fans, while several industrial fans turned up in the Spurs' locker room.

It was rendered moot after the Spurs won the final three games of the series with James healthy. After a 17-point loss in Game 5 that avenged the Spurs' loss to Miami the season before, it was clear who the better team was regardless of temperature.

In the locker room, Shane Battier, who'd been a crucial addition to the team three years earlier, announced his retirement. Ray Allen then surprised when he hinted he was considering retirement after an eighteen-season Hall of Fame career. He never played another game.

Rashard Lewis, a veteran of fifteen seasons who started four of the five Finals games, was soon forced into retirement because of knee issues. Greg Oden, who was on the team but didn't play much, was forced to retire from the NBA for the same reason.

The team's doctors were quite busy during the season as Wade missed 28 games, mostly due to knee pain or to rest his knees. He had problems in both. His left knee had been an issue for years, dating to his Marquette days when he had his meniscus partially removed, a procedure doctors nowadays avoid as much as possible because of its long-term effects. He needed several more surgeries, including one to his left knee before the 2012–13 season. Before Game 7 of the 2013 Finals, which the Heat won over the Spurs after a heroic effort from James, Wade needed to have the knee drained. He was also suffering in his right knee, where he'd dealt with pain for months because of bone bruises and irritation.

So it was an old, battered, and tired Heat team, and the final loss felt more like a going-away party. James outclassed the rest of his teammates, scoring 31 points with 10 rebounds and five assists in Game 5. He did not share in the feeling of relief.

As the Spurs celebrated with champagne and planned an all-night party at a nearby Italian restaurant, James arrived at the postgame press conference. Within moments he was asked about his future, as he had an opt-out clause in his contract with a decision due in fourteen days. His answer ended up being telling.

"I'm not disappointed in any of my teammates, just wish we could have come through, played a better series," he said.

He hadn't been asked about his teammates. Perhaps they had given their best, but at that point, even after two championships and four consecutive Finals trips, it was not enough. That answer made it clear that when thinking about his future, James was thinking about his teammates, the ones who would even be left.

Three days later, Heat president Pat Riley called his own press conference back in Miami. These were traditional at the end of every season and often celebratory. Not this one. Riley sat down and immediately slammed his hands against the table.

"You want to trend something, trend this," he said, referring to social media. "I'm pissed. So go ahead, get it out there." He proceeded to go on a diatribe in which it slowly became clear he wasn't just speaking to the media and the fans but also to his players. "Everybody needs to get a grip. Heat players, organization, all of our fans, get a grip!" he said.

He talked about his time with the Los Angeles Lakers, during which the team won five titles over twelve years. "That means seven times they didn't win. They didn't run, they didn't win!" he said. "This stuff is hard. You have to stay together if you've got the guts. You don't take the first door and run out of it." He compared the just-finished season to a Broadway show, saying it sort of "ran out of steam."

It was strange for Riley to be so cranky. He was a man who typically presented a front that things were under control and everything happened for a reason, whether it was the truth or not. He'd been through so many events in his career, there were few things he didn't have a personal history dealing with and a story to grease the message he needed to deliver. He also usually had a plan, and often that plan was good. One of his greatest talents was his sales pitches, whether it was to players he was coaching, free agents he was trying to sign, or executives who paid tens of thousands to hear him speak.

In 1987, at the rally celebrating the title, he famously guaranteed the Lakers would repeat as champions. It was brash and, with his custom shirt and designer sunglasses, unquestionably cool. But it was part of a plan. The previous two times he'd coached the Lakers to titles they'd come back flat the following season and hadn't defended. Riley wanted to motivate them with his words. The Lakers got the repeat in 1988. Riley reacted by secretly filing a trademark for the phrase "three-peat."

Even when Riley didn't win he was often spectacular in his efforts. Once, in 2000, he was hoping to sign major free agent Tracy McGrady. When McGrady came to Miami to visit, Riley arranged for him to board a boat at Heat star Alonzo Mourning's house and then speed across Biscayne Bay to Riley's waterside mansion to receive the contract offer. McGrady signed in Orlando, but that presentation beats the greatest PowerPoint in boardroom history.

It was in a boardroom where Riley closed the deal on James in 2010, appealing to his desire to win championships by placing his seven championship rings on the table to illustrate he knew how to get them for James. By the summer of 2014, Riley had nine and James two.

So there was an assumption that Riley again knew what to do. That he'd looked ahead and had a plot ready to make sure James would be staying with his ring-producing machine. But the fiery press conference hinted he did not. All he had was a challenge to James's manhood.

Riley's aggressive nature exposed several previously unknown things. One was that he and the organization were nervous about James's free agency and keeping the team together. The second was that Riley felt the need to give this message via the media instead of in person. He admitted his postseason meeting with James was brief and they didn't discuss these themes in depth, as James was looking to leave on a head-clearing trip to the Bahamas.

While Riley's message—that even great teams don't win every year and failure often is a part of establishing a dynasty—was sage and even reasonable, his tone and methods seemed misplaced, especially for a player he was supposed to have a relationship with. A little more telling was that he announced in the press conference that James and his wife were expecting a third child, their first girl, that fall. James had taken steps to keep that information private in the previous months, something media members who knew him had been well aware of, and Riley mentioning it seemingly off the cuff was surprising.

Five days later, James opted out of his contract, a week earlier than he was required to. There was no other comment made, but other teams started to believe the rumors they'd heard, that James might be considering leaving after all.

A day after he opted out, James, Wade, and Bosh got together for a late afternoon meeting at Soho Beach House, a private and secluded hotel in South Beach, where they discussed their situation. After ordering watermelon salad, chips, and guacamole, they talked about free agency. All three of them had opt-out clauses in their deals, but only James had exercised his at that point. They'd had a similar summit in 2010 before joining together to play for the Heat when they'd agreed to align their decision making. They'd also had more informal discussions in 2006, when they all believed they should sign three-year contract extensions rather than the typical five-year deals when they all played for different teams. It was expected this type of meeting would take place again.

Only this time was different. There would be no decision or even a consensus. James had different representation, and he, Wade, and Bosh wouldn't be operating with all of them aware of the others' moves. Options were discussed, especially about the changing landscape in the league and how that might affect contracts. But James didn't know for sure what he was going to do, and he told them. In retrospect, Wade and Bosh would later say his indecision said everything. But at that place and time it just came off as uncertainty. When it was over, Bosh went home, as he and his wife, Adrienne, were planning a long worldwide trip with his children. James and Wade went to Sun Life Stadium to attend a concert by friends Jay-Z and Beyoncé, who were kicking off a tour.

James's tone was relayed to the Heat offices. Their reaction played out quickly. Owners of the 26th pick in the NBA draft the following night, the team began calling around looking for ways to move up in the draft. Their target became known. They were chasing Shabazz Napier, the undersized point guard who'd led Connecticut to the national title that spring. Napier fit into the type of player Riley often likes—he was older after four years in college, had championship experience, and he was American. Riley typically didn't draft international prospects. Napier's résumé resembled those of many other Riley picks, from Wade, who played three years at Marquette and went to a Final Four, to the team's current point guards, former NCAA tournament hero Mario Chalmers and four-year collegian Norris Cole.

But there was another motive, and it was tied to James. During UConn's title run, James had marveled at Napier's playmaking. "No way u take a PG in the lottery before Napier," he wrote on his Twitter account during the title game where Napier scored 22 points to lead his team to a win over Kentucky. The Heat obviously took notice. Even though they needed help at the wing positions after Battier's and Allen's statements, they traded two second-round picks to move from the No. 26 pick to the No. 24 pick to get Napier. It was pricey for such a modest move up, but the Heat clearly had motivation, and it wasn't just to get Napier.

"Why not?" Riley said that night. "If LeBron and I have the same taste in talent, so be it. But he didn't call me on the phone, or he didn't make a point to me about it."

This was true. James had not discussed it with the Heat and they had not talked on the phone since his opt-out. Riley would later criticize James for misleading the Heat when it came to Napier, who ended up being traded away after one unsuccessful season in Miami. The larger point was to get James's attention. On that front, it clearly worked.

After the Heat made the trade, James went back to Twitter, writing, "My favorite player in the draft!"

It gave the impression James and the Heat were on the same page. It also gave Riley some momentum and some hope for a mission he planned for the next night. That was at a wedding in the Coconut Grove section of Miami for Mike Mancias, one of the Heat's trainers, who was extremely close to James.

James and Riley were both in attendance, along with numerous other Heat personnel. In a more relaxed and celebratory atmosphere, Riley hoped he would be able to go off into a corner with James and be able to have a conversation about the future. A veteran motivator and dealmaker who'd won James over in the past, he was hopeful he could do it again. It certainly had seemed to the Heat the move the day before to get Napier had energized James, and if nothing else it would be an excellent conversation starter.

But there would be no meeting. James kept his distance and wanted to do no business. Paul also attended the wedding but did not meet with Riley. James and Paul had agreed they would have a systematic approach to this free agency. There would be a process and Paul would be leading it. There would be no end runs or backroom sessions. It would be handled in an orderly fashion, and it would be handled after July 1.

There was a perception that Riley and James had to have some sort of falling-out for it to reach this point. It wasn't that black-and-white. Despite Riley's efforts, the two had never really had a falling-in. They'd had talks, they'd shared meals and drinks, they'd embraced after titles. Riley always believed these moments created bonds for life. For James, it was always a business relationship. Riley could switch to business easily. He'd traded franchise cornerstones Tim Hardaway, Shaquille O'Neal, and Alonzo Mourning. He eventually let Wade walk over a monetary dispute. And in the end, he cut Bosh loose when the sides weren't on the same page on a medical issue.

James had many warm moments with Riley, but he'd never lost sight of the reality. He knew Riley could be ruthless. He eventually began to resent he'd given the Heat a contract discount only to see them cut some corners on salaries later. Ultimately, James's circle was small and tight and Riley was never in it. That reality caught Riley, and much of the Heat organization, by surprise.

James did have a few special audiences at the wedding that night. One was with Zydrunas Ilgauskas, who had flown into town because Mancias had befriended him when working for the Cavs and Heat. That night Ilgauskas told James he had decided to leave the Cavs organization. But they spent time talking about the status of the franchise, James kept asking questions about the roster and about the team's plans. But while Riley waited for his chance, James stepped into a private room for an important duty. Along with the bride and groom, Mike and Heather, he became the official witness in signing their marriage certificate.

As it would turn out, it was the only contract he'd sign in Miami that summer.

Chapter 4

"I'M COMING HOME"

Midnight on July 1 is the most frenzied moment on the NBA calendar, the official opening of free agency. After midnight on July 1, 2014, Rich Paul's phone went hot with calls and texts. Within a few hours, all thirty teams had made contact, letting him know they were interested in his client. In the league, where due diligence is demanded, it's not uncommon for a team to express interest in dozens of free agents after midnight merely to test the waters. In many cases, talks start directly or indirectly days or even weeks earlier despite rules against contact before July 1.

Over the previous ten days, James had several serious conversations with Paul and Maverick Carter, his friend who heads many of James's off-court ventures, and Randy Mims, who travels with him throughout the year. These three and James's wife, Savannah, are essentially his inner circle, and they would be the ones involved in making this major choice. Also involved was Adam Mendelsohn, who had been James's media strategist since 2011.

James knew for some time that he was going to exercise his option to become a free agent. And he had spoken with Paul, Carter, and family members about moving back to Ohio to play for the Cavs again at some point in the future. The reason the Cavs had even gotten their hopes up was because these feelings had trickled to them in various forms over the previous eighteen months.

But it was not a decision James had reached by the start of free agency. Just a few weeks earlier the Heat had been tied with the San

Antonio Spurs 1–1 in the Finals after two games. Going home, with the home court advantage, it seemed like a third consecutive title was within reach. Had that played out, James would likely have elected to stay in Miami to defend another title. Instead the Heat lost three straight games and looked old and emotionally spent in doing so.

The outcome of the Finals had helped push going home to the front of James's mind. And that meant the hometown Cavs—even if they didn't know it, and all of their actions showed they didn't—were in the lead. They were there because James felt a pull to come play at home, where he could live in his Akron mansion and send his kids to Akron-area schools near all of his friends and family and his wife's friends and family. And he could try to change the course of his career by trying to lead the woebegone Cavs to a championship. He'd followed the team and its moves, and he thought it would be possible.

But everyone involved in the choice maintains when midnight struck on July 1, the race was still very much in progress. With a decision of this magnitude, more consideration was needed.

In the wake of how the process played out, not everyone believed this. Certainly not the Heat, who in retrospect felt like what happened over the next week and a half was a damaging wild-goose chase. But James maintained he wasn't fully sure if another option might be better. He also still wasn't sure if he could work for Cavs owner Dan Gilbert again.

By 2 p.m. on July 1, Paul had returned every call. There were twenty-four "thanks but LeBron is not interested" messages. Six teams were told James would consider them—the Dallas Mavericks, the Los Angeles Lakers, the Phoenix Suns, the Chicago Bulls, the Miami Heat, and the Cleveland Cavaliers. By July 2, Paul had explained James's general timetable and invited most of the teams to Cleveland for presentations beginning the next day, Thursday, July 3.

Not only did these calls slow these teams' free agent moves, they effectively halted the market. It jammed players like Gordon Hayward, who went from a recruiting visit to an afterthought after a phone call expressing James's interest.

At Paul's suggestion, James made it clear he was going to stay physically removed from the process. A few days before the start of the frenzy, he left on a family vacation to the Caribbean. Using social media, he let the world know he was away. As the finalists for James learned they'd made the cut, he posted a short video of his oldest son, LeBron Jr., reeling in a nice-sized blackfin tuna off the back of a boat James had rented for a family fishing trip.

When he was a first-time free agent in 2010, James hosted six teams at his business office in Cleveland over a three-day period in early July. The meetings quickly became public and led to a media horde surrounding the building. Cameras were ready at the airport, catching owners and executives filing off planes. Reporters knew the order of the team's pitches, and video of their arrivals and departures was on *SportsCenter* every night.

This time there would also be meetings in a Cleveland office, that of Klutch Sports, but it would be different. Minimal leaks. No waiting cameras. And no James. Paul and Mark Termini would hear the pitches and secrecy was requested. Representatives from teams began quietly arriving on July 3. Some surprised each other in the lobby of the Ritz-Carlton, where most visiting NBA personnel stayed in Cleveland. Gilbert, ironically, owned the hotel.

The Lakers were represented by general manager Mitch Kupchak. Suns owner Robert Sarver came with his front office. So did Mavs owner Mark Cuban, who inadvertently was spotted sitting in Public Square, which is adjacent to Klutch Sports' offices, drinking iced tea. The photo quickly made its way across social media. Cuban, who the night before had hosted free agent Carmelo Anthony in a pitch meeting at his home in Dallas, tried to cover it up and announced he was in town on business as part of his television show, *Shark Tank*. The Bulls were led by Michael Reinsdorf, son of owner Jerry Reinsdorf, and front office leaders Gar Forman and John Paxson, who had come four years earlier to pitch James as well.

All of them had presentations explaining their plans for their roster and their teams going forward. Paul and Termini revealed nothing, taking notes and keeping their thoughts to themselves. The billionaires and executives tried to probe for info or read them. They got very little.

Beyond the team's shows, Paul and Termini had two topics to discuss. Each team got the same two. First, all were told James would only be accepting a full max contract. Unlike in Miami, where he'd taken less than the premium number, there would be no discounting, no matter how much it might help the team in building its roster. And this contract might range from one year in length to the maximum of four. While a four-time MVP still in his prime getting the highest salary possible may seem like a foregone conclusion, that was not necessarily the case.

Anthony, who is one of James's closest friends, said even before he became a free agent that he might be willing to take less than a max contract to help build a team—essentially, the James/Dwyane Wade/ Chris Bosh Heat plan from four years earlier. The New York Knicks, Anthony's team, seized on this statement.

"He's the one that opened that up that it wasn't about the money," said Knicks president Phil Jackson, who didn't take any discounts when he signed on to run the team for $12 million per year several months earlier. "So I challenged him on that because I want our fans to see he's a team player"—the implication being that a "team player" would take less money.

Beyond maximizing James's earnings during his prime years, it also appealed to him to set a tone. If he accepted less than a max contract—again—it would set a precedent that was hurtful to his fellow stars. His doing so four years earlier had already affected the way fans and teams approached negotiations, as Anthony's situation showed.

Cuban, who had never been afraid to pay and pamper talent, hinted in interviews before free agency that he didn't anticipate giving out any max contract offers that summer, even though he was soon to pitch Anthony and James. The Bulls, with high-priced stars Derrick Rose and Joakim Noah on their roster, didn't have enough cap space to offer any player a max deal without making trades. Yet they also pitched James and Anthony with less than the max slot, which was slated to be $20.7 million that year.

The second topic from James's reps involved the NBA's luxury tax, which attached a monetary penalty for teams spending beyond established thresholds. Each team was asked whether they would be willing to pay the luxury tax and the repeater tax. In 2011, new rules were ushered in that made high payrolls more costly. The repeater tax was an even more punitive levy that was reserved for a team that paid the tax in four out of five years. As a result, teams had become more cautious in spending, especially the best teams with the highest payrolls.

It certainly affected the Heat. Owner Micky Arison was one of just five owners who voted against the new rules and he publicly said he felt it was unfair to his team. While he still paid the luxury tax in three of the four years (a total of $34 million) James played in Miami, he'd curtailed spending and the Heat made a series of moves to shave payroll over James's last year there. James and his team believed competing at the highest level meant owners would have to eventually pay the luxury tax, and so he made it a prerequisite of his signing.

On July 4, Cavs general manager David Griffin drove over to meet with Paul and Termini. His presentation was more informal. He talked about locking up Kyrie Irving on a five-year deal. He talked about how Andrew Wiggins, the prized No. 1 pick, could be an ideal partner for James. He talked about the extra draft picks the team had, a cupboard stocked by previous GM Chris Grant, that could be used as bait to trade for veterans.

Yet as he delivered it, Griffin still wasn't sure the Cavs were truly in the running. Indeed, there had been some contact between Paul and the Cavs on this matter. Gilbert and Paul had direct discussions with each other, and at one point, Gilbert was a guest at Paul's Cleveland home. There were positive feelings and the impression of once bolted doors being unlocked. But nothing close to a promise. The Cavs, having been burnt by James in the past, were cautious in making any sort of leap. Griffin, a brand-new GM, had a brand-new coach and a franchise player with a brand-new contract, and none of them had to be tied to James at all.

That's why Griffin had been proceeding with other free agents. In addition to staying in touch with Hayward, he'd made some progress with the agent who represented Chandler Parsons and felt the Cavs could structure a deal that would enable them to have a chance to sign him. Griffin still was hedging that James probably would go back to the Heat, likely on a one-year contract, and he believed this meeting might lay the groundwork for 2015 when James could be on the market again.

During the meeting, Griffin was given the same two bullet points as those before him. He was easily able to commit to owner Dan

Gilbert spending. Gilbert had spent $43 million in luxury taxes during James's first tenure. His willingness to lay out cash was legendary within the NBA, whether it was on players, coaches (both current and fired), or even tossing money into trades as a sweetener. The Cavs facilities and services were among the best in the league. Their training facility on a wooded hillside overlooking the Cuyahoga River valley is five-star even by NBA standards. From multiple chef-cooked meals per day to having someone to start players' cars in the middle of the night so they'd be warm when the team plane arrived home from road trips in the winter, Gilbert left no frontier unexplored when it came to pampering his team.

But the second issue, the max contract, was a factor. At the time of the meeting, the Cavs didn't have enough salary-cap space to pay James the max. In another example of how the team wasn't expecting to really get James back, they'd added some salary around the draft two weeks earlier and weren't in position to sign him to the big number at that moment. Griffin told Paul and Termini that if James were to commit to coming, he'd make trades to create enough room. This was not well received. Griffin was told if the Cavs wanted to stay in the game, they had to have the cap space. It was like poker and this was the ante.

After the meeting with Griffin, Paul called co-owner Nate Forbes and asked him to help arrange a face-to-face meeting between Gilbert and James. James and Gilbert had hurt each other, and they hadn't spoken for four years. James had flown back to Miami from the Caribbean the night before, and Gilbert was in Detroit for the July Fourth weekend.

When he left the meeting, Griffin still didn't fully know where his team stood. When he got back to the office he huddled with his team and they started brainstorming ideas on how to trade players to create cap space. They had laid the groundwork with some other teams to make cap-space-clearing trades, but they had been exploratory talks. Now it was time to get serious. And it was time for Gilbert to book a trip to Florida.

On Sunday, July 6, Gilbert boarded his Gulfstream IV jet at a suburban Detroit airport and took off for Fort Lauderdale. As he was in the air, a Cleveland radio host tweeted that he was flying to South

Florida. Within minutes, reporters and fans had found his plane and its destination on tracking websites and speculation started flowing. Gilbert was going over what he planned to say to James as the plane traveled south when he heard the secret was out. His first move was to try to squash it, and he posted a lie on social media, saying he was actually in his backyard. Then he instructed his pilots to change the jet's destination from Fort Lauderdale–Hollywood International Airport to the more exclusive Fort Lauderdale Executive Airport, thirteen miles to the north.

"I had a bunch of notes that I was going over on the plane. I really needed to make sure I knew what we could do with the roster and everything and how much cap space we had," Gilbert said. "Then it got out and I was talking to the pilots on how we could change airports. There was some drama."

Gilbert took a car to a condominium where Paul had set the meeting. Paul and Termini had flown to Miami ahead of it. Gilbert came alone, as was requested, and wasn't sure who would be there to meet him other than James. Only James's inner circle was there.

It was not a time of tearful apologies. It was a part of the process Paul and James had decided needed to be done. There were no promises made. There were no contracts offered. It was a look-each-other-in-the-eye clearing of the air.

The night James left the Cavs in 2010 was discussed. James's *Decision* show where he announced his intention to sign in Miami had insulted and deeply offended Gilbert. Gilbert's angry letter later had insulted and deeply offended James. Gilbert used a line he'd crafted, telling James they'd had five good years together and one bad night. Then he shifted to the future, talking about the talent on the team, the new coach he'd hired, the new deal Irving was about to sign, and his promise to surround him with talent. The two shook hands. Paul said he would be in touch. Gilbert went back to the airport and flew home. The next day, he had his plane blocked from public tracking services.

"I had no idea how long we'd have to talk about the past. The answer was not long, maybe ten or fifteen minutes," Gilbert said. "I'd gone over this in my head many times, and it was more comfortable than

I thought it would be. We talked for two or three hours and that was it. I felt good about it and I thought we had a chance to get him to come back, but I didn't know what else he was doing or who else was bidding. When you're in something like this, you're always concerned about what you don't know."

On Monday, July 7, James filmed a commercial in Coral Gables, where he'd lived since moving to Miami. Later, he flew to Las Vegas, where he was planning to attend his annual Nike camp, the LeBron James Skills Academy, for top high school and college players. He was joined by Wade and some friends at Lavo, a pricey Italian restaurant inside the Palazzo hotel on the Strip. The fascination with their meeting was intense and the restaurant took advantage, putting out a press release saying they'd ordered steak and sea bass. In reality, it was not a strategy meeting but actually a large group that later adjourned to a nearby nightclub where one of James's other friends was DJing. There was no free agency discussion.

Meanwhile, back in Miami, the Heat made their first two moves of the offseason. As they waited on the decisions from their big free agents they agreed to a four-year, $23 million deal with free agent forward Josh McRoberts, who had played against them in the playoffs as a member of the Charlotte Bobcats that spring. They also signed veteran Danny Granger, a former All-Star forward whose career had been derailed by knee issues. These were seen as supplemental adjustments to replace some of the Heat role players who were retiring.

Paul remained in contact with the Heat but didn't invite them to Cleveland for meetings as he did the other teams. Because James had played there for the past four seasons, he didn't need to have as in-depth a presentation. Instead, the Heat were invited to come to Vegas for an in-person meeting with James that week during James's camp. The meeting was set for that Wednesday, July 9.

The Heat were uncomfortable as the days passed and their stars remained on the market, but Riley was always confident he could close. The Houston Rockets had made getting Bosh, a Texas native, a priority and offered him a four-year, $88 million max contract over the previous weekend. Bosh had been in Dubai riding camels, relaxing at a resort in the Maldives, and posing with elephants in Sri Lanka, and he had flown to Ghana to take part in a camp for NBA Africa. He waited for James's decision before making his own. Like everyone else in the process, he had guesses but no hard information from James and therefore had to leave his options open.

The Heat felt some relief when James started spending time with Wade, who intended to re-sign in Miami. James and Wade worked out together the day after their dinner at James's camp, which was held at a convention center north of downtown Vegas. James routinely worked out alongside high school and college players at his camp and often brought star friends to play in pickup games. Wade was still nursing sore knees but was able to spend time with James. Like everyone else, however, Wade was left to guess and try to read the situation as James was keeping his thoughts on free agency mostly to himself. Even though Wade had developed into an extended family member, he was not part of this decision. For his part, Wade decided he wouldn't actively attempt to recruit James to stay with him in Miami. By then, these two knew each other well enough that such a move would've felt shallow. James knew how Wade felt.

Paul let some of the other interested teams know that James was moving on from them. Within twenty-four hours, the Mavericks finalized a deal with free agent Chandler Parsons. Meanwhile, Hayward agreed to a four-year, $63 million deal with the Charlotte Hornets. Because he was a restricted free agent, the Utah Jazz matched the offer and retained him. Which probably would've happened with the Cavs as well. The Bulls, who had also pitched Anthony, started focusing on signing free agent Pau Gasol.

After the workout, James went to the Wynn, the hotel where he'd gotten comfortable as his base in Vegas over the years because that was the home for USA Basketball when he played with the team over four summers between 2006 and 2012. There he continued to seriously discuss the upcoming decision with Paul and Carter.

A topic throughout the process was how this choice might end up defining his legacy. Could going back to Cleveland put him in position to change the way millions felt about his career? It was also a type of challenge that he hadn't faced before—to be a part of the building of something and not just a hired gun, like he sometimes felt he was with the Heat. As they examined the options—which had essentially become Miami or Cleveland—the phrase that started to be used by the group was that going back to Cleveland would be "a legacy play."

James had paid close attention to the Cavs' moves. He knew a lot about their roster. One of the little hints he dropped was the previous fall when the Heat made a visit to Cleveland for a game. Miami won as the Cavs were off to a bad start in what would become a lost season, but James went out of his way to compliment the team. He praised Irving as "an incredible talent," and talked about how the Cavs "have some really good pieces." He knew that if he chose the Cavs he would have input on the roster, and his team started talking about those choices.

James didn't have much of a relationship with Irving. They'd been together at Team USA training camp in 2012 and both were represented by Nike. But Irving was more drawn to Kobe Bryant, whom he idolized. Nonetheless, James believed he could succeed with Irving because of his immense talent, and he believed he could mentor him. James never sought much counsel from older players when he came to the NBA but had come to enjoy mentoring younger players, whether they wanted it or not. Most did, as James had been in the league eleven years and many young players had grown up as fans of him.

But James felt he'd need a big man who could shoot to help him on the Cavs. The trio of him, Wade, and Bosh, a power forward who could defend centers and open floor space by shooting from outside, had been a championship fit in Miami. James and his friends discussed who could be that player in Cleveland with him. They came up with three names: LaMarcus Aldridge, Kevin Love, and Carmelo Anthony, who could play as a forward alongside James.

Aldridge was under contract in Portland and it wasn't clear the Cavs could trade for him. Anthony was in the process of a national free agent tour, visiting Chicago, Houston, Dallas, and Los Angeles. But James didn't think he'd leave New York, much less come to Cleveland. That brought them to Love, who was coming off his best season and was available on the trade market. And James knew the Cavs could get him. The concept had been brought up by Griffin and Gilbert. But they needed Love's support, something James thought he might be able to deliver.

The Cavs remained hopeful but were getting nervous. Channing Frye, another of their free agent hopes, agreed to a contract with the Magic. They were thrilled to be in it with James but nervous that they'd be left with no one to sign if he re-upped with the Heat. Meanwhile, the James camp's communications were giving them nothing solid. Instead, they kept asking why the Cavs hadn't cleared cap space for a max contract yet.

As the process was unfolding, Mendelsohn reached out to Lee Jenkins, a feature writer for *Sports Illustrated* who had done several cover profiles on James over the previous few years. In the spring, Jenkins and Mendelsohn had discussed how James might announce his free agency choice. Several months earlier, Jason Collins had used a first-person essay in the magazine to become the first active NBA player to announce he was openly gay. In addition, rookie-to-be Jabari Parker wrote an essay in *SI* announcing he was leaving Duke and turning pro.

Regardless of what James would do, handling the announcement was of paramount importance. James had been badly burned by the *Decision* broadcast in 2010, even though he and his team still believed it was a forward-thinking idea that put the power in the player's hands. It had raised seven figures for charity and changed the nature of the way athletes looked at making big announcements. The execution, however, was obviously flawed. In what had become a 140-character and soundbite world, James's utterance of "I'm taking my talents to South Beach" defined the entire ordeal and destroyed the chance to give the choice context. The handling of the drawn-out broadcast was also a mistake. Mendelsohn, who built his career working in the political arena, had worked with James to consider a way to improve on the presentation with the lessons of 2010.

Jenkins was asked to come to Vegas from his home in Los Angeles, though he wasn't told why or even promised an interview with James. If James decided to re-sign with the Heat, it might not have been seen as a choice that needed explanation. If he chose the Cavs, James knew he needed a way to explain his feelings with some depth and space. Jenkins booked a flight and took the forty-five-minute trip unsure of what he was going for.

On Wednesday, July 9, the Cavs finalized a three-team trade with the Boston Celtics and Brooklyn Nets. They traded Jarrett Jack and the remaining three years on his contract to Brooklyn. Jack had been a failed signing the year before, and getting his money, $6.3 million, off the team's books had suddenly become a priority. To do the deal, the Cavs had to pay with their 2016 first-round pick, which went to Boston. Also the team traded Tyler Zeller and Sergey Karasev, two of their young prospects, to shed salary. When the dust settled, the Cavs had dumped $9.5 million and reached enough cap space to sign a max player. Their ante was finally and officially in the middle of the table.

Shortly after the deal, Paul finalized a meeting with Gilbert and Forbes in Vegas the following day. Gilbert was in Sun Valley, Idaho, at the annual Allen & Co. Media Conference. This was a transitional place for Gilbert and James. The event for billionaires, CEOs, and politicians is one of the most exclusive gatherings every year. In 2009, Gilbert had arranged for James to be invited—Allen & Co. had helped arrange the Cavs purchase for Gilbert in 2004—and hoped to use the time to talk to James about a contract extension. The meeting didn't happen. The following year, Gilbert was in Sun Valley when James announced he was going to Miami, and he'd written his hot-blooded letter from there. Now here he was in Idaho again on the verge of getting him back.

That afternoon, Riley and Heat general manager Andy Elisburg arrived for their meeting with James. This was Riley's chance to make his personal case to James. His message included selling the stability of the Heat organization, which is almost unmatched in pro sports as Riley was in his twentieth year with the team, Elisburg was in his twenty-sixth, and coach Erik Spoelstra was in his nineteenth. The Cavs, meanwhile, had their third coach in three years and third GM in six years. Riley also talked about how he saw McRoberts and Granger, the new signees, fitting into the team alongside James's favorite player in the draft, Shabazz Napier.

As the meeting was going on, two large semis pulled up to James's mansion back in Coral Gables. They were from an Orlando-based exotic car transport company and they were there to load up some of James's cars to be shipped north, including the red Ferrari that he loved to drive around the city. James shipped some of his cars to Akron every summer, but with tension building as his free agent choice lingered, it jolted Heat fans.

When the meeting wrapped, James and Paul gave no hint to the Heat of their intentions. This unsettled Riley, who had hoped to close the deal. In the wake of it, both sides would have separate viewpoints. Riley felt like he'd wasted his time flying to Vegas when James had been in Miami for several days the previous week. There were also indications the Heat felt James had already made up his mind and was attempting to make Riley grovel. ESPN media personality Dan Le Batard, who is close with Riley, later said on his Miami radio show that Riley was offended that a World Cup soccer game was on television in James's hotel suite during the meeting and Riley felt he didn't even have everyone's full attention. In a press conference a year later, Riley made a vague but pointed reference to his opinion of James and his team's behavior during this period, saying it had been "smiling faces with hidden agendas."

Bottom line: Riley felt disrespected.

From James's perspective, Riley had been afforded a chance that no other team had. James didn't meet face-to-face with any of the other front offices. The Gilbert meeting didn't include Griffin. And James wanted to give Riley a chance to go last. In the immediate aftermath and years into the future, James and Paul insisted no final decision had been made when the Heat arrived for the meeting. James was indeed seriously considering a Cleveland return but was giving the Heat a final chance to make a compelling case, which supposedly Riley had always wanted.

Bottom line: James felt this was paying Riley respect.

Here was a reality that wasn't arguable: The years of competing for titles had exhausted the Heat of many of their assets to build a team. They were older, thinner, and had few options to add players. Especially when compared to the Cavs. Miami was at this disadvantage because it'd pressed so hard over the previous four years to surround

James with a championship team. But the Heat were not going to be given favored status for these past actions.

At that stage of his career, James had become all business when it came to his decision, the same way an organization might look at a once valued player who was cut or traded when he passed his prime. From James's perspective, he was holding the Heat to the same standard. In short, there was no home team discount being offered. Riley and Elisburg believed they could manage these challenges and keep the team in position to reach a fifth consecutive Finals. That was a feat that hadn't been accomplished since the 1960s, by the Boston Celtics, and with good reason—it's very hard to keep refreshing a team without taking a step back. But Riley and Elisburg's track record was strong and they had reason to believe in their plan. At that point, because of the circumstances, James needed to be blown away. Unlike in 2010, the Heat simply weren't able to do so. It wasn't the Heat's fault; they were competing for titles over the previous four years, while the Cavs, who had the worst cumulative record in the NBA over that span, were restocking. But it was the situation.

On July 10, 2014, James called a morning meeting in his hotel suite with his inner circle. After the Heat meeting the previous day, he told his friends that he was close to making up his mind but wanted to sleep on it. The group spoke for forty-five minutes, going over the situation one final time. At the end, James came to his choice. He would return to Cleveland.

The meeting broke up. James called his wife to tell her. Mendelsohn called Jenkins, who was in his room below. Jenkins took the elevator up to James's suite on the fifty-eighth floor. For the next twenty-four hours, he was going to be brought into the circle of trust.

As James ate breakfast, Jenkins interviewed him. James would assemble a first-person essay that would be published in *Sports Illustrated*, and Jenkins would help him write it. The goal was for James to be able to explain himself in full and not be subjected to chopped-up highlights from a press conference. In fact, he had decided there would be no press conference. Jenkins is a gifted and award-winning writer, but the thoughts were James's. He talked about how his four years were like a college experience, one he never had. He discussed what it was like to grow up in Northeast Ohio. He discussed his emotions the night he announced he was leaving Cleveland. Jenkins recorded the conversation, and it didn't last long. He immediately went to his room to transcribe James's words and start putting together the essay.

As Jenkins was holed up, James went to check in on his Nike camp. When he arrived, Wade was with him. Their presence there together a day after Riley had personally given his pitch suggested he was headed back to Miami. Just as the Cavs' deal the day before had rattled the Heat—there were questions about whether the Cavs had gained a commitment from James before making the deal—seeing Wade and James hanging out again left the Cavs wondering where they stood.

As James and Wade watched the teenagers, Gilbert and Forbes arrived at the suite and had a four-hour meeting with Paul. In particular, Paul told the Cavs what type of contract James would be signing. He would sign a one-year deal for $20.7 million and would retain a player option for a second season at $21.5 million.

This move stopped Gilbert and Forbes cold. It meant that James would retain not just maximum flexibility but maximum leverage. If he was unhappy with the Cavs or if they broke a promise—such as spending on the payroll—there was no long-term commitment to protect them. He could walk in a year. It was a massive power move, one made because of James's financial security and his realization of the market. Termini, who specialized in contract negotiation and construction, had intensely studied James's choices and believed projected increases in the salary cap for the next few years meant locking into a long-term deal in 2014 might cost James money. It might not be wise to be locked in for 2016, when a new television deal was expected to flood the league with new revenue and push salaries upward.

In 2012, after James's departure had reached the acceptance stage and Gilbert had a chance to do a postmortem, the owner believed he'd made a costly mistake. He accepted some fault that the franchise had been devastated when James left. He vowed he wouldn't let it happen again.

"The big lesson was if a player is not willing to extend [his contract], no matter who they are, no matter where they are playing, no matter what kind of season you had, you can't risk going into a summer and having them leave in unrestricted free agency and get nothing back for it," Gilbert said at the time. "It's not the player's fault. That's on ownership."

Now here he was, just a few years later, and Paul was telling him James would only be giving a one-year promise. No negotiation. Those were the terms. Gilbert and Forbes talked about it and tried to understand it. But ultimately the two veteran businessmen realized in this situation they had no leverage, and they agreed they'd be willing to do such a deal. At that point, Gilbert felt like he was on the verge of getting James to come back, and several times Gilbert pressed Paul to give him an answer so the team could start making preparations. Paul remained mum. Gilbert still didn't know for sure. James had already made his mind up—the Cavs were getting him back. Jenkins was writing it up. Paul still did not tip his hand.

"Rich was the best poker player ever. We had no idea what was really happening, and he played it straight down the middle," Gilbert said. "He said to me, 'Dan, we're in the decision cave right now.' I said, 'Rich, what's the decision cave? Is that next to the bat cave?'"

Downstairs, Jenkins toiled on the biggest assignment of his career. He wanted to make sure it was in James's voice. When James talked about his Heat teammates he used their nicknames, calling Udonis Haslem "UD," Bosh "CB," Mario Chalmers "Rio," and even Riley "Riles." He'd never written anything like it before, because the two most important paragraphs were at the end.

> In Northeast Ohio, nothing is given. Everything is earned. You work for what you have.
> I'm ready to accept the challenge. I'm coming home.

Jenkins finished the first draft of the essay within four hours, sent it to James's team, and waited for revisions and comments. He went to the hotel lobby to get some food and felt like he was suddenly in some sort of spy movie. He pulled his San Diego Padres hat down low over his eyes, concerned that he might bump into a reporter he knew and it might tip his hand.

While he was on his way back to his room, an attractive woman stopped him. She asked if he would be interested in having her tuck him into bed. Jenkins froze, his mind raced, and he started to think this was some agent sent to try to steal his secret. Maybe to try to drug him and grab his laptop. He had to shake himself to get back to reality—she was just a prostitute propositioning him, as happens all the time in Las Vegas. He took the snacks to his room, not the woman.

After watching the afternoon sessions of his camp, James went to McCarran International Airport and boarded a Nike-owned jet. Its destination was Miami, and Wade joined him on the flight, which had been previously arranged as he got a ride back home. Two days later, on Saturday, he was scheduled to go to Rio de Janeiro for the conclusion of the World Cup as part of a Nike promotion. On the plane were Nike personnel, some of James's staff, and Wade. As the plane traveled east as night fell, James reviewed and made some changes to Jenkins's first draft. But Wade was still not told.

"You can't ask Dwyane to carry that [secret]," Paul said. "He couldn't. It would've put him in a terrible position."

They arrived in Miami late and Wade and James hugged before getting in separate cars. A local Miami TV station captured footage of the arrival on the tarmac and fans immediately tried to break it down like the Zapruder film. Wade, however, felt James's distance and began to believe that indeed he was leaving to return to Cleveland. But like Gilbert, Griffin, Riley, and others, he went to bed not knowing for sure.

Back in Vegas, Jenkins worked through the night to finish the essay as a select few *Sports Illustrated* editors began preparing the release. A photo that had previously been used as a cover when James was named the magazine's Man of the Year in 2012 was repurposed with the headline "I'm Coming Home." Paul and James had a protocol they had to go through in the morning to inform people. A release was planned for around noon eastern time on Friday, July 11, 2014.

That morning, James called Wade and told him what his plans were. He sent a text to Bosh in Africa telling him. After he was criticized for his impersonal delivery of the bad news to the Cavs in 2010, James personally informed Arison and Riley what his intentions were, an interaction that would end up being burned into his brain for years.

At just after noon Eastern, Jenkins was advised that James was ready. Jenkins had the link. He was at the airport for a flight to Cleveland, where he would be working on a follow-up story. He'd barely slept. His fingers were shaking as he typed a tweet into his phone. At 9:17 a.m. in Vegas he tweeted the news and James's essay. Then he turned off his phone and boarded the plane.

Just as he'd done four years and three days earlier, Paul called the Cavs to inform them of James's decision. Gilbert was overwhelmed. At the end of the call, Gilbert asked Paul how James was going to announce the news.

"Don't worry, Dan," Paul said. "It's already out."

Chapter 5

ALL YOU NEED IS LOVE

By Vegas standards, July 11, 2014, was mild. It was still below 100 degrees in the morning when Trent Redden, the Cavs' assistant general manager, made a three-mile run from the team hotel in the Mandalay Bay complex down the perimeter of the airport to the Thomas & Mack Center on the UNLV campus. As is his tradition, he ran to Summer League practices and had given his phone to assistant coach Phil Handy as the team bus departed for the gym. A short time later, Redden arrived at UNLV, sweating and disconnected, to some excited staff members.

Mark Cashman, the team's longtime equipment manager, looked at Redden and raised his eyebrows. For a man who rarely shows emotion—Cashman's nickname is "Cobra"—this meant something was up. Koby Altman, the team's director of player personnel, held up his own phone and asked Redden, "Is this real?" Redden sprinted onto the floor to get to Handy, interrupting a drill he was running, and asked for his phone. It was ringing. Nate Forbes, the part owner who only a day before had left a meeting with James's agent unsure of what would happen, was calling.

Yes, it was real. Then came the screams.

Eighteen hundred miles away inside Cleveland Clinic Courts, the Cavs' suburban practice facility, David Griffin found himself on his knees inside his office. The building was mostly empty, as all the coaches, staff, and front office members were in Vegas for the start of Summer League games that night. A television was tuned to

SportsCenter, which was reading James's letter. The walls around him were made out of magnetic whiteboards that were covered in plates with players' names and scenarios written in grease marker. Some of them were dreams. Dreams for this moment.

Griffin was still trying to come to grips with the news and what the next steps would be, sending texts and talking to staff, when a call came in. It was from Jeff Schwartz, Kevin Love's agent. The Cavs had been making trade pitches to the Minnesota Timberwolves for Love for more than a year. At that moment, the Timberwolves were in negotiations with the Golden State Warriors surrounding him. Cleveland hadn't been a realistic option. But the world had just changed.

As Love, like the rest of the NBA world, was digesting the huge news James had just made, he too got an unexpected call. It was James. The two knew each other from their time together during the 2012 Team USA experience, a typical two-month crash course that creates fast bonds because international travel and security keep the players together virtually all the time. Love and James weren't particularly close. James palled around with Chris Paul and Carmelo Anthony in London, while Love spent time with his UCLA teammate Russell Westbrook, among others. In fairness, Love wasn't particularly close to many of his teammates throughout his career, a personality trait that sometimes led to criticisms of him as an ineffective leader, as the Wolves never made the playoffs with him on the roster. The bottom line was Love and James weren't friends but they had a relationship. More important, they'd played and practiced together and had some understanding of each other's games.

James told Love he wanted him to come to Cleveland and that he felt they could be great complementary pieces. Many in the NBA would've quickly agreed, a good-shooting big man is an ideal teammate for James, as Chris Bosh had proven the previous few seasons in Miami. Also, Love's strong rebounding and ability to throw excellent outlet passes to start fast breaks seemed like it could add an element James had never enjoyed before. Of course, a trade would have to be arranged, and that was not an insignificant hurdle. But before that could even get serious, Love and James needed to have this conversation. And it was James who was instigating it.

Love had been displeased with several things in his six seasons in Minnesota. Though the rules somewhat forced their hand, the Wolves prioritized the future of young guard Ricky Rubio while in contract extension talks with Love in 2012, leading him to sign a three-year extension instead of the five-year deal he wanted. That moment essentially started his slow march out of town over the following seasons. Previous general manager David Kahn bungled a number of draft picks, trades, and free agent moves, which disillusioned not just Love and many fans but even the owner, who put the team up for sale. But the Wolves became frustrated at Love's injury history, including when he broke two bones in his hand doing knuckle push-ups at his house the fall after signing his extension. Questions about that injury lingered longer than the breaks did.

While Love had deep West Coast ties—he grew up in Oregon and played collegiately in Los Angeles—he tried his best to make it clear that what he really wanted was to be on a winning team. That would be a case he'd have to repeat numerous times, but it was a stance he never dropped. And the call from James was a transitional moment in his life.

"I'm in," Love told James on the phone.

The Cavs' situation had been dramatically altered in just a few hours. Their team with a single and still-developing franchise player in Kyrie Irving, an experimental coach brought over from Israel in David Blatt, and a collection of young prospects and future draft picks was now transformed. Now they had one of the best players in league history coming back and working to bring another All-Star with him. The team's plans and timelines were shoved into the garbage. A completely new reality was staring them in the face.

The excitement from the fan base was of course extraordinary—season tickets sold out within ten hours of James's announcement—and the NBA began remaking its schedule with its television partners to turn the Cavs into a feature attraction. There were headlines across the world, and quickly the concept that Love could be coming too made it into the media, with *SportsCenter* using graphics and salary-cap experts to illustrate exactly how the Cavs could construct a trade to bring him in. Those trades all included Andrew Wiggins, who that night was making his debut wearing a Cavs uniform in a Summer

League game against the Milwaukee Bucks, who were debuting No. 2 pick Jabari Parker.

James's *Sports Illustrated* letter, which quickly received heavy praise for its tact and tone, included references to a number of Cavs teammates he was looking forward to playing with. Wiggins's name was omitted. James's team attempted to quell speculation that a Wiggins-for-Love deal was implied by this omission, saying there was no such message intended. But that was not entirely true. James was interested in playing with Wiggins and hoped the Cavs would find a way to trade for Love without needing to trade Wiggins. But that was unlikely and James and his agents knew it. James had rushed to call Love. He never spoke to Wiggins. And therefore Wiggins's name was not in the letter.

Below the layer of hype, the Cavs front office was trying to come to grips with what exactly they'd been presented. Though James's words about coming home were moving, he was essentially signing a one-year contract. Love was now only under contract for one more season, and trading the No. 1 pick for him plus other assets was an unacceptable risk. One thought that came up was if Love wanted to play with James, as he was now saying, why not wait until the following summer when the Cavs might be able to clear enough cap space to sign him outright as a free agent?

In James's letter he wrote, "I'm not promising a championship. I know how hard that is to deliver. We're not ready right now. No way. Of course, I want to win next year, but I'm realistic. It will be a long process, much longer than it was in 2010. My patience will get tested. I know that."

But here was James looking to bring in Love and yet only committing to a one-year deal. That was not a process, that was a mandate: Let's go now! Griffin, Gilbert, Forbes, and the rest of the Cavs front office had to grapple with this sudden situation. This is what they said they'd wanted, to accelerate the team's makeover. Now they were mainlining jet fuel but were tentative on tapping the afterburners, worried going too fast came with dangers. If this all blew up in their faces, a year later they could be right back where they were in 2010. They were elated at James's decision, but there were still only the seedlings of trust. And as for Love, there was no relationship there at all.

As Griffin sat in his office and conferenced in his staff and his bosses, he soon realized what must be done. He'd talked again to Flip Saunders, the Wolves' president, and quickly understood the landscape. The Wolves thought they had a deal with the Golden State Warriors as they advanced in discussions to trade Love for a package including young star Klay Thompson. A deal was nearly finalized when team adviser Jerry West threatened ownership he'd resign if the Warriors ownership allowed such a trade. New coach Steve Kerr was also against a deal. It threw Love back into limbo and left him on the market.

Just as he wouldn't bend on Thompson, Saunders was only willing to trade Love if he got Wiggins in a package back. The Cavs had to pick a path; they could not straddle the fence. And James was yanking them toward going for broke now. They'd gotten themselves in James's poker game, and now they were on the verge of going all in.

Before committing, the Cavs asked if they could have an in-person meeting with Love. Usually something like that would've been prohibited by league rules. But the Wolves, getting excited at the prospect of landing Wiggins as the foundation of their rebuilding process, granted formal permission. And so yet another vital step to the Cavs' future was planned, and once again it went down in the NBA's summer capital, Las Vegas.

The next few days turned into a whirlwind. James finalized his contract the same day the letter came out, signing it in Miami before reboarding the Nike jet to fly to Rio for a weekend of appearances around the World Cup final. Meanwhile, in addition to Love, James started doing full-time recruiting elsewhere. When Griffin had pitched James's agents the week before, James had a list of free agent shooting specialists he thought would be a good fit. He'd contacted many of them during the free agent process.

One of them was Mike Miller, the veteran wing who'd played with James for three years in Miami. A year earlier, Miller had been released by the Heat in a cost-cutting move and because he'd been injury-plagued, needing five surgeries for hand and shoulder issues plus back problems. When he was put on waivers by the Heat, the

Cavs seriously considered claiming him and bringing him to Cleveland. Not just because he was a veteran shooter, but because then general manager Chris Grant was launching his "get LeBron back" plan, and having Miller, a close friend of James, might've helped.

Miller, though, wanted no part of Cleveland. His own powerful agent, Arn Tellem, asked the Cavs not to claim him. Miller even leaked a story to the media that he might need back surgery, which wasn't true, to try to deter the Cavs from grabbing him. Ultimately the Cavs decided to pass and Miller went on to sign as a free agent in Memphis, where he had a great season and played in all 82 games.

Now, a year later, Miller was on the verge of signing with the Denver Nuggets, and Griffin didn't think he had enough money left at that point to outbid them. And he wasn't sure Miller wanted to play in Cleveland. After a call from James, however, things quickly turned. By the end of the weekend as James was getting ready to come home from Brazil, Miller was agreeing to a deal with the Cavs.

A day later, Griffin closed a deal with James Jones, another veteran shooter whom Griffin had a relationship with from when both were with the Suns. Jones had also become close with James over the previous four years with the Heat. Nicknamed "Champ," Jones was highly respected in the league not so much as a player but as a leader—he was a high-ranking member of the players' union—and a tone setter. A diligent worker, he was always one of the first to arrive and the last to leave the facility, plus he was always willing to pull younger players aside.

While Griffin was happy to make the deal, Jones was also a symbolic signing. He is from Miami, played in college at the University of Miami, and played with the Heat for the previous six years. In 2010, he restructured his contract to help the team make salary room for James. He was seen as a future coach or front office member, perhaps with the Heat. And he was coming to Cleveland with James. The Cavs roster was filling with talent, experience, and James's influence.

The next step was important. Love, his agent, Griffin, and Gilbert assembled in Vegas for a sitdown. Love wanted to come play with James. The Cavs wanted him, seeing the formation of a "big three" with Irving. This was the formula that had been winning titles for teams for decades—three stars at different positions. But what to do about the situation, with Love headed into the last year of his contract? How could the Cavs be comforted that Love wouldn't leave in a year to play for the Lakers or the Suns or the Blazers? How could Love be sure to protect himself in case the fit wasn't good?

As soon as the meeting opened, Schwartz made one position clear: Love would be expecting a max contract offer from the Cavs the following year if a trade went through. The Cavs understood the position, though they legally couldn't agree to the terms at that point. The team had its preference, but stopped short of making it a demand.

Love had a player option for the 2015–16 season in his contract, which was for $16.7 million, and the Cavs wanted him to pick it up as part of the trade process so he'd be under contract for the following two seasons. Something similar took place back in 2011 when the New Orleans Hornets traded Chris Paul to the Los Angeles Clippers. The Clippers wouldn't do the deal without Paul picking up his player option, ensuring he was under contract for the following two years. The Cavs felt they had precedent and, with the price being asked and Love's apparent quest to play on a (suddenly) winning team, that it was a reasonable ask.

But Love and Schwartz weren't willing. Much of it was purely economic; projections for increases in the salary cap showed that Love might cost himself $3 million or more by opting in and not becoming a free agent and signing a brand-new deal. These projections were also the central reason why James only signed a one-year deal with the Cavs. As for Love making a "promise" he'd re-sign with the Cavs in a year, that was out as well.

It's strictly against league rules for players and teams to come to agreements on contracts before they are free agents. So-called "wink-wink" deals certainly take place. But if those making them are caught, the league has been known to hand down franchise-destroying penalties. In 2000, the Wolves were caught in an under-the-table deal with former No. 1 overall draft pick Joe Smith, where the two sides inexplicably signed a document that was later unearthed in a lawsuit between agents. Minnesota was stripped of five first-round draft picks, fined $3.5 million, and the owner and general manager were suspended for a season. So this was not an option for the Cavs and Love, especially given how high-profile this situation was.

Outside of the accounting, though, Love expressed his future commitment to the Cavs. In his mind, he wasn't coming to Cleveland for a year, he was coming for the long term. He was sincere, or so it seemed, and focused on wanting to be on a championship contender and playing with James. So, while no explicit agreement was reached and taking care to stay within NBA rules, they reached an uneasy and unofficial understanding. Love expressed that he didn't want to leave the Cavs high and dry; if things didn't go well during the 2014–15 season, he said he'd be willing to revisit picking up the player option, which he had until the following June to do. If the parties wanted to part either during the season or the next summer, this would give the Cavs a chance to trade him. Under the challenges presented, this was probably the most reasonable scenario.

"I asked a lot of people what we should do and some people just came up to me," Gilbert said. "When I was in Las Vegas for the meeting, I was at dinner and a college coach I didn't even know came up to my table. He said 'Love is a no-brainer, you have to do it.' There were people making the argument to me to keep Wiggins. We thought he was going to be a stud and he brought us things we didn't have, especially on defense. Ultimately it was Griff's decision. You have to go with your basketball guy. He's been doing it twenty years. He felt Love was the way to go."

The Cavs had one additional request, and it was a hard one for Love to accept. They didn't want him to play for Team USA that summer, a year when the 2012 gold medalist was a lock to play on the team that was going to Spain to play in the World Cup of Basketball. Love cherished his time with Team USA in the Olympics two years earlier. But now with so much riding on the 2014–15 season, there were concerns an injury would totally derail their plans.

Love ultimately agreed and USA Basketball ended up putting out an odd and opaque statement saying Love was pulling out "because of his current status," without saying exactly what that status was. It was really because of his informal future commitment to the Cavs, even though he was still a Timberwolf at the time. A week later, Indiana

Pacers star Paul George suffered a horrific broken leg during an exhibition game while playing for Team USA. Everyone felt terrible for George. The Cavs privately were relieved they'd requested Love stay home.

All this was happening as Wiggins was playing games in a Cavs jersey at the Vegas Summer League. As the top pick, he was a marquee attraction, and he was being asked in interviews about playing alongside James. After he was drafted, the Cavs requested that they hold off on signing him because it gave them some salary-cap benefits. Wiggins agreed and the Cavs took out insurance to make sure he was covered in case of any injury before signing. Now the fact that he wasn't signed was suddenly extremely relevant.

Six days after James signed, on July 17, rumors that the Cavs had made Wiggins available in trade talks with the Wolves hit the media. The report was a little premature; the Wolves had only granted permission for the Cavs to speak to Love.

It was clear Wiggins believed the rumors. In a moment that would repeat itself several times in the future, Wiggins seemed mad in a game that night against the Houston Rockets—mad, it seemed, at the Cavs for deciding to trade him. He relentlessly attacked the basket and repeatedly drew shooting fouls.

At one point, after he'd turned the ball over on another quasi-reckless drive, he sprinted full speed down the floor to swat what looked like an easy basket in a "chasedown"-style block that James had made famous. With Summer League in its dog days, it was striking to see Wiggins play at a different speed than everyone else. When it was over, he'd set a Summer League record by getting to the foul line 20 times. It turned out to be the last game he would ever play in a Cavs uniform. As the trade became realistic, the Cavs pulled Wiggins from their last Summer League game to protect him from any injury that could've halted what was now a full-speed train to get Love to Cleveland.

Wiggins's agent, Bill Duffy, went to his client and told him he was about 90 percent sure he was going to be traded. Duffy had been working with Saunders all summer. Duffy and Saunders were close, Saunders once hosting Duffy on a recruiting visit at the University of Minnesota when both were teenagers. Duffy also represented the

Warriors' Thompson, and he'd been on the front lines of those discussions involving Saunders. So when Saunders felt he was in range on making a deal for Wiggins, Duffy was well aware.

"It was a way for Andrew to understand that he now was in the business of basketball," Duffy said. "He knew that at the end of it he was going to be playing professional basketball and he was going to get his contract. He also knew that he had to act like a professional and not talk about it publicly, which is what he did."

The haggling lasted another few days, and soon a package was agreed to. Anthony Bennett, the 2013 No. 1 overall pick who'd had a miserable rookie year, would go to Minnesota. Wiggins, the Cavs' prized pick who only a few weeks ago was being counted on to be a foundational piece, would be traded with him. Cleveland would also send the Wolves the Miami Heat's 2015 first-round pick, the last piece of silver the Cavs had from the James sign-and-trade deal back in 2010. It was symbolic in a way that the Cavs were using something they got from the Heat to help rebuild the team around James, and a fact that only rubbed salt in the wounds in Miami.

It was an excellent haul for the Wolves but not something the Cavs were focusing on. It came with a tinge of melancholy, losing Wiggins, plus what they were going to have to put him through over the following month.

Never before had anything like this ever happened, a No. 1 overall pick traded just a few weeks after being selected. Making it more difficult, the rules and pacing of the summer schedule weren't designed for such a situation, which ended up making it miserable for the nineteen-year-old Wiggins.

The Cavs had explored trades where they could have executed the deal immediately, but the Wolves wanted to take back as little salary as possible. That meant the Cavs would need to sign Wiggins so his salary could be used to make the trade work under league rules. NBA trades require the exchanging salaries be within 25 percent of each other, and draft picks who haven't signed don't count. There is another rule that says draft picks can't be traded until thirty days after they sign.

Finally, on July 24, Wiggins signed a four-year, $24.8 million contract with the Cavs knowing that he'd never play for them. The Cavs then did what James had essentially done with his letter two weeks earlier—they scrubbed Wiggins from as many promotional materials as possible while at the same time refusing to publicly discuss Love. Within a week, Wiggins's Cavs jersey had been discontinued at the NBA's website.

In early August, Wiggins had to go through an uncomfortable week at the league's rookie transition program in New York, wearing Cavs jerseys for photos even though he knew he was being traded. He attended a required photo session for the league's official trading cards despite the fact that the pictures would soon be obsolete. He did an interview with *SportsCenter* and had to deal with the uncomfortable questions. He summed it up by saying, "I just want to play for a team that wants me. So, whichever team wants me, I'll play for."

By the second week in August the pretense that Love wasn't already a Cav had essentially been dropped. Glen Taylor, the Wolves' owner, said in an interview that Love would be traded on August 23. Though he didn't say where, that was the first date Wiggins was eligible to be dealt, and it was clear.

When the deal was official, Taylor fired off a few salvos to kick Love on the way out the door. "I think he's around a couple guys who are awful good," he said. "Now, I'm not saying that Kevin's not good, but I think where maybe he got away with some stuff, not playing defense on our team, I'm not sure how that's going to work in Cleveland. So I would guess they're going to ask him to play more defense. And he's foul-prone. I question if this is going to be the best deal for Kevin because I think he's going to be the third player on a team. I don't think he's going to get a lot of credit if they do really well. I think he'll get the blame if they don't do well. He's going to have to learn to handle that."

Taylor also questioned the Cavs for being interested in a player who missed 112 games due to injury in his six years in Minnesota, though he averaged 26 points and 12.5 rebounds per game in his last season there.

On August 8, James took part in a formal welcoming party when more than 25,000 fans attended a rally at the University of Akron's football stadium. The event was wrapped around James's annual foundation gathering, which was aimed at keeping at-risk children in his hometown in school. It was his first public appearance since re-signing with the Cavs.

The evening was emotional and highly produced. After several speakers, James emerged like a boxer with his family as an entourage as he performed a slow lap around the stadium waving to fans. Awing the crowd, singer Skylar Grey suddenly appeared onstage with a grand piano to play her hit song "I'm Coming Home," which had become an anthem of sorts for James over the previous month.

James then took the stage and made a speech, which he concluded with "I love you, I'm back." He dropped the microphone on the stage and immediately a fireworks show started over the stadium, completing the moment.

But he also made it clear that night that he'd soon have a new teammate, Love, even if it was supposed to be a forbidden topic, openly saying, "I'm going to be very excited to have him."

Meanwhile, Love kept a low profile and wasn't able to talk to anyone about what was happening. To pass time, he started working through a list of the 250 greatest movies of all time, watching 40 of them. He watched every episode of *Seinfeld*. He later said he felt like he was in purgatory.

The ruse mercifully ended on August 23 as the Cavs and Wolves made the deal official. It had been settled for so long that the Wolves had already agreed to trade the draft pick the Cavs were sending them to Philadelphia for veteran forward Thaddeus Young, another player who found himself caught in bureaucracy of waiting for the moment when Wiggins was eligible to be traded.

Three days later, Love arrived for his press conference wearing a dark three-piece suit with a lavender tie. He'd been in Cleveland for days already. He had already found a place to live, an apartment in a high-end downtown building, because he'd had weeks to look. Smiling with his new jersey, No. 0, Love said he was committed to being in Cleveland for the long term, a mantra he would repeat over and over for the next eleven months.

It had been a hundred days since the end of the season, a little over three months since Griffin had officially been made the general manager. Only weeks earlier the team was getting told no by their top coaching candidates, and were politely told to forget about trading for Love. They'd even put their elaborate plan of getting James on a back burner.

"We seem to be doing quite a bit of these this summer and I think it's a good thing," Griffin said with a smile as he kicked off Love's introductory press conference. "This is an exciting time for the franchise. This is really special for all of us."

The memory of Griffin sitting in the same spot explaining why the team had fired another coach and talking brashly about the team's plans had already faded from memory.

Target acquisition mode indeed.

Chapter 6

IN THE DARK

On the first day of training camp in September 2014, LeBron James asked new coach David Blatt if he could hold a players-only meeting before practice. Blatt hadn't planned for it and it put him behind in his practice schedule for his first day. But he granted the request, and for more than a half hour, Blatt and his coaches and staff wandered around the floor killing time as James spoke to his new teammates.

James had two primary messages. One was to set a tone that when issues came up during the season, it was vital to keep them in house. He knew from experience there would be intense media coverage and essentially wanted no leaks. James himself, though, didn't always follow this mandate. Then he went player to player and told them what he expected their role to be on the team. Role definition is important in the NBA; players desire clarity. It's not uncommon for roles to be discussed in front of the group, and the veterans had been through these sessions before. Only never was a player leading the meeting, it was always the coach. James had put a lot of thought into his comments, and he had a role for everyone, even the young camp invitees who were there primarily as practice bodies.

James never would've attempted something like this in his first tenure with the Cavs. It was his way of showing confidence and leadership. Whether he intended it or not, though, it also sent a message about the coach. James didn't wait to see if Blatt was going to say these things; he did it first.

After he'd signed, James spent almost no time with Blatt during the summer. They didn't meet face-to-face for nearly a month afterward. It happened on the set of the movie *Trainwreck* in New York City. James talked with Blatt between scenes. He told him that he'd been watching film of Blatt's offense on YouTube.

James's early days with new coaches had sometimes been trying. His first weeks with Mike Krzyzewski, who coached him over four summers with Team USA, were rocky. His first months with Miami Heat coach Erik Spoelstra were a challenge, and even after they'd won two titles together, their relationship remained sensitive. James was hard on coaches, even those with lots of NBA experience.

James also was great for them. He'd been a reason they'd gotten contract extensions, awards, or their next job. Not to mention rings and medals. Generally, most found it a palatable and profitable bargain, even if some days were miserable. Mike Brown, who coached James for five years, said he appreciated James "allowing me to coach him." He was questioned for that sentiment and called weak in some circles. But it was a comment based in reality.

During Summer League the previous July, Cavs executives had been impressed with Blatt's coaching, both in games and practices. He had a different yet skilled way of teaching and running plays, and it was refreshing. After games when the front office would have debriefing sessions at Vegas restaurants, they started to believe they indeed had found a possible difference-making coach. Then again, he was coaching rookies and free agents, and the star he'd tried to bond with, Andrew Wiggins, had been traded.

Blatt thought his forays into almost every league in Europe prepared him for anything. But he'd never dealt with a force like James, and it became evident that first day. As Blatt struggled a little bit in the early going, he sometimes made it worse with behavior that ruffled players, and he and James failed to develop a reliable working relationship.

Just two weeks into camp, the team departed on what promised to be a bonding experience. After a home preseason game, the team took a chartered 777 from Cleveland on an overnight flight to Rio de Janeiro. But instead of sleeping, many players gathered around the first-class cabin in the wide-body jet telling stories and laughing for much of the ten-hour trip. Kevin Love later described it as being like the first day of school.

Their first morning in the city found James exercising along Copacabana Beach in what looked like a shoe commercial coming to life. Here was James running along the coastline with a pack of joggers, some perhaps recognizing him and others just wondering what the commotion was, growing behind him. He followed it with a beach workout with Tristan Thompson and Dion Waiters, the team's mercurial guard, whom James had made a personal project.

The Cavs were in Brazil to play an exhibition as part of the NBA's Global Games series, where they export teams each preseason. But it was awkward—the Miami Heat were in town too. James had broken some of the ice a month before when he attended Dwyane Wade's wedding at a castle in Miami with most of the Heat franchise also in attendance, but it was still uncomfortable.

As he evaluated his former teammate's new situation, Chris Bosh gave it a dose of knowing skepticism. Bosh, who re-signed with the Heat after James left, was closely watching Love's situation. Bosh's game is similar to Love's, and in some ways so is his laid-back demeanor. He predicted Love would be in for some challenges, much like Bosh was when he was thrust from a starring role into a supporting role next to James four years earlier.

"It's going to be very difficult for him," Bosh told Bleacher Report in an interview that week. "Even if I was in his corner and I was able to tell him what to expect and what to do, it still doesn't make any difference. You just get your entree and that's it. It's like, wait a minute, I need my appetizer and my dessert and my drink, what are you doing? And my bread basket. What is going on? I'm hungry! It's a lot different."

It echoed the warning Timberwolves owner Glen Taylor issued when he traded Love to Cleveland. Taylor predicted Love would be a target for blame as the third wheel.

Running practices in an antiquated Rio gymnasium that reminded him of some of the dank spaces he used to work in at his lesser stops in Europe, Blatt seemed to be at ease. The early returns from the players on Blatt, just as with Cavs management, seemed positive. Players had prepared themselves for some of the authoritarian Blatt they'd heard about from European contacts, but that wasn't who they were encountering.

Blatt had gone to Princeton, where he studied literature and played under Pete Carril, who is credited with perfecting the Princeton offense with all its backcuts and ball movement. Blatt was not a stand-out player by any means; his stats were anemic and he couldn't even shoot free throws. But Carril trusted him and he knew the game. Blatt was named captain as a senior.

In the first weeks of the preseason, Blatt was teaching his players what essentially could be termed a modified Princeton-style offense, which used some of Carril's principles but was geared for more talented players. Though the Princeton offense is hardly a revolutionary concept, players hadn't quite seen anything like it.

"His offensive stuff is borderline genius," Mike Miller said after a few days of practice. "It takes a little time, but you see why he's done such a good job leading teams to championships. He's a good coach."

"People always say the Princeton when you have four guys above the free throw line. A lot of teams have played it in the past," James said. "There's a lot more options to this than I'm used to seeing."

During the preseason game in Rio, the Cavs ran some of Blatt's plays to perfection. Much of the action was set up that night for center Anderson Varejão, the Brazilian native who was being honored during the team's time in his home country. Varejão joined the Cavs in 2004 and quickly made a name for himself as a hustler and rebounder but also as a flopper. He was one of the best in the league at exaggerating contact. He'd been with the team for ten years now and was popular for his style of play and his mop of curly reddish-brown hair.

At one point during the game James appeared for a moment to forget which team he was on. While playing defense, he jumped out and essentially screened new teammate Matthew Dellavedova while former teammate Norris Cole had the ball as he'd done hundreds of times over the previous few seasons. Dellavedova was certainly caught off guard. But James said it was just a miscommunication on a basic defensive maneuver—which was certainly possible—and mocked anyone who thought differently.

"Non-basketball people, they like to critique everything that I do," James said. "It's stupid."

James's experience told him, however, the critiques were just beginning and plenty more would be arriving when the team got back to the United States. And he was right.

The first game of the 2014–15 season was momentous. The restaurants and bars in Cleveland were packed. ESPN set up a stage on West 4th Street, a popular pedestrian plaza, for a day full of coverage. A new ten-story-tall Nike billboard featuring James was installed across the street from the arena four years after the previous iconic banner was quickly disassembled after James's free agency departure. On the new one, James's arms are spread with his back to the street and "Cleveland" across the back of his uniform. During the day, hundreds of fans posed for photos in front of the football-field-sized structure. The energy in the arena at tip-off, where James caused a frenzy when he brought back his once signature move of tossing chalk into the air, was extraordinary.

The game, however, did not live up to the moment. The Cavs played sloppily and were out-executed by the visiting New York Knicks. Carmelo Anthony, who had re-signed with the Knicks the previous summer, outplayed his friend James and the Cavs lost, 95–90. James had 17 points, well below his standard, and turned the ball over eight times, including two in the fourth quarter that crushed his team's chances.

Then, in an event that would become commonplace, James and Blatt seemed to be on different pages when it came to reviewing what happened. Blatt suggested, reasonably, that the emotions of the night had affected James negatively. James, a veteran of many emotional games, denied it and said unfamiliarity with teammates caused most of the issues.

The team flew to Chicago after the game for the next night against the Bulls. Late the next morning, the team had a breakfast meeting in a hotel ballroom, standard for such situations. As the team went over film and that evening's game plan, Blatt chided the players for their poor play the night before. His tone was harsh and perhaps a bit aggressive for it being the second day of the season, but not something out of the ordinary for a coach upset over a poor regular-season performance.

That night, the Cavs did play much better, starting with James. He was more under control and confident, scoring 36 points as the Cavs won, 114–108, in overtime. The Bulls were expected to be a team that would compete with the Cavs to win the Eastern Conference. So this was a quality victory, even though the Bulls lost star Derrick Rose with a sprained ankle.

James waited for Blatt at the final buzzer and congratulated him on his first win with a hug. When Blatt arrived in the locker room he praised the team for executing much better than the previous game and concluded his remarks with "good for you" as he turned to leave. In unison, players called for him to stop. Irving had grabbed the game ball and had it ready for Blatt. The players gathered around him as Irving presented it and they began rubbing Blatt's head in a sign of congratulations.

"That was a big win for him," Thompson said. "We messed up his hairdo."

"That's his first NBA win," Irving said. "He deserves the game ball. It's his first time in the NBA. I call him the virgin of the NBA."

Blatt did not feel like a virgin, though. Not at all. A few moments later he stepped into the hall to meet with the media and attempted to fix his hair.

"You know, I didn't even think about it," he said regarding his first win. "That was so beautiful what LeBron did right after the game, what the team did in the locker room."

He could've left it there. It was a nice gesture from team to coach, a bonding moment. But Blatt had something he wanted to point out and he did.

"You know, the funny thing about that is, not all of you know me that well, but I've probably won about 700 games in my career. Just none of them have been here," he said. "So, it was a little bit odd on one hand, but that's the first NBA game and that's a bit of history for my friends and my family, and I'm glad I did it with the Cleveland Cavaliers."

Since the day he'd been hired, Blatt had routinely pointed out how his experience in Europe was applicable to the NBA. He frequently told players how certain situations were similar to those in Europe. While these were valid points, in general European accomplishments were not valued greatly in the NBA. Not only did few fans or players track what happened in the EuroLeague, but it was regarded as a lesser league. This was in part because over the previous decade numerous players who'd been stars in Europe had come to the NBA and struggled. Blatt's European success, fair or not, was deemed to have been achieved in a minor league.

Blatt's sentiment somewhat undercut what the players had done to make the night special. The divide between him and the players on this issue ended up becoming symbolic. Players viewed Blatt essentially as a rookie NBA coach. Blatt saw himself as experienced as any of the head coaches in the league—actually, one of the most experienced in the world.

Then Blatt said something else that would become a touchstone. He said he'd ripped into the players during that morning meeting at the hotel and that the team had "responded beautifully" to his lashing. When the locker room opened for interviews, instead of the focus being the bounce-back win and how the team had celebrated earning the coach his first victory, players were being asked about how Blatt's morning speech had led to their better play.

"He got on us from the time we started our meeting to the time we left. And it's great. For a team like us, we need that. I love constructive criticism," James said as he soaked his feet in ice after the game. "I never took it personal. It's just an opportunity for us to get better, and it definitely put a fire into us."

James and others were diplomatic. But privately they wondered how the subject had become Blatt's speech from twelve hours earlier. The joy of victory in the league is often fleeting, part of the nature of the relentless schedule, and the Cavs were facing a three-game western trip. But the joy of this win diminished more quickly than usual and players were wondering about the way Blatt handled what should've been a good night.

That too proved to be an indicator of things to come.

The team flew to Portland to open their first long trip and were blown out, 101–82, by the Trail Blazers. As the game unfolded, James

began to disconnect from his teammates. Irving and Waiters kept taking shots out of the flow of the offense and at times essentially stopped
making passes. James watched with growing dismay and eventually
started what looked like a boycott. As the Blazers built a huge lead,
he started standing in the corner, a few feet from the Cavs bench,
watching Waiters and Irving bomb away. He didn't say a word and
sometimes would run to the spot without even looking back to see if
someone wanted to pass him the ball.

Blatt called several timeouts, but nothing he said in the huddle
seemed to change anything. When it was over, James had gone score-
less in the second half and taken just four shots. He finished the game
with 11 points, his fewest in a regular-season game in nearly six years.
Irving had taken 10 second-half shots, missing eight. Waiters had
taken nine, missing six. Neither had an assist. Of the team's six assists
in the second half, James had three of them.

James didn't display anger in the locker room. The mood was downtrodden. Dellavedova sat on the training table getting his knee examined. He'd sprained it. James looked around and made some rather
somber proclamations as he tried to explain why he'd been so passive.

"It's going to be a long process, man. There's been a lot of losing
basketball around here for a few years," he said. "There's a lot of bad
habits; a lot of bad habits have been built up over the last couple of
years and when you play that style of basketball it takes a lot to get it
up out of you."

James had just witnessed what had driven coach Mike Brown
mad the year before: Irving and Waiters ball hogging and not playing together. The preseason was devoid of these sorts of moments.
Waiters, whom James had been trying to mentor, had been on better
behavior. Now James was giving a lecture to both Irving and Waiters
and doing so in front of the microphones.

"I'm here to help and that's what it's about," James said, brighten-
ing a little. "For me, it's like building a car from scratch. I've done that
before. I hated the process, it got on my nerves, I sent it back to get
repainted a hundred times, and it came back and it still wasn't done
right. Once it was completely finished, you're excited about it. So that's
what it feels like."

James was the last out of the Cavs locker room, the bus to the airport waiting for him in the loading dock. The Cavs flew to Salt Lake City, not landing until after 2 a.m. as they faced having to play another back-to-back against the Utah Jazz that night. On the flight, James pondered what he needed to do. Already, he was feeling problems. He'd already become perplexed by his coach. And he was already resorting to tough love for Irving and Waiters. He was beginning to realize this was going to be a tougher job than he'd first thought, breaking this team of bad habits.

The next night, he went through his extensive pregame stretching routine, being twisted, turned, bent by trainer Mike Mancias. As they went through the process, James kept his eyes closed and bounced his head as he listened to music through a pair of customized Beats headphones. Three months earlier, Apple had closed its $3 billion purchase of Beats. James had equity in the company and realized more than $35 million personally out of the transaction. It was a reminder that even on tough days, James often comes out the winner.

"I've had two games where I've played a little passive and been more of a setup guy and it's resulted in two losses. And I've had a game where I've been very aggressive and we won," James said as he put on his uniform, explaining what was going through his head. "It's a fine line. Is winning the ultimate thing? Is being the best we can be as a team or winning one game better? It's something that's going on in my mind right now, I'm trying to figure out."

James was asked if he'd talked to his teammates about it, especially after he'd gone public the night before with rather pointed quotes that seemed to be fingering Irving and Waiters for hogging the ball.

"I don't know if the guys saw it, but I continue to preach it and they will get it," he said. "No need to tell them. It's not the time for it."

He was then asked if he'd talked to his coach about the issues he was seeing and dealing with.

"I didn't look for his guidance," James said.

From the first day of practice, James had set the tone that he planned to operate independently of Blatt at times. It's not unusual for a star and a coach to be on different wavelengths, but it was also clear Blatt wasn't being made a partner as James was evaluating how to go about sending messages. The coach was left to read James's quotes and try to guess like everyone else.

"I think what he's referring to is just having a winning tradition to hang your hat on and to be able to get through things because of that," Blatt said. "I really think that's what he's referring to more than anything else. You got kids? Then you know the answer. I've got four, I taught a lot of them. You watch. You show. You speak. You use examples. You hug. You never hit. But you do admonish. How's that?"

Blatt smiled as he said it, happy with his metaphor but also with a little acknowledgment he was trying to sell the concept to the media he knew exactly what James was doing. In fact, he did not. There was no doubt he recognized the issues James was talking about. At the film session that morning he'd stressed the need for the Cavs guards to set up the forwards, James and Love. And that night he took Waiters out of the starting lineup for good and replaced him with respected veteran Shawn Marion, whom general manager David Griffin had brought in to add experience.

Waiters went to the locker room during the national anthem and starting lineup introductions that night. It looked like a form of protest, though he later gave several conflicting reasons why he'd left the floor. A few days later Blatt dismissed questions about Waiters losing his starting job. In a type of exchange that would become commonplace, where Blatt would pick seemingly needless fights with the media, he said that Waiters wasn't a bench player.

"We didn't move him to the bench," he said. "I never saw guys that play as many minutes as Dion played as bench players. To me they're just second starters."

No matter how Blatt wanted to rebrand the concept of benching a player, Waiters never started another game in his time with the team.

The starting lineup became trivial when the team then suffered a brutal defeat to the Jazz. Gordon Hayward, the young forward whom the Cavs had been courting the previous summer before James made his move, made a jumper at the buzzer to win the game. James was guarding Hayward but got caught in a screen, as was the Jazz plan, and lost him. Thompson had scrambled and switched onto Hayward and was able to challenge the shot. Hayward just made a great shot, and the sold-out crowd thundered in response. The Cavs dragged themselves back to the locker room with a 1–3 record.

James was angry. But he was not angry about the loss. He was not angry that his man had scored the game-winning basket, though he grumbled Thompson needed to be quicker. He was not angry about his 31 points or Irving's 34. Irving had made some fantastic plays as the team tried to pull off a second-half comeback; he scored 12 points in the fourth quarter alone.

No, what James focused on was seeing zero assists under Irving's name. He'd had no assists in the second half in Portland. The Cavs had just six as a team for the entire game, the lowest in the history of the franchise, and James had four of them.

James approached Irving in the locker room. The night before, he'd tried to send a message through the media. Irving, it seemed, hadn't gotten it. The 34 points were impressive, but what James perceived as continued ball hogging was a bigger issue. Irving seemingly had ignored Blatt's strategy session too, but James wasn't interested in involving the coach.

"He came up to me and was like, 'One, you can never have another game with no assists. You can damn near have just one, two, three, but you can't have zero.' And I was like, 'All right, cool, it won't happen again,'" Irving told Cleveland.com.

James made it clear he did not re-sign with the Cavs because of the team they had, he did so because he felt a calling to come home and to change the viewpoint on his career. Privately, he believed Irving's potential was attractive, but Irving's re-signing to stay in Cleveland for five more years didn't affect his feelings on his choice. However, the reality was James joined a team where Irving was the established star who had been at the centerpiece of everything.

James knew Irving was a potential superstar who could help him win, and, like he'd done in Miami with Wade, he was committed to finding a way to make things work. But it didn't fully work in Miami until Wade willingly took a step back to allow James to be the central figure. Wade was older than James and already a champion with a secure legacy, none of which the much younger Irving had. Irving hadn't made the choice to play with James as Wade did. When Irving signed his extension the previous July it was after he'd been sold on a vastly different scenario. Though playing with James had undeniable advantages, it was something that was forced on Irving. That awkwardness was manifesting itself quickly.

Leading up to the season, James and Wade had talked with each other about this dynamic. They were closer friends and had played together several times on Team USA before becoming Heat teammates. And yet there were still plenty of nights when they left the locker room upset with each other as they went through the process. Irving and James had no such background to lean on and they came from different eras. James grew up idolizing Michael Jordan, who ruled his teams with an iron hand and led by example and brute force. Irving grew up idolizing Kobe Bryant, who led by sheer will and often viewed his teammates as inferior and so just took what he felt was needed. It was clear the two Cavs had a journey to go together and the turbulence was arriving quickly.

"You know, LeBron can do it again, because he's a little younger, but I wouldn't want to do it all over again. That was a grind, man," Wade told Bleacher Report about James having to go through another assimilation process with a fellow star. "It was a great grind, because we got success out of it. But I wouldn't want to do it all over again. More kudos to him for doing it all over again. You've got to go through the same process, you know."

As James left Salt Lake City, next stop Denver, he had some clarity. The fine line he was considering over the first week of the season got a little bolder in his mind. If Irving couldn't be counted on to share the ball and if trying to force it with passivity didn't work, James would move into active mode. It had started with his scolding of Irving in Utah and was soon to be followed up.

Irving did show a different mind-set in the game against the Nuggets; in fact, he broke his streak of 70 minutes without an assist just 90 seconds into the game when he set up Love for a basket. He only tried one shot in the first quarter and didn't score. But James also grabbed the wheel. That night, a 110–101 win, James essentially took over much of the point guard duties from Irving. He had six assists in the first quarter alone and 11 for the game.

After the game, Blatt and James explained it was a strategy decision because of the style of defense the Nuggets used that night. It was one of the few things the coach and player agreed on over the following few weeks.

After the win in Denver, the Cavs launched into a four-game win streak. Irving kept passing the ball—he even had a nine-assist game—and it appeared the team was finding some rhythm. To get there, however, Blatt was riding his stars with heavy minutes. He slashed the playing time for Waiters and Mike Miller and started giving more to rookie Joe Harris, the team's second-round pick from the previous summer. With Dellavedova out with the knee issue and Miller, Waiters, and even Marion struggling, the Cavs started to look like they had depth problems they hadn't expected.

The winning streak ended with a sluggish home loss to the Nuggets, a team that had been 2–7. It kicked off a losing streak and a period of growing tension between James and Blatt as they traded a series of barbs.

After the loss, Blatt said the team "didn't come with the proper mind-set and with the energy level that we had the other night and have had the last several games."

James refuted Blatt's analysis, saying, "I didn't feel that. It's easy to say that after the fact."

The next day, James raised the issue of his minutes. This was often an evolving topic for him—for years he would express concern at minute totals, but he'd also sometimes not want to come out of games when he was on a hot streak. At that moment, though, he thought Blatt was playing all the stars too much. A few weeks into the season, James was third in the league in minutes at more than 41 a game. Irving and Love ranked fourth and fifth in minutes played. Some of the veterans James had brought in, specifically Miller and James Jones, weren't playing much.

"I think we have to give our guys on the bench more of an opportunity. I looked at a stat and myself, Kyrie, and Kevin are three of the top five guys in the league in minutes per game," James said. "That has to come down. I don't want to do that all year... You want to be smart about it."

Blatt again was on a different page. "Right now LeBron has said and has told me that he's feeling good and he's starting to feel his real game shape," he said. "So this is not the time to think about resting him. He's feeling good. Let's not overlook the fact that he's been playing great basketball and he looks good physically. He looks excellent. So for the foreseeable future we're going to ride that."

In a game that was deemed to be a possible Finals preview, the San Antonio Spurs came to Cleveland and beat the Cavs by two points. Blatt had heard LeBron's comments and slashed his minutes to 34 after playing him more than 40 in seven of the previous nine games. But his rotations were all off as he sat James, Irving, and Love all at the same time, which didn't make much strategic sense, and it twice led to Spurs runs. He played the rookie Harris the final 18 minutes of the game without substituting him, perhaps forgetting about it. Harris was gassed at the end and the Spurs' Manu Ginobili beat him to score the game-winning points.

Late in the game, Blatt called several timeouts in succession. During one, James was talking with players without Blatt in the huddle. At one point, Blatt had to force his way in. This visual soon became a talking point, especially for those who remembered Blatt throwing players off the bench when they attempted to talk over him in the Olympics.

Eventually, the Cavs ran out of timeouts. Early in the season, Blatt relied on top assistant Ty Lue to help manage timeouts, which are handled differently than in Europe because some are compulsory at various stages of the game, tied to television commercials. There's an art to it and some experience is needed, and Blatt was learning. Spurs coach Gregg Popovich, one of the most experienced coaches in the world, perfectly managed his timeouts and had three available in the final minute.

On the deciding play of the game, James had to try to push the ball up the floor after a rebound with nine seconds left instead of perhaps using a timeout that could've been saved for such a situation. He turned the ball over and the Cavs lost.

After the game, when questioned on his timeout usage and his substitution patterns, Blatt hinted he shouldn't be the one blamed for the loss. "I don't take all the credit for anything," he said. "I'd like not to take all the blame for everything, but that's part of my job so I have to do that."

James did take the blame for the turnover, but things were quickly getting to the point where James and Blatt appeared to be bickering via the media. They were having conversations before, after, and during practice, but it seemed both were satisfied in sending at least some messages indirectly. The chill started to become more clear.

The veteran Popovich was watching and, gracious in victory, he waved away the suggestion the Cavs were having problems. "They're going to be one hell of a team. But it's a new system, new bodies, and it doesn't happen quickly," he said. "I'm glad we played them now. They'll be a whole lot tougher later on in the year."

Then he reflected on what it was like when he was a first-year coach, as Blatt was dealing with, and he put it very succinctly. "You either know what you're doing or you don't," Popovich said. "You either can develop or garner respect from players or know how to deal with a group and be able to lead it or not."

Two days later, the Cavs were blown out by the Wizards in Washington. The body language of the team sagged, including James, who became visibly upset and didn't run back on defense once when Waiters took an ill-advised three-pointer. Love scored just eight points, his fewest in two years. The Blatt offense that had flourished and been praised in the preseason was unrecognizable.

"We're a little bit in the dark," Blatt said, "and we've got to find our way out."

As the Cavs rode the bus to Dulles International Airport for their charter flight home, James posted a message on his Twitter account that quoted Martin Luther King Jr.: "The ultimate measure of a man is not where he stands in moments of comfort and convenience, but where he stands at times of challenge." It didn't exactly defuse the situation or help calm nerves that it was still so early in the season.

A day later, the Toronto Raptors blasted the Cavs by 17 points back in Cleveland, dropping their record to 5–7. The team's reserves were outscored 91–25 over the two games. The front office had already started to realize the team wasn't as deep as projected. General manager David Griffin believed he might have to make a trade during the season to add to the bench. That timetable looked like it had to be moved up. As Waiters had another subpar game—he scored just six points—Griffin and his staff began to discuss how they might be able to trade him.

James spent the last six minutes of the Raptor loss on the bench, staring out on the floor as Blatt stood silently. This wasn't going how any of them thought.

"We're a very fragile team right now. Any little adversity hits us we shell up," James said. "But I'm very optimistic. I'm very positive, more positive than I thought I'd be right now."

James was positive because as he'd sat there on the bench he'd gotten closer to making a decision. He was about to make a change. He was about to execute a bloodless coup. His star teammate, Irving, didn't know it. Neither did his coach.

"Nah, I can do it on my own," James said later. "I'm past those days where I have to ask."

LeBron James was just eighteen years old when he began his first stint with the Cleveland Cavaliers after being selected with the No. 1 pick in the 2003 draft. (Bob Rosato / Getty Images)

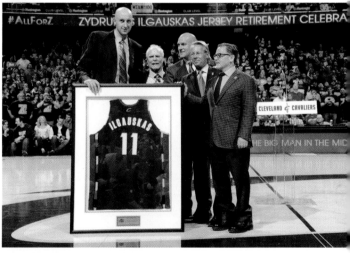

The jersey-retirement ceremony for Zydrunas Ilgauskas (left) during the 2013-14 season allowed the Cavs ownership group led by Dan Gilbert (right) to test the waters for a potential LeBron James return to Cleveland. (David Liam Kyle / Getty Images)

Heat president Pat Riley's (middle) "If you've got the guts" message during a June 2014 press conference may have alienated LeBron James on his way out the door. James was also frustrated that Heat owner Micky Arison (left) slowed spending on the roster. (Garrett Ellwood / Getty Images)

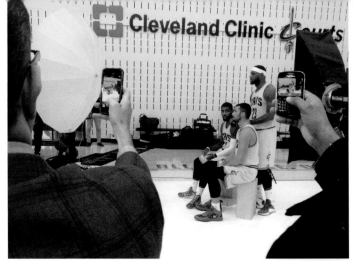

The new big three of James, Kyrie Irving, and Kevin Love were under the media's microscope from their very first day together. (Dave McMenamin)

LeBron James shared a flight with friend and former teammate Dwayne Wade from Las Vegas before making his final decision to return to Cleveland. They were opponents on Christmas Day a few months later, but their in-game fraternization would upset Cavs officials. (Issac Baldizon / Getty Images)

Irving scored a career-high 57 points in an overtime win for the Cavs in San Antonio in March 2015. "The kid is special, we all know it, we all see it," James said afterward. (Dave McMenamin)

James and head coach David Blatt huddling up prior to a team shoot-around at The Palace of Auburn Hills. (Dave McMenamin)

James, shown here at the United Center in Chicago, has long played in the shadow of the legacy of Michael Jordan. (Dave McMenamin)

"To be honest, the play that was drawn up, I scratched it," LeBron James said after hitting the game-winning shot that tied the 2015 Eastern Conference Semifinals series with the Chicago Bulls 2-2. (Jesse D. Garrabrant / Getty Images)

A fractured left knee-cap suffered by Kyrie Irving in Game 1 of the 2015 NBA Finals seriously jeopardized the Cavs' chances of winning the title. (Ezra Shaw / Getty Images)

Blatt, before his last game coaching the Cleveland Cavaliers. He was fired the next day after beginning the season with a 30-11 record. (Dave McMenamin)

"This is not an indictment of David Blatt as a coach," Cavaliers general manager David Griffin said at the press conference to announce Cleveland's coaching change. "And it's not to say that Ty Lue is a better basketball coach. He's a better basketball coach for this team today." (David Liam Kyle / Getty Images)

After taking over for David Blatt at midseason, Tyronn Lue became the first rookie head coach in league history to start his playoff career 10-0. (Ronald Martinez)

J.R. Smith (far left) holds the 2016 Eastern Conference championship trophy and stands next to Tristan Thompson at the Air Canada Centre in Toronto as the pair await the finish of the big three's press conference recapping the team's second consecutive trip to the NBA Finals. (Dave McMenamin)

LeBron James later described his chasedown block on Andre Iguodala in Game 7 of the 2016 NBA Finals as the "defining play of my career." (Joe Murphy / Getty Images)

Kyrie Irving's 3-pointer with 53 seconds left in Game 7 over back-to-back MVP Stephen Curry broke an 89-89 tie and propelled Cleveland to the championship. (Ezra Shaw / Getty Images)

any Cleveland Cavaliers players, LeBron James included, burst into tears upon completing the comeback from 3-1 down in the Finals to capture the first professional sports title for Cleveland in half a century. (Ezra Shaw / Getty Images)

"Cleveland! This is for you!" James exclaimed shortly before accepting the Larry O'Brien Trophy on stage. (Garrett Ellwood / Getty Images)

Smith was seen shirtless so often during the Cavs' championship celebration that even President Barack Obama joked about it. (Dave McMenamin)

A scene many thought would never happen after the fallout from "The Decision" in 2010: Gilbert presenting James with a championship ring. (Ezra Shaw / Getty Images)

Love shows off the Cavs' 6.5 carat championship ring, encrusted with more than 400 diamonds. (Dave McMenamin)

More than 1 million flocked the streets of Cleveland for the Cavaliers' championship parade. James mimicked his pose of the iconic 10-story Nike banner hanging from Sherwin-Williams' global headquarters located across from Quicken Loans Arena. (Dave McMenamin)

Chapter 7

"WHAT OTHER COACH DO WE HAVE?"

The sideways glances met each other around the huddle. David Blatt was sitting in the middle, sliding a pen over his grease board, instructing Shawn Marion where to go on the important offensive set that was about to take place. Marion, however, was not in the game and had not been told to check in. Blatt had simply lost track.

The players noticed things like this happening during the coach's first few months on the job. Sometimes he would have the same player in two places when he drew up plays, or assign the same man two different assignments on defense. Other times his hands were shaking as he drew the lines, sometimes he let assistant coaches come to the center of the huddle to draw the plays. There would be times when LeBron James would dispute the strategy. Blatt didn't just have to make a choice on what to run, he had to sell it to James. And mental mistakes, especially as they piled up, did not help the pitch.

During practice scrimmages when coaches called fouls—a naturally controversial situation—players noticed Blatt sometimes clammed up when there were arguments. In Europe when the coach made a ruling, whether it was a foul call in a scrimmage or who was taking the last shot in a playoff game, his authority was almost never questioned. Blatt, who was revered in Europe and adored and massively supported by Israeli fans, was used to authority. This was not the case in the NBA, where power is fleeting for many coaches, especially those without accepted experience.

James was ultracompetitive. At times he'd have a meltdown over losing a scrimmage or drill. In frustration in losing, he was known to take the ball and heave it 80-plus feet to the other end of the building. When he didn't agree with a foul call, be it in the final minute of a playoff game or in a routine end-of-practice run, he would protest. When he would slow practice down ranting and raving about some call, Blatt would become a wallflower. Sometimes it took assistant Ty Lue to step up and tell James to shut up, it was a foul and go run the next play.

Within weeks the players, notably the wing of veterans, started to whisper. They had begun to believe that Blatt, who arrived with a reputation as a short-fused taskmaster, was actually afraid of James. In retrospect, perhaps Blatt should've told James on the first day to hold his requested meeting later. It might've upset him, but it might've fostered respect.

Many of the Cavs players liked Blatt personally. He was generally good-natured and many liked his personality. They just didn't really know what kind of coach he wanted to be. The veterans were aware he was in a challenging spot, but they weren't sure of the identity he wanted for the team. The older players preferred that he'd be more communicative. The younger players, like Irving and tough-nosed guard Matthew Dellavedova, seemed to bond with the coach more easily.

Opinions on the early days between James and Blatt are varied—different people on the team saw different angles. There were times when Blatt did show some of his trademark mettle and times when James was supportive and fell in line. But there was no disputing Blatt was in a tough situation. Frequently James didn't offer support within the team and in public. Within weeks it seemed James wasn't completely invested in his coach's success. Combined with Blatt's sometimes shaky poise, it was not the best recipe for developing a bond between the coach and best player.

So as the Cavs sat with a 5–7 record as Thanksgiving approached, James felt he needed to make changes, and he didn't feel Blatt was vital enough to be wholly included in the process.

"I have a low tolerance for things of this nature," James said as he evaluated the Cavs' record. "So it's something I'm working on as well, which I knew from the beginning that that was going to be my biggest test to see how much patience I've got."

Starting with a game against the Orlando Magic, James effectively took control of primary ball handling, pushing Irving to play mostly off the ball when they were on the court together. The concepts Blatt had installed in the early season were gone. And the offense came to life. The Cavs rolled off eight straight wins, turning their prospects around thanks to James's playmaking.

They beat the Magic by 32 points and James racked up 29 points and 11 assists. They avenged their loss to the Wizards, pounding them by 26 points as James registered 29 points and eight assists. They beat the Indiana Pacers by 12 as Kevin Love had one of his finest games, scoring 28 points with 12 rebounds. Love had 27 points, Irving had 28, and James had 26 points and 10 more assists as the team beat Milwaukee. Irving had a huge game in Madison Square Garden as he put up 37 points to beat the Knicks, James repeatedly setting him up as the de facto point guard with 12 more assists. James had 13 assists in a revenge win against the Raptors, then he scored 35 points the next week when they beat the Raptors again.

The winning streak eased tensions and enabled James to focus elsewhere. On one memorable night in Brooklyn during the streak, the team executed a protest and mingled with dignitaries. In warmups, Irving and James wore shirts that read "I Can't Breathe," a reference to an African American man named Eric Garner, who had been killed as police attempted to arrest him on Staten Island. The tragedy was captured on video, where Garner could be heard telling the police he couldn't breathe. It created a national reaction. James and Irving violated NBA protocol by wearing the shirts and showing support after other athletes had done the same.

Once the game started, focus turned to the royals as Prince William of England and his wife, Kate Middleton, arrived while on a rare visit to the United States. They sat courtside next to Jay-Z and Beyoncé, making for an irresistible moment that had photographers craning and the crowd too transfixed to watch the game, which the Cavs won yet again as James led the team in assists. Afterward, James met with the Duke and Duchess of Cambridge.

"The stuff that you read about, people like them are only in books growing up. And to hear that they're coming to town to see me play and they want to see me do what I do best, it's a huge honor," James said.

As the Cavs left New York, James posted to social media a picture he had taken with the royals and said it would be going on his wall. In the photo he'd posed with his arm around the Duchess, which was frowned on immediately by the British press because it defied protocol that no one is to touch the royal family. Such is a day in the life of LeBron James.

The royal family mini-gaffe reinforced that nothing early in the season could be drama-free. Sure enough, the Cavs' winning streak came to an end in Oklahoma City when James had to pull himself from the lineup with a sore knee. Then during the first half, Irving landed awkwardly on his left leg after defending a shot attempt by Russell Westbrook. He crumpled to the ground and yelled, "Call Steve!" to his teammates, meaning athletic trainer Steve Spiro. Irving feared he'd done something to his left knee. He avoided serious injury, but the scare derailed the team.

A week later they didn't dodge the injury bullet. Anderson Varejão tore his Achilles' tendon as he reached for a rebound in a home game against the Minnesota Timberwolves. He would be lost for the season and face a grueling recovery. It was a blow because the team was already thin at the position and because for a player in his thirties, an Achilles' tear is devastating. The team had just signed him to a three-year, $30 million contract extension in October. The news of the MRI came down on Christmas Eve as the Cavs were about to fly to Miami.

Then there was the Waiters issue. After losing his starting job, Waiters had been pouty at times and insufferable at others. Always known as a shoot-first guard, he had grown frustrated by his lack of playing time and lack of shots. Sometimes he'd physically jump up and down when he was open, demanding the ball, and then slump his shoulders like a child when he didn't get it.

Waiters's South Philadelphia neighborhood was immersed in violence as he grew up, and it had a profound impact on him. When he was eight, he and his mother were caught in the crossfire of a shoot-out in a park and he escaped bullets by falling to the ground. When he was fourteen, one of his cousins was shot and killed. When he was fifteen, a close friend and teammate was shot more than ten times and died. Another of his cousins was murdered a few months earlier. In the spring of 2016, Waiters's brother died in a shooting in his old neighborhood.

When Waiters committed to play at Syracuse before his sophomore year of high school and at age nineteen became the No. 4 pick in the draft, it was not only a remarkable success story, it was a remarkable survival story. His past shaped his game. He played with anger and like it could all be taken from him. There wasn't much finesse, there wasn't much nuance. He was often at his best trying for the impossible. He didn't always excel in doing the mundane but needed tasks.

James had hopes of molding him, but had quickly given up at Waiters's insistence on playing his preferred style. Knowing Waiters was hoping for a contract extension the following year, Griffin had met with him and talked about the role he could fill next to James that could make him valuable to the team. This also failed.

The veterans like James Jones, Mike Miller, and Brendan Haywood tried to counsel Waiters. They told him he needed to play differently with James, to cut off the ball to get open or to run the floor with him and offer himself as an option. Waiters flat out told teammates that wasn't the way he played. Whether his points were valid was immaterial; at best he was going to be the team's fourth offensive option. This was a fact even if he didn't want to accept it.

Blatt was playing him less than 10 minutes a game some nights. The front office stepped up their efforts to trade him. Players started to whisper that his days were numbered, and the media's attention on his plunging playing time grew.

The loss of Varejão was worrisome because he was one of the team's true quality defenders. The defense, which Blatt had wanted to make a calling card, often lagged. This was a challenge, because Irving, Waiters, and Love were not good defenders and the Cavs didn't have a classic shot blocker to guard the rim. In addition, the team's lack of depth on the wings continued to be an issue.

Meanwhile, Kevin Love had started to show some signs of frustration. He went through a period where he only averaged 10 shots a game over a two-week period, nine fewer than he'd averaged the previous season. He knew his touches would drop, but the process was starting to get to him. Sometimes he would show exasperation at not getting the ball. It was as Chris Bosh had forewarned.

All these developments made the team feel like it was on a losing streak even though they came into Christmas having won 12 of 15 games. James admitted he had some butterflies returning to Miami. Wade, attempting to be magnanimous and to help his friend, gave several interviews before the game asking the fans to be respectful to James. "I think he should be received very well at the start of the game," Wade told Bleacher Report.

The fans booed James, but it was nothing like when he returned to Cleveland after signing with Miami in 2010. Midway through the first quarter the Heat played a video tribute to James's four seasons and the crowd gave him a standing ovation. James waved and appeared to get a little emotional. Had the Cavs tried to show a video tribute in 2010, there might have been a riot.

As for the game, the Cavs played poorly and were beaten soundly by the Heat. James had 30 points and Wade had 31, a duel that delighted the audience. Luol Deng got some revenge on his old team, scoring 25 points. In the second half, Love tried to throw a long pass to James and, summing up the day, overshot him. James tried to chase the ball and ended up going into the stands. He leapt over the first row of seats and landed hard, and pain shot up his left knee, which had already been bothering him. He went to the locker room and was done for the night. Late in the game, Irving aggravated his left knee that he'd tweaked in Oklahoma City. All in all, it was a miserable Christmas for the Cavs.

"We're not that good right now," James said, summarizing everything surrounding the team.

The next night the Cavs were in Orlando. James played, though maybe he shouldn't have. Irving did not, his knee aching. Upset about the team's play in Miami, upset about the defense, upset about Waiters, and cranky because of his knee, James was disconnected for much of the game. Some at courtside were taken aback at how he ignored Blatt during the game, sitting off by himself during timeouts.

Midway through the third quarter, James was guarding Magic forward Tobias Harris, a young player James had no history with. Harris whipped around and his elbows just missed James's face. James backed up and glared and the two started yelling at each other, with Harris finishing by barking "Stop flopping!" to James. Though he's one of the most physically imposing players in the league, opponents had been annoyed with James's knack for exaggerating contact over the years, something that was commonplace for the whole team when he played in Miami.

In an instant, James's demeanor turned. No longer floating and uninterested, he went on the attack. He scored 18 of his 29 points over the last quarter and a half and smothered Harris on defense, holding him to one basket. The Cavs ended up winning by nine.

"The words that he said, that got me going," James said. "I was actually in chill mode tonight, but chill mode was deactivated after that."

The incident was a great way to spice up the game, but it overshadowed two things. One was James essentially admitting he was taking a game off—chill mode—and the other was that Blatt benched Love in the fourth quarter because of defensive issues. At one point Blatt asked Love if he wanted to go in, but he'd sat so long, he just waved him off.

Griffin had been talking to teams about trading Waiters for weeks and was getting traction with the Thunder, who were seeking a way to bolster scoring in their backcourt. Separately he'd also been talking to the Knicks about trading for one of their available guards, free-agent-to-be Iman Shumpert. When Varejão went down, the front office had to start looking for centers as well. For months the team had been trying to get the Denver Nuggets to trade them Timofey Mozgov, a huge 7-foot-2 center whom Blatt knew well from his time as the Russian national team coach. The Nuggets had resisted or asked a huge price.

But Griffin had another problem. Ownership had gotten jittery about Blatt, and conversations about whether there needed to be a change had been taking place. Griffin was against it. He knew the team was a little banged up. He also knew he hadn't given Blatt the kind of depth he needed. The veterans he signed were struggling and Blatt didn't have many live bodies to bring off the bench, especially when Dellavedova got hurt.

Two days after the game in Orlando, the Cavs were pounded at home, losing to the Pistons by 23. Irving missed another game. As a Detroit native and resident, Gilbert didn't take well to losses to the Pistons. The Cavs played lifelessly and the rhetoric afterward was as bad as it had been all year.

"We're not a very good team," James said, echoing what he said at Christmas. "We're still trying to find our way."

Blatt admitted he wasn't doing the best job but said he wasn't concerned about losing the team, which was now 18–12. The next day, ESPN reported that his job was in jeopardy. Blatt reacted negatively to the report, saying that it was "unfair." When James was asked about the news, he gave an evasive answer.

"Yeah, he's our coach. I mean, what other coach do we have?" James said. When asked if he should give Blatt an endorsement, he made it clear it wasn't up to him: "Listen, man, I don't pay no bills around here."

Irving, on the other hand, defended his coach: "I would do anything for Coach Blatt."

With the pressure building, the team was dealt another setback. As the Cavs prepared to play in Atlanta, a sore back James had been dealing with worsened. His knee was also still bothering him. Shortly before the game, the Cavs scratched him from the lineup and he spent much of the first half down in the Hawks locker room in their whirlpool trying to loosen up his back. It was his thirtieth birthday and this wasn't how he wanted to spent it. He was feeling his age as he watched his team fall down by 10 on their way to another loss, his cursing echoing off the walls and throughout the locker room area, catching Hawks employees off guard.

The next day, New Year's Eve, James went to the Cleveland Clinic to get an MRI. It showed significant inflammation in his lower back. This at least explained why he hadn't looked like himself physically for the previous few weeks. Team doctors recommended he get a power-ful anti-inflammatory shot to help the issue, a treatment that would sideline him for two weeks. He had never missed more than a week due to injury in his career.

James had fought advice to rest for several weeks, but now couldn't do it any longer. He got the shot and skipped that night's game with the Milwaukee Bucks. So did Kevin Love, whose own back had seized up on him. The team was crushed by 16 points, their fourth loss in five games.

It was the close of a trying week for Griffin, who was holding off a push to fire Blatt while pulling together a complex trade. He'd found a home for Waiters in Oklahoma City but was trying to get his hands on Shumpert as part of a three-team deal.

The Knicks wanted a first-round pick for Shumpert, but Griffin didn't want to give it. He needed his picks to get Mozgov; the Nuggets were demanding two first-round picks. The Knicks also wanted the Cavs to accept J. R. Smith in a trade. A volatile shooter who had been a darling in New York when he won the 2013 Sixth Man of the Year Award, he'd fallen out of favor with new president Phil Jackson after two suspensions over the previous year and for his love of the New York nightlife. Griffin wasn't in favor of trading for Smith. He was the type of player the Cavs needed, a wing with good size who could shoot, but he was so prone to bad decisions that much of the NBA considered him toxic.

As he did the summer before when he was mulling the Love trade, Griffin asked the Knicks for permission to talk to Smith. They had a phone call. Smith had been offended when he heard how the Knicks were basically attempting to give him away and attach him to Shum-pert like a bad debt. He told Griffin he'd "walk to Cleveland."

Griffin brought the topic to James. Smith and James were just a year apart and had gotten to know each other as teenagers. After James's first season in 2004, Smith came to the NBA right from high school, and the Cavs considered drafting him but instead took a more seasoned player, Luke Jackson. Ever since, Smith had wanted to play with James, and several times he came to Akron in the summer to work out with him. With the team badly struggling and in need of a talent injection, James told Griffin he should make the deal for Smith. When Griffin expressed further concern, James said he'd take on the responsibility of keeping Smith in line.

Griffin met with his front office and ownership, specifically co-owner Nate Forbes, who was always involved in such matters. They were still shaky on Smith, but James's reassurance and the call had turned them around a bit on the issue. Shumpert was in the last year of his deal and Mozgov had a team option for the next year; those investments were safer. Smith had a $6.4 million player option, which had the Knicks turned off. If Smith was a bad fit, the Cavs would be on the hook and wouldn't be able to get rid of him. Ultimately, with Forbes's and Gilbert's support, Griffin decided Smith would be on a short leash and they'd just release him and pay him off if the plan didn't work.

Finally with some clarity, Griffin and his front office started finalizing the details of the trades. They were trying to assemble a four-team deal with the Thunder, Knicks, and Nuggets that would send out Waiters and a first-round pick and land Shumpert, Smith, and Mozgov.

The mechanics of such a move are complex, but Griffin still had another fire to put out regarding Blatt. With James out and the Cavs headed for a long West Coast trip, Griffin knew things were probably going to get worse before they got better. But he also believed Blatt deserved a chance to work with a more complete team. Over the previous summer it was Griffin who was skeptical of Blatt but Gilbert who wanted him. Now here was Griffin making the case for Blatt to get more time. With the trades about to come down, Griffin was able to calm the storm and get agreement to give Blatt a chance after the trades.

So on a Sunday morning, January 4, Griffin called an impromptu news conference before an afternoon game with the Dallas Mavericks. He blasted the concept that Blatt's job was in danger and made it clear that he would not be fired. It was a classic vote of confidence even though Griffin tried not to package it that way.

"Coach Blatt is our coach, he's going to remain our coach," Griffin said and chided the media for stories attacking Blatt in the previous days. "Do not write that as a vote of confidence. He never needed one.

It was never a question. So don't write it that way. That narrative is done. No change is being made, period."

Without James, the Cavs responded by losing to the Mavericks by 19, with Irving pulling himself midway because of back spasms. Griffin, though, wasn't paying attention. He spent much of the game on the phone in his office next to the locker room trying to put together his deal. The final piece was when the Knicks dropped their demand for a first-round pick and agreed to take a second-rounder because Smith was in the deal. As Griffin was finalizing trading him away, Waiters went 4-of-14 shooting in the loss to Dallas. He missed one three-pointer so badly that it hit the top of the backboard, prompting boos from the crowd.

Griffin felt like he was on the verge of fixing the roster. He thought his strong comments to the media backing his coach would end that drama until James could get healthy and the new players would turn things around.

On January 5, 2015, Waiters was excited because he was making his first start in two months and it was going to be in front of dozens of friends and family members at Wells Fargo Center in Philadelphia, not far from where he grew up. Irving and James didn't make the trip to Philly because of injuries, and Waiters was promoted to starter. He was announced and was removing his warmups when Raja Bell, the Cavs' director of player administration, mysteriously arrived on the bench and told him he had to come with him to the locker room immediately.

The Cavs had been plotting this trade in one form or another since the previous August. In addition to Waiters and the draft picks and bench players Alex Kirk and Lou Amundson, the Cavs used something called a traded player exception to execute the deal. It functioned like a gift certificate created by previous trades. Team director of strategic planning Brock Aller and team counsel Anthony Leotti hatched a multilayer plan that involved five trades with four other teams. Every few days over the summer, the Cavs had made minor transactions that barely went noticed because they mostly involved swapping future second-round picks and end-of-roster players. But it ended up becoming crucial to the team in completing the deal.

Another factor in the trades was owner Dan Gilbert agreeing to take on $9 million in additional salary as part of the swaps. The moves put the Cavs into the luxury tax, meaning it would cost Gilbert around $15 million in actual additional dollars. The previous summer the team had gone nearly $23 million under the cap to sign James, and now were nearly $15 million over it. The league had never seen a swing of spending like it. It fulfilled a promise Gilbert had made to James that he'd spend to put a team around him.

Griffin's relief was short-lived. As the team trumpeted the arrival of the new players, there was another dustup. It became public James had gone to Miami to work on his back and knee rehab on his own. It made sense, James going to the warm weather to help his back. On the other hand, the optics were terrible. The Cavs were struggling and had just been beaten by the Heat, and James, who was only on a one-year contract, was back in Miami and spending time with old friends. The Cavs had cleared the trip but hoped it would stay secret.

"That was by design," Blatt said, forced to explain the situation. "He hasn't been around per orders of the doctor."

After losing with the depleted roster in Philadelphia to a team that was 4–28, the Cavs lost again by 12 points at home to the Rockets. Irving came back and looked great, scoring 38 points. But Mozgov hadn't yet arrived, Shumpert was nursing a shoulder injury and wouldn't be back for two weeks, and, in his first game, Smith shot 0-of-5. The Cavs were about to leave on a five-game trip to the West Coast. Even though James was feeling better and nearing a return, the Cavs had lost six of seven games and were in free fall.

Chapter 8

FIT OUT, FIT IN

When LeBron James returned from his midseason Miami vacation, his back was feeling better and his activity level was ramping up. He'd rejoined the team in San Francisco, the start of their longest road trip of the year, but wasn't ready to play yet. As the team prepared to depart for a morning workout ahead of that evening's game with the Golden State Warriors, the elevator doors opened and a giant human being ducked his head out.

David Griffin brought Timofey Mozgov over to James and made the introduction. James cursed at the size of the man. He'd played against Mozgov for years but had forgotten just how big he was. As the team left, Mozgov went to Stanford Medical Center, where the team had arranged for him to have his physical to complete the trade. When Mozgov got on the treadmill he was too tall and a ceiling panel had to be removed so he could stand and run. Alterations made, he passed and the deal was finalized.

The team opened the road trip with an 18-point loss to the Warriors, who were blitzing through the league with a 29–5 record. The concept that the two teams would be possible playoff combatants in the Finals felt far-fetched at the time. Smith had a terrific game in his first start, scoring 27 points and showing some of the flashes that the Cavs were hoping might come from their gamble.

Mozgov, whom teammates quickly began calling by the nickname "Timo," started at center two days later and immediately played well, scoring 14 points with 12 rebounds. But the Cavs were still deep in a funk as they were miserable defensively in a 19-point loss in Sacramento. It dropped the team to .500 at 19–19 and happened against a Kings team that was in the midst of losing 11 of 13 games. With James and Irving in and out of the lineup, Love had put together several games with good stats. This was another one, 25 points and 10 rebounds, but he was being transported back to his Wolves days when he put up big numbers on a bad team.

At this point, despite James still being out, the questions were growing about what was going on. Defensively the team remained lifeless, and Blatt remained unable to shake them from the slump. He was asked afterward how a team that still had two healthy maximum-salary players, Irving and Love, was unable to play better.

"Kevin's not a max player yet, is he?" Blatt said.

These sorts of exchanges had become typical with Blatt, who often challenged reporters' questions. But this was not the best answer, because indeed Love was earning a max salary for that season. Whatever Blatt meant to say, it came off sounding like the coach disputing Love's salary and standing as one of the league's best players.

Love also had been getting crushed defensively during the losing streak. Kings power forwards Rudy Gay and Carl Landry combined to score 34 points on 67 percent shooting that night. So Blatt had underlying reasons for being lukewarm on considering whether Love was playing like a star. But in the delicate world of dealing with NBA players, that was a needless slipup. With Love headed for free agency, media and fans seized on such commentary and it quickly became a topic on talk shows.

It was a comment that the Cavs ended up having to address internally. After the game, the team flew to Phoenix. The next afternoon before practice at Grand Canyon University, Blatt met with Love and tried to smooth over his comment. He then gave a half retraction, explaining that his words had been taken out of context.

"I was simply saying that with our team, he does not have a max contract because we aren't allowed to talk to him about anything until after the season is over," Blatt said. "I just wasn't clear in what I meant, but I hope he now understands exactly what I meant. Kevin Love for me is a player of the highest order."

Again this was not accurate, because Love was indeed playing at that very moment on a max contract. The exasperation with Blatt not simply openly admitting he'd insulted the player, on purpose or not, only furthered some growing angst.

"I wanted to get the context of it all," Love said. "He's right. We can't talk about anything about this summer or contracts or anything of that nature so I just let it roll off."

All of this was a distraction. While Blatt was trying to clean up the mess, the team had one of its best days in weeks. James returned to practice and for the first time took the floor with Smith and Mozgov. The rest and treatment clearly had made a difference as he looked explosive. For a team that had lost eight of nine games, it was uplifting.

James announced he would return the next day against the Suns and then hurried out a back door to go to the airport, where he'd chartered a jet to fly to Dallas and watch the college football national championship game between Ohio State, his favorite team, and Oregon. He was a guest of Dallas Cowboys owner Jerry Jones and sat in his suite.

James's return was an unhappy one. That night the Cavs lost again to the Suns to fall below .500 on the season, giving up 53 percent shooting. Midway through the second quarter, James was called for an offensive foul and Blatt stormed onto the court to protest. James came over and pushed Blatt back toward the bench so he could argue with the referee. Under another circumstance, the act might've been ignored. But with James's public dismissiveness of his coach throughout the season, it came off looking to some like another belittling act.

"Coach Blatt was getting a little fired up about it and he was on his way to a technical foul. So I just got him up out of the way before he got a T," James explained. "Just protecting my coach."

Explained Blatt, "I just thought my guy was taking a lot of hard hits and I didn't like it and I was expressing my opinion, and LeBron stepped in to I guess protect me in that situation, which is more than fine. But what I really wanted to do was protect him."

It illustrated just how off course the season had gone. James and Blatt were both trying to protect each other, but because of all the team's unrest it became another controversy.

As the Cavs tried to make a comeback late in the game, Blatt once again chose to bench Love throughout the fourth quarter. It was a tactical move that helped, since Love's defense was again an issue. Suns power forward Markieff Morris scored 35 points in the game and Love struggled against him. But because of the events of the previous two days, it again took on a political layer. All the things that Griffin had tried to defuse with his public vote of confidence for Blatt were coming up again.

Moments after the game ended, Love and Griffin held an impromptu meeting. The two went into the practice court next to the Cavs locker room, Love still wearing his uniform. One of the Suns' players, Miles Plumlee, came to the practice court to work on his shooting after not having played in the game. He ran into Love and Griffin in the middle of the discussion and immediately turned around and left, knowing he'd just accidentally walked in on something.

When it came to talking about it, Love stuck to James's edict from the start of the season and kept it in house. "If you told me I was going to sit out the fourth quarter, maybe I would have thought it would have been tough. But we had a great rhythm going tonight. I thought the group that we had out there was doing a great job of getting us back into the game," he said.

Amid that sideshow, James looked excellent. He had 33 points and three explosive dunks, saying, "I couldn't make those moves two weeks ago." Smith, in his first game playing with James, drilled eight three-pointers. Had Love played a little better on defense or Irving, who had eight turnovers, played just average, the story might've been different. Instead, it was another stressful night.

After the game, the Cavs made the short flight to Los Angeles. They scheduled a practice for the next afternoon. When the team boarded the bus at the Beverly Wilshire, the players were expecting to go to Westwood to practice at UCLA as teams had done on off days in L.A. for decades. But they went toward West Hollywood instead and pulled up at a bowling alley. In an effort to blow off some steam, Blatt as a surprise had set up a team bowling trip instead of practice. It was well received by the players, who hit the lanes.

Later, this day was referred to as a turning point. The laughter and bonding was a relief, but of course it was more complex than that. As guys in basketball shorts threw gutterballs, they discussed a rumor that was going around. The origin was unclear, but the players were hearing it from their agents: If the Cavs didn't turn things around in their two games in L.A. to end the road trip, Blatt was going to be fired. Whether or not it was accurate, the players were discussing it, and how they responded would be an indication of where they were with their coach.

The team, however, was feeling positive. Getting James back was a major boost, and the new players were delivering. In addition, in practices on the road trip Blatt had been installing a new defensive strategy. With Mozgov and his rim-protecting ability, the team was working on changing its scheme. Some of it was aimed at making things easier on Love, who had been getting roasted as the previous strategy required him to cover more ground than he was used to.

When the team arrived at Staples Center they were confident they'd end the losing streak. They did, beating the Lakers by seven points. James looked healthy and active again, racking up 36 points. Irving bounced back as well, scoring 22 points. During the game, Cavs players openly discussed with some Lakers players the prospect of their coach possibly being fired.

Late in the game, there was a pivotal moment in a timeout huddle. After sitting much of the second half, Kobe Bryant had scored seven quick points and the Lakers had cut the lead from nine to four. Blatt wanted James to switch over to defend Bryant, who had been scoring on Shawn Marion. James declined. Blatt was silent. Assistant Ty Lue stepped in and barked at James, "Bron, you take him. Shut that water off!" James reversed course and agreed. The Cavs closed out the game without more damage from Bryant.

Moments like this had been happening for weeks: Lue stepping in at practice to calm a situation; Lue stepping in during a film session when Blatt ignored a mistake James had made; Lue helping Blatt with substitution patterns and timeout management.

It was a crucial win and everyone had a piece—even Love, who was still dealing with a sore back. He suffered another bout of spasms during pregame warmups but played through it and scored 17 points. In the fourth quarter he made a key defensive play, taking a painful charge when the Lakers' Jeremy Lin ran over him. He would end up sitting out the next night because of the back issue.

But the Cavs won that game too, beating the Clippers, 126–121, for their best victory in weeks. James had a third straight strong game with 32 points and 11 rebounds. Irving scored 37 points, nailing five three-pointers with five assists.

At the start of the season, Irving and James clearly lacked chemistry playing together, and then James purposefully reduced Irving's ball handling. It was a frustrating time for Irving, who was being shoehorned a bit into a role he wasn't familiar with.

Over the following months, Mike Miller had spent time with the young guard and they had many conversations on how to play alongside James and where to pick his spots. Miller wasn't having a good season. The Cavs were thinking he was going to provide a significant contribution as a shooter off the bench after he'd hit 46 percent of his three-pointers the season before and didn't miss a game. But he didn't arrive in great condition—neither did their other veteran pickup, Marion—and he was having the worst season of his career.

But Miller's easygoing personality helped him connect with teammates throughout his career and he'd become someone for Irving to lean on—that was where he was making a contribution. Miller and Irving became regular dinner companions on the road. Miller knew the challenges of learning to play with James, of finding ways to succeed with star teammates. As Irving spent more time with Miller and more court time with James, he clearly started making progress.

Now that James was getting over his back issues and Irving's knee was feeling better, they were getting traction playing together. The one-two punch they delivered against the Clippers was the best example yet of their budding partnership starting to form.

In the final minute there was once again some intrigue in the huddle. With the Cavs ahead by four, Blatt drew up a play for Irving where James would be a decoy. James wanted to change the play, saying he wanted to take the ball out and inbound it to Irving. Blatt agreed. When the play went in motion, James looked to Irving and froze the Clipper defense, which allowed Tristan Thompson to make a backdoor cut. James fired a perfect pass to Thompson, who scored and was fouled to finish off his own 24-point night. It was a perfectly executed play that sealed the win.

James immediately pointed to Blatt, letting everyone know he was to get credit. This was quite a moment, because they both came up with the play and it was James who'd made the great read. Blatt had been the subject of so much undercutting by James, both within the team and in the media, that it was a surprising turn—all part of the seesaw experience of coaching James.

"The play was good, the pass was much better," Blatt said. "LeBron made the play."

The two wins made the long flight home enjoyable. Blatt had been pulled back from the edge, the pressure around him easing, James's public praise helping. The changes Griffin had made were starting to bear fruit.

After two days off, the Cavs opened a homestand by crushing the rival Bulls. In his first game in Cleveland as a Cav, Mozgov had 15 points and 15 rebounds and was an effective defensive presence. Smith nailed six three-pointers as the crowd started to like his ability to get hot.

The three-game win streak had Blatt pulling back his shoulders and rediscovering some confidence. After going into a bit of a shell during the losing streak and the faux pas with Love, he began to exude confidence again. His turn in attitude was personified by his return to admonishing the media for negative stories during the team's struggles.

"Despite all the crap that has been said and written, a lot of it unfair and a lot of it ugly, we stayed the course and didn't pay attention to that and locked in on basketball," Blatt said. "Eat all that crow."

Over the next several weeks, the Cavs started ripping off victories and piling up momentum as their new players and new schemes started taking hold. Love, James, and Irving combined for 63 points and Mozgov had 16 points and 11 rebounds in a win over the Jazz. Smith nailed seven three-pointers in a victory over the Hornets in which Shumpert made his debut. The Cavs beat the Thunder as James had a duel with Kevin Durant, James scoring 34 points and Durant 32. At a game in Detroit, Irving put up 38 points and James had 32 as they continued to demonstrate their progress learning to find ways to succeed playing with each other.

James missed a game with the Trail Blazers because of a sprained wrist. Irving missed his first seven shots and it appeared the winning streak might be coming to an end that night. Then he had one of the most impressive shooting runs in NBA history as he made 11 three-pointers and showed all of his offensive mastery. His wizardry with the ball on dribbles, change-of-direction moves, and quick releases had the crowd delirious. He made two three-pointers in the final 75 seconds, one to tie and one to win with six seconds left over the much taller Nic Batum. He'd scored 55 points, a new career high and one off James's franchise record, set in 2005. The 11 three-pointers were a franchise record. He even had five assists, leading the team.

James sprinted to meet him after the game-winner as Irving flexed at center court. As he drove home, James tweeted about what he'd just seen. "Just watched one of the greatest performances by a person and he happens to be my teammate/runningmate/brother Kyrie Irving," he wrote.

The Cavs ended up winning 12 in a row. Their defense was improving. The Shumpert and Smith additions had provided a huge lift on the perimeter, and Matthew Dellavedova, recovered from his own knee issue, was turning in quality performances. James and Irving were racking up numbers and both were selected for the All-Star team in New York in February.

This was closer to the situation that James had envisioned when he made the choice to return to Cleveland—his supporting cast executing their jobs. He had prepared himself for a breaking-in process both with teammates and coaches, but it had been worse than he expected. He didn't realize how many bad habits there were. Not just in actual performance within games, where he had to try to break them of what he saw as selfish streaks, but in how few of his teammates acted as professionals. In his mind, there wasn't enough extra work being put in after practice or in the film room, not enough guys taking care of their bodies in the weight or recovery rooms, and—this might've bothered him the most—a lack of punctuality. Time was one of James's most valued possessions, and he hated, hated it when people were late and made him wait. It also miffed him that some of his younger teammates were slobs, leaving the locker room a mess and letting the attendants clean it up.

James hadn't counted on dealing with his own injury issues. He'd never missed more than five games with an ailment, his durability being one of his greatest traits. When the knee and back slowed him down, it slowed the assimilation process he'd been trying to force through. He'd also not predicted spending so much time and effort with leadership. Perhaps he was overstepping conventional bounds with Blatt, but he was doing it because he felt it had to be done. In truth his plate had never been more full. He told people he felt like he'd already played two seasons because of how dramatic the transition had been.

His statistics suffered, with his shooting numbers sagging backward. James had been proud, at times obsessed, with becoming a more efficient player as he matured. He loved that he'd improved his shooting percentage in seven consecutive seasons. But this year the challenges had knocked him off his routines—he loved routines—and the injuries had hurt his performance. He always said he didn't care about stats as long as he won, but that wasn't true. He did care about stats, dearly, just not more than wins. Now that the wins were coming and he was feeling healthier, he was easing off a little. But he didn't see a complete product.

One area where James and the rest of the team hadn't made much progress was with Love. When the winning streak ended in Indianapolis, Love had just five points after getting only eight shots. Even as the Cavs found some success after half a season in a morass, Love often wasn't much a part of it. Even as they ripped off victories, the loss to the Pacers was the fourth time in the previous 10 games that Love had failed to score 10 points. At times he was a major part of the game plan; the night before the Indiana loss he scored 24 points in a home win over the Clippers. But he was averaging nine fewer points and six fewer shots per game than a year before.

The Indiana loss was a low point for Love, who'd gotten frustrated with his role. Often the game plan would be to feature him, and it would happen for the first 10 or so minutes. He racked up shots and stats in the first quarter, only to be forgotten by the fourth. He'd stand in the corner waiting as James and Irving went to work. When he got yanked for his defensive shortcomings he wasn't surprised. If they weren't going to involve him on offense, it wasn't worth having him out there.

"I think it's one of the toughest situations I've had to deal with," Love said after the game in Indianapolis. "There's no blueprint for what I should be doing."

Once again, the sentiment drummed up attention, because Love was a free-agent-to-be. He'd repeatedly said his future was in Cleveland, but he wasn't thriving. The team took the next day off, but James, having read Love's quotes, sent a message. It was done again in an odd and indirect way: on social media.

"Stop trying to find a way to FIT-OUT and just FIT-IN. Be apart of something special! Just my thoughts."

It appeared on James's twitter account late in the evening. The phrase was strange and it made its origin easier to identify. During the preseason, Love had used the same wording when explaining how he was trying to adapt to his new situation. "I'm comfortable and just not trying to, I guess, fit in so much," he said after a preseason game. "I had a talk with the guys...and they told me to fit out. Just be myself."

At the time, Love said he'd laughed at the concept because it didn't *fit* the classic team-first approach players are usually taught. "You always say check your egos at the door, but we also need to bring our egos with us, because that's what makes us so great. We wouldn't be here without them," he said.

But Love hadn't really followed this advice. He spent much of the season becoming a wallflower, drifting at the edges. His personality had been tough to read. When he made a mistake on the court, he frequently looked down and avoided eye contact with teammates or coaches. The same went for some interview sessions when he was uncomfortable with the questions. It was hard to get to know him, which made it hard to help him.

Love had a cutting sense of humor and a broad set of interests. His background was fascinating. The son of an NBA player and the nephew of one of the founding members of the Beach Boys, he split his youth between the pristine suburbs of Portland, Oregon, and the basketball courts of Los Angeles. Obsessed with basketball history, he studied the style of 1970s star big man Wes Unseld, a contemporary of his father's. When he was at UCLA he took advantage of access to Bill Walton and John Wooden, delving into conversations with both as often as possible. He later gave the university $1 million to help fund a basketball facility. Doughy as a kid and young adult, Love had devoted himself to training and remade his body, shedding lots of weight as he spent summers conditioning in the mountains near Park City, Utah.

Repeatedly when the topic of Love's disappearance from offensive strategy was brought up, James or Blatt would reference how he needed to "demand" the ball more or "make himself more available" by getting teammates' attention. It would seem like they wanted Love to "fit out" and not just go with the flow that often bypassed him.

It wasn't that Love was having a bad season. His numbers were good, and frequently he was a major force in wins. But he was not the dominating player the team and perhaps James expected when it made a major trade for him. Some of this could've been because Love was dealing with rolling periods of back pain that kept him out of games intermittently throughout the season. When it came time to announce the All-Star reserves, the coaches passed on voting him onto the team. He'd been an All-Star three times in Minnesota when he was facing stiff competition among rival power forwards in the Western Conference like Dirk Nowitzki, Tim Duncan, and Blake Griffin.

James's tweet seemed like a nefarious jab, one that wasn't just opaque but came off as passive-aggressive—a James trait that sometimes was irksome.

The day after the tweet, Love exploded for his best game of the season, scoring 32 points with 10 rebounds in a victory over the Lakers in Cleveland. He hit seven three-pointers, three of them assisted by James. Irving had 28 points, making five three-pointers, and a season-high 10 assists. James had 22 points, meaning the three had combined for 82 points in the type of performance the entire enterprise was supposed to be about. Fitting in, fitting out, whatever—this type of triple threat had the Cavs looking like a championship-level team.

James admitted he was aiming the tweet at Love, which now seemed like a nice story with him responding so strongly. The only thing was Love said he hadn't even seen it—it was an afternoon game and he hadn't been asked about it earlier in the day. Then James put out an odd denial, reversing course.

"If I have a problem with a teammate or anyone I'll say to their face and not over social media. That's corny and wack!" James wrote in another tweet.

As he'd done throughout the season, Love took the high road. "I truly feel if LeBron had a problem with me or needed to talk to me, for good or for worse, he would have come up and talked to me," he said. "There's no problem with us. I'm going to keep saying that I'm trying to help this team. That's all that matters. I don't need any validation."

The merry-go-round kept moving, eventually it led to wins in 18 of 20 games. Whatever James was trying to accomplish with the fit in/fit out message, it didn't change much. Love continued his inconsistency. Though he had a few impactful games as the season went on, his teammates passed him the ball even less but he avoided complaining. The team just kept winning.

Timo Mozgov kept putting together nice performances. He scored 20 points in a blowout of the Heat. They blasted the Wizards by 38 points as J. R. Smith and Iman Shumpert combined for 27 points. The team put up 127 points that night, Love, James, and Irving combining for 68. It was 51 points more than the previous trip to Washington.

Smith had 17 points in a triumphant return to Madison Square Garden. Love made eight three-pointers in a win at Detroit, with James assisting on five of them. The Cavs then added veteran center Kendrick Perkins to the roster, another veteran voice in the locker room from someone with a championship ring.

It culminated with an 11-point home victory over the Warriors, who'd become the championship favorite with Stephen Curry, who'd become the MVP favorite. James scored 42 points with 11 rebounds and five assists, his most forceful game of the season. The Cavs moved through March by winning 14 of 17 games. After once falling to as low as seventh in the Eastern Conference standings, they leapt into second place.

When the Cavs arrived in San Antonio for a nationally televised game against the Spurs, James's world was totally different than when he walked out of the building after Game 5 of the Finals the previous June. He was on a new, younger, and up-and-coming team, and they were coming together in such a way that he was feeling good about his decision to leave Miami. Irving was hot, he was healthy, and he'd found a way to play with James that had both fulfilled and growing. The team's new players, Shumpert, Smith, and Mozgov, were all thriving.

And Blatt was being Blatt, his bravado expanding with each win. His team was 23–5 over the previous two months at that point. Headlines in the Israeli media, which were closely charting the Cavs' progress, were championing his efforts in turning the team around.

Before the game, Spurs coach Gregg Popovich was reminded that he'd predicted the Cavs would eventually get themselves together. As he had in November when Blatt had coached a mess of a game in a close loss, Popovich praised his peer.

"I know what his system is, and if he had a group that was willing, I knew it would turn," Popovich said. "But it takes a while to have a coach institute a system and have everybody buy in, understand it, feel good about it, gain confidence. He's a good one. He knows what he's doing. The guys figured that out and they're playing great basketball."

A few minutes later, down the hallway, Popovich's remarks of praise were repeated to Blatt. Instead of just accepting Popovich's compliment, Blatt again took an offensive posture in repeating his biography.

"I came back to the United States after thirty-three years speaking the same language," Blatt said. "Don't forget I coached in Russia, Italy, Turkey, Greece. That was a lot harder. Those are different languages, different cultures, and different worlds." He said he was "one of the more experienced coaches in the world" and then compared his accomplishments to the Spurs' success—five titles over the previous fifteen years—to the various championships he'd won in Europe.

On a roll, Blatt was asked when he knew he'd found his footing as an NBA coach as Popovich indicated he'd observed in recent months.

"The day after I signed," he said.

As hot as the Cavs were running by then, Blatt felt safe doing some gloating. It did take some savvy to manage all the obstacles that had been put before him, and he was leading a team that was improving by the week. But those involved with the team, the people who were at practice, in film sessions, and around the bench, knew there was an elephant in the room no one really talked about. James did follow Blatt at times, but he frequently freelanced without concern. Blatt had yielded, perhaps out of survival, and operated around it. Meanwhile, James, and many of the other players, still seemed to connect better with Lue.

James had another good game in San Antonio, scoring 31 points. Yet he was relegated to a sideshow. Irving had one of the most remarkable games the NBA had seen in the previous decade, putting on a shooting and scoring display that was breathtaking and record-breaking.

He made 20 of 32 shots, all seven three-pointers he attempted, all 10 free throws he attempted. He again had five assists. He scored 14 straight points in the second quarter. At the end of the fourth quarter with the Cavs down three points, James acted as the inbounder and Irving got free to nail a three-pointer at the buzzer that forced overtime. The clutch shot was over Kawhi Leonard, the freakishly long-armed and giant-handed defensive beast who'd won Finals MVP the year before and was a month away from winning Defensive Player of the Year. Irving would eventually score 15 straight Cavs points in the fourth and overtime.

The Cavs eventually won, 128–125, and Irving totaled 57 points. It broke James's franchise scoring record. It was the most points a James teammate had ever had. It was the most points a Popovich-coached team had ever allowed. It was the most points scored against a defending champion since Wilt Chamberlain put up 62 on the Boston Celtics in 1962.

It was a moment to celebrate Irving, but it was also graduation day in certain respects. His career had been knocked to a different track when James arrived and his mental preparations for it weren't enough. Beyond the mechanics of going from the team's primary scorer to operating alongside one of the greatest scorers of all time, Irving had struggled with James's leadership maneuvers. Tough love, real love, coded messages, being caught in the middle of the James-Blatt seesaw—it had been a challenging season for Irving to find his place.

He had always been a player who followed his instincts—usually, do whatever is necessary to get your team a basket—and he was suddenly in a world where there were so many more layers.

Slowly he'd found room to flourish. James wanted him to, he was invested in making it a partnership, but they were so different—their ages, their styles, their experiences—that it was a daily challenge. He hadn't totally figured it out, but Irving's willingness to work at it had won James over. And as he drilled shot after shot on the Spurs, he got something from James that he almost never showed. Awe.

"The kid is special," James said. "We all know it. We all see it. For him to go out and put up a performance like he did was incredible."

"As long as my elbow's pointed at the rim, I feel like it has a great chance to go in," Irving said, explaining how he'd hit some circus shots. He also was the beneficiary of Mozgov, who acted like a road grader in leveling Spurs point guard Tony Parker with screen after screen that allowed Irving to eat up the Spurs' defensive scheme.

Irving gave teammate Miller, who'd become a valued mentor, supporter, and friend, his shoes from the performance as a gift, complete with autograph, date, and the number 57. Miller cradled them like a baby as he boarded the team bus.

As for the James-Love dynamic, that remained more of a work in progress. After a victory in Milwaukee a few weeks later, James gathered some teammates for a group photo in the jetway as the team was about to board their plane to head home. James, Irving, Shumpert, Smith, Mozgov, Tristan Thompson, and the newly signed Perkins were together. Again, James's Twitter feed became a news item when he posted the photo along with the caption: "Clique Up."

The implication was this was James's clique on the team. That wasn't even truly the case, as James Jones and Miller, two of James's most adored teammates in his career, weren't in the photo. But the focus immediately was on Love's absence after he'd had another less-than-stellar game, scoring just nine points with three rebounds. Once again, relationships and the future were thrust to the forefront as chatter enveloped the team.

The next day, Love had scheduled a round of morning radio interviews as part of a marketing deal he'd signed to promote chocolate milk. Love, who had been guarded in so many interviews all season, was refreshingly honest in the discussions. As expected, his relationship with James came up.

"You know, we're not best friends, we're not hanging out every day, but we see each other every day," Love told Mike Greenberg and Mike Golic on ESPN Radio. "If we have a chance at the end of the year to hoist that Larry O'Brien Trophy, then it's all been worth it. There's been times this season...that I fought [my role], but then seeing the end result it kind of changes everything. Had it been different, maybe I would've felt a different kind of way."

Later, on Dan Patrick's national radio show, Patrick asked Love who would get his vote as MVP. Curry and the Rockets' James Harden were candidates, with the Cavs' strong second-half surge making James an option too.

"Time spent on the court—LeBron took a couple weeks off. They're both having an MVP-type season, but I'm going to go with Russell Westbrook because every single night you're looking at his stat sheet," Love said. "I think Russ is arguably having the better season."

Love's viewpoint was reasonable. Westbrook had been carrying the Thunder after defending MVP Kevin Durant was lost for the season with a foot injury. Love had been teammates with Westbrook at UCLA, and they had a long-standing relationship. Love also once again repeated he wanted to be a Cav long-term.

That didn't matter. Headlines took off because Love's comments were on the heels of James's tweet. Love giving an honest answer instead of defaulting to saying his teammate should win MVP became fresh chum on the talk show circuit. Love's 22 points and 10 rebounds on 10-of-13 shooting in the next game, yet another Cavs blowout win in Memphis, didn't quell it much.

"I don't really think too much of it, really," James said, trying to defuse the matter. "Kevin has his own opinion, who he believes is MVP, no one should fault him for that."

Several days later, though, James got in a playful dig. When he was asked for who he'd vote for in the MVP race, he smiled.

"Who would be my vote?" he said. "Kevin Love."

Chapter 9

TIMEOUTS AND FIGHTER PILOTS

The Cavs finished the season 53–29, going 34–9 after the night in Phoenix when they'd fallen to 19–20, to capture the No. 2 seed for the East playoffs. They sacrificed a few games at the end to rest players, or the record might have been even better. After dealing with back, knee, and wrist issues, LeBron James was healthy. After dealing with knee issues, so was Kyrie Irving, and frequently playing brilliantly alongside James. Love was battling back problems but was able to play through it most nights. The rest of the team was in good shape. They were going into the playoffs with star power, depth, health, and momentum, all a team could ask for.

Just before the end of the regular season the Cavs beat the Bulls, who had a strong finish to the season to surge into the No. 3 seed. James had played well, posting his first triple double of the season. But the Bulls, who lost three of four games to the Cavs, were in it until the end despite star Derrick Rose missing the game with a minor injury.

As they lined up for a potential showdown in the second round of the playoffs, the Bulls thought the outcome proved they'd fare well against the Cavs in a possible playoff series.

"It would be great to play them in the playoffs," said Bulls team leader Joakim Noah, who had a healthy personal rivalry with James after seeing him in three playoff series over the previous five years. "It would be very, very exciting. Something that I really hope happens."

At the first postseason practice, James had brought some show-and-tell material. He pulled out the two diamond-encrusted championship rings he'd won with the Miami Heat to show to his younger teammates.

Over the next few days, the Cavs' three stars smothered the outclassed Boston Celtics through the first three games. In Game 1, James, Love, and Irving combined for 69 points, with Irving putting up 30 and Love pulling down 12 rebounds as he led a punishing of the Celtics' big men on the boards. In Game 2, the three scored 69 again and again Love helped smash the Celtics in the trenches. In Game 3, the Celtics tried to push back on their own floor, going to the traditional underdog game plan of playing physical.

Celtics guard Evan Turner slammed James down and was called for a flagrant foul. Jae Crowder, Boston's young and tough forward, leveled Irving on a drive to the basket, causing Timofey Mozgov to retaliate by shoving him. Later, Tristan Thompson got under the skin of Gigi Datome after a rebound battle and the two men went face-to-face. Celtics coach Brad Stevens was excoriating his team during timeouts to fight, and they were, but the Cavs were just stronger.

By Game 3, Irving looked a little off, not moving as well as normal. He'd say after the game that his acceleration was missing. What he didn't say was that he'd sprained his right foot and it was affecting him. It didn't matter. Love nailed six three-pointers, his most in two months, and scored 23 points. For Love, who'd waited for seven seasons to make the playoffs, it was a highly satisfying moment. It was the type of performance that made the drama of the previous nine months—the trade demand, the reduction in stats, the various controversies—worth it. That went for everyone.

"Kevin's been highly criticized this year," James said. "I know why. When you have a Big Three, they've got to find someone. When I was in Miami, Chris Bosh was that guy at one point. I've seen it before. They've got to find somebody. Kevin was the guy they tried to find and tried to tear him down. The one thing about him, he's always stayed positive. I've always believed in him."

This, of course, wasn't true. There were times when James openly doubted Love. Others on the team did as well. But with the Cavs' three stars averaging a combined 68 points a game over the first three games of the series, no one was complaining.

As the first quarter of Game 4 unfolded, the Cavs were playing beautifully as a unit. They jumped out to a 10-point lead, executing some of their smoothest offense of the season. James and Irving were playing together seamlessly, the product of months of work. Love was making an impact as a third scorer and combining with Thompson and Mozgov to create a relentless front line. J. R. Smith and Iman Shumpert were playing their roles perfectly, finding ways to contribute at both ends. David Blatt had found game plans that seemed to take advantage of his players. His defensive changes when the mid-season reinforcements arrived proved to be effective.

Then Crowder missed a long three-pointer badly and the ball bounced toward Love, who was about to get yet another rebound. As he moved into position by boxing out Celtics center Kelly Olynyk—one of the players Stevens had been ripping into about the Cavs' rebounding dominance—Olynyk got his right arm tangled with Love's left arm.

The ball was to the right and Love was reaching to control it. Olynyk pulled Love to the left, grimacing as he yanked Love's arm down and away from his body. The official called a foul on Olynyk, stopping play. James, Irving, and Smith turned and started heading up the floor. The crowd hissed at the call. But Love was yelling in pain.

He immediately started running toward the tunnel to the visitors' locker room, his left side lower than his right. His left hand was in a fist, the arm motionless. As he passed the team bench, the players saw what appeared to be a dent in his shoulder area. Several covered their mouths as they saw the damage. Olynyk had dislocated Love's shoulder. The team's momentum was crushed.

The incident instantly elevated the animus. Late in the first half, Kendrick Perkins, who was the Cavs' de facto enforcer, buried his forearm in Crowder's neck on a pick and the teams ended up in a scrum at the center of the floor. When the team got to the locker room, Love was in a sling and irate at Olynyk, telling his teammates he was convinced it had been done on purpose. The replays helped convince them.

Less than 90 seconds into the second half, Smith and Crowder got tied up fighting for positioning on a rebound. Crowder's style of play had gotten on the Cavs' nerves over the four games. When he shoved Smith in the back, Smith reacted violently, swinging his arm back and hitting Crowder in the jaw. Crowder crumpled, falling awkwardly and injuring his left knee. Smith was quickly ejected. As Crowder was carried to the locker room he screamed at Smith, telling him it was "a bush-league play."

At that point the Cavs were up 19 points and the series was effectively over, but the body count was piling up. It was certain Love was going to be out an extended period. And it looked likely that Smith was headed for a suspension that would spill over into the next series. Meanwhile, Irving again wasn't himself. The foot was bothering him and he ended up making just 11 of 30 shots over the final two games of the series. The Cavs had just finished a sweep, but there were no smiles.

"I have no doubt in my mind that he did it on purpose," Love said about Olynyk. "Oh, the league will take a look at it and it better be swift and just."

The league would also be taking a look at Smith. "This is a situation that I put my teammates in, and it's a selfish act because I don't want anything that we do collectively to be taken away by one individual," Smith said. "My team is going to pay for it. I'm nervous as hell to see what could come out of this."

The league ruled the next day. Olynyk was suspended for a game the following season. Smith was suspended for the next two games and hit with a $116,000 fine, his record of 27 previous suspended games certainly hurting his case. Perkins was fined $15,000 as well. But by the time the announcement was made, Love was getting ready to have surgery that ended his season.

The team had eight off days before facing the Chicago Bulls in the second round. It was the fourth time in six years that James would face the Bulls in the postseason, including his time in Miami, and the Bulls felt like they had a legitimate shot to finally beat him. Especially with Love out and Smith suspended.

And indeed Chicago got off to a good start, winning Game 1 by seven points. The rest had helped Irving's foot—he scored 30 points— and Shumpert was excellent in moving into Smith's spot in the starting lineup, scoring 22 points. But Rose ripped the Cavs, especially as he burned them with the same play over and over late in the game, setting up teammate Pau Gasol for baskets.

In an effort to deal with the personnel losses, Blatt altered his game plan to a style the team hadn't used all year. Compounded by the fact that he tried some lineups that hadn't ever played together, the Cavs looked lost for the first time in months. Blatt's failed strategies became an issue, and grumbling that hadn't been heard from the locker room for a while started to return.

James rallied the team to a 15-point victory in Game 2 as he scored 33 points, but he took 29 shots, the most he'd taken in a playoff game in six years. As the talent level dropped and the stress mounted, James kept ending up with the ball. It was not the style the team had worked on. Shumpert played strongly again but suffered a groin injury and was wrapped in ice in the locker room after the game.

Yet with the series 1–1 and going to Chicago, the Bulls were in a great position. Smith came back from suspension and made four three-pointers, but Shumpert was diminished in Game 3. James played poorly, missing 17 shots and committing seven turnovers.

At one point, James was called for a technical foul for taunting Noah. James and Noah had battled for years. Noah had once ripped James for celebrating too much, James barking at him from the foul line while Noah was on the bench. When James was in Miami, Noah called the Heat "Hollywood as hell," his way of calling them phony. This time he called James a "bitch" after a play and it set James off.

"I love his emotion as a competitor. But I think the words that he used to me was a little bit too far," James said. "I'm a father with three kids. It got very disrespectful."

Noah was stunned. He'd called James much worse to his face at other points within the same game. "Disrespectful?" he said. "I got mad respect for LeBron. We're just two players trying to win a game. That's all. I don't know what he's talking about."

Beyond that, the bad news for Cleveland was Irving reinjured his right foot. He stayed in the game and played on it, limping at times and putting more weight on his left side. "I just tried to stay out there for my brothers," he said. "And use myself as a decoy."

It was the first time it appeared as if Irving's injury was serious, and it came at a bad time. Despite the challenges, the Cavs were tied in the final moments and hoping for overtime. With three seconds left, they defended perfectly, breaking the Bulls' inbounds play. Rose threw up a desperation shot at the buzzer with the much taller Thompson challenging the shot, and the ball banked in off the backboard, winning the game and giving the Bulls a 2–1 series lead.

Rose just stared ahead as teammate Taj Gibson lifted him into the air while the crowd in his hometown screamed in glee at one of the biggest shots of his life, the last of his 30 points. Thompson bent over as if someone had punched him in the stomach. When he got to the locker room, his teammates consoled him as he broke down and started to cry for not having been able to defend the shot.

Thompson is a relentless competitor who has a sensitive side, which has always made him endearing. His parents are Jamaican, but they moved to a suburb outside Toronto, where he grew up. At the urging of his parents, he played soccer as a child, which helped him develop good footwork. He became more interested in basketball after attending some Raptors games where he saw Vince Carter star. As he grew, eventually to 6 foot 10, his footwork proved to be valuable. It's a talent few big men have.

He moved to North Jersey in high school so he could play against better competition. When his school, St. Benedict's, lost a high-profile game to St. Patrick and a young star named Kyrie Irving, Thompson got in a fight with his coach and quit the team. That is not Thompson's personality—he's usually even-tempered. The Cavs drafted him with the fourth pick in 2011, three picks after they'd taken Irving.

He can get emotional, and it can be an aid—he had developed into a relentless rebounder and worker. When he struggled with free throw shooting after his first few seasons in the league, he stopped shooting left-handed as was his nature and instead shot right-handed.

As Thompson and the rest of the team collected themselves after the brutal loss, James remained calm. He'd been here before. The year he won his first title in Miami, the Heat had been behind in three consecutive series and rallied back to win them all. He'd won elimination games on the road. So being down 2–1 wasn't devastating. But with Love out, Irving shaky, and now Shumpert limping, a feeling of unease surrounded the team. James preached calm, even if he wasn't.

The Cavs got a break in Game 4 when Gasol was scratched because of a pulled hamstring, but Irving and Shumpert were a mess. They combined to shoot 3-of-18 and limped through it, especially Irving, who labored through 40 minutes. The Bulls had a seven-point lead going into the fourth quarter and looked to be on the verge of taking a 3–1 lead.

The Cavs rallied back, Smith hitting four three-pointers, and had a two-point lead with 27 seconds left. Then the team seemed to go into a collective brain freeze. They called three timeouts during the next possession, once because they couldn't get the ball inbounds. Referees advised the Cavs bench that they were out of timeouts.

The timeouts appeared to be wasted as the Cavs struggled again to execute the inbounds and James was quickly trapped. Without a time-out, he tried to get free and was called for an offensive foul. It was his eighth turnover over the game. He was carrying a heavy burden but he was far from playing his best.

Moments later the Bulls tied the game when Rose left the hobbled Shumpert in the dust and scored on a layup. There were 9.4 seconds left. Matthew Dellavedova, who'd been pressed into more service with Irving's injuries, went to inbound the ball. Blatt, inexplicably, started walking onto the court to call timeout. A timeout the Cavs didn't have.

It was perhaps ironic that it was in Chicago on the second night of the season Blatt stood outside the locker room and reminded everyone he was not a rookie head coach. He had become furious months later when media questioned why Lue was seen signaling for and managing timeouts from the bench. It was this loss of composure in the heat of the game that had shaken his players' confidence in him. And it all came to a head in that moment. Had Blatt been given the timeout, the Cavs would've been called for a technical foul and the Bulls would've gotten a free throw and the ball in a tied playoff game with less than 10 seconds to go.

Lue immediately saw Blatt's mistake and reached out and pulled him back to the bench. Veteran referee Scott Foster looked at the Cavs bench as Blatt was asking for time, but he didn't stop the game. It was a near miss, a moment of infamy avoided.

"I almost blew it," Blatt said.

James ended up going to the basket and missing, again, having his shot blocked out of bounds. He thought he was fouled, but he was also going one-on-three—he didn't trust any of his teammates to shoot and the Bulls knew it. Shumpert was standing alone in the corner, wide open, as James forced the shot. Then the Cavs caught another break. The officials had to look at replays to determine how much time should be left. It was a free timeout to design a play. Blatt got into the middle of the huddle.

Blatt wanted to have James inbound the ball and for Irving to take the final shot. Irving hadn't been in the game and Blatt wanted him to sub in. Blatt's reasoning was sound. James was the team's best passer and the Cavs had just struggled massively to get the ball inbounds against the Bulls defense moments before. Several times during the season, Blatt made James the inbounder on crucial plays and it worked.

James heard the play and stopped Blatt as he was drawing it up. He said he would be taking the final shot. He drew up a simple play where he'd fake going to the rim and then pop out to take a jumper. It was not a high-percentage play. It was also not unusual for a superstar to overrule his coach at such a moment.

With 1.5 seconds left, James made his move and shook his defender, Jimmy Butler. As he popped open right in front of the Bulls bench, coach Tom Thibodeau jumped back as he almost made contact. He wasn't expecting the James move either. James launched the shot from 20 feet, his toe on the three-point line. He fell into the bench and watched it drop through the net shoulder-to-shoulder with Bulls players.

It was salvation and a moment of redemption from James, who had been a big reason why his team nearly lost. It might have saved the Cavs' season. It is impossible to know what would've happened had his team gone down 3–1, but it seemed unlikely they'd be able to recover. It was also one of the biggest shots in a career that was already filled with them.

After the game, Blatt explained the last play design, which featured Dellavedova inbounding. "We wanted Delly to throw it right in over the shoulder. And with that amount of time on the clock let LeBron take a shot and he did. Great play."

When asked for his side of the huge event, James told a different story. "To be honest, the play that was drawn up, I scratched it," he said on the interview podium as he gave a little smile. "I told Coach, 'Just give me the ball. It's either going into overtime or I'm going to win it.' I was supposed to take the ball out. I told him there was no way I'm taking the ball out."

In the locker room, the players added to the lore. "At first Coach had LeBron taking the ball out. I'm like, 'Are you sure?'" Smith said. "Then he went, 'No, no, no, no, Bron, you get it.' I'm like, 'Okay, we need to switch it up.'"

In the corner, Irving sat with not only his ailing right foot in ice but also his left knee, an ominous development that was just starting to present itself. He was favoring his right leg because of the foot, and now the left knee was barking and he was concerned he'd seriously hurt it.

Over the next twenty-four hours, three highlights kept running: Blatt trying to call timeout, James hitting the game-winner, and then the sound bite with James declaring, "I scratched it." In what was supposed to be a triumphant moment, Blatt was having to defend himself. The issues from the season's first few months were rushing back, Blatt's fitness for the job and James's trust issues with him again in the forefront.

"A near mistake was made and I owned up to it and I own it," Blatt said. "A basketball coach makes 150 to 200 critical decisions during the course of a game, something that I think is paralleled only by a fighter pilot."

Blatt comparing himself to a fighter pilot created a new cycle of reaction both for his supporters, who loved the brashness, and his critics, who seized on the arrogance. Coaches make mistakes, and it was expected in their playoff experiences. But Blatt's attitude during the season and repeated declarations of his experience had eroded some sympathy. James didn't much help when revealing the details of the final huddle.

While that was all happening, Irving was in an MRI machine having his knee looked at. The results came back showing no damage. Irving was relieved. He wasn't just dealing with pain, he was having a mental battle while playing huge minutes through an injury that needed rest.

"This has been the biggest mental challenge of my career thus far, just because I want to do more," he said. "I want to be that guy for my

teammates as well as for Bron. We built a dynamic of me and him playing off one another extremely well. When you can't do that, and you are
limited to certain things, you have to come to grips with it."

The tide had turned, though. James was due for a good game, and
he found one in Game 5. He scored 38 points with 12 rebounds, six
assists, and three blocks with no turnovers. Irving played with more
confidence on his knee and scored 25 points. The Cavs won by five and
took the series lead for the first time.

With 10 minutes left in the game and the Cavs up 10 points, the
Bulls' Gibson hit Dellavedova with a clean but hard pick. A few seconds later, Gibson knocked Dellavedova to the ground as they scrambled for rebounding position.

Already a popular player in Cleveland because of his hustle plays, Dellavedova was spending more time on the floor and his style of play had
irritated the Bulls. As he was lying on the ground, Dellavedova leg-locked
Gibson, who reacted by kicking him to get free. Officials ejected Gibson,
who was enraged because he felt it was a dirty play. It certainly was a
unique one. As the replay was shown on the scoreboard, James and Mike
Miller howled with laughter on the sideline at Dellavedova's unconven-
tional move. "I've never seen that in my life!" James screamed to Miller.

The Bulls were angry and they were defeated. The Cavs came back
to win the series in Game 6 in Chicago, pulling away for a 19-point
win. It was costly. Irving landed on Thompson's foot in the second
quarter and tweaked his left knee again, forcing him to leave the game.

Thompson, who had been victimized by a few shots in the series, had
a strong game, scoring 13 points with 17 rebounds. Dellavedova, filling
in for Irving, finished with 19 points in his best game of the season.

James missed a triple double by a single rebound and vanquished
the Bulls yet again. Several days later Thibodeau was fired and the
team began a multiyear restructuring. James had effectively ended
a once promising era of Bulls basketball, not unlike the way Michael
Jordan had with many teams in his career in Chicago. That included
beating the Cavs three times in the playoffs, Jordan's series-winning
basket in Game 5 in 1989 being one of the great moments of his career.

The Cavs had five days off before starting the Eastern Conference
finals against the No. 1 seed Atlanta Hawks, who assembled a 60-win

season despite largely being in the shadows because of all the attention on the Cavs.

Smith made eight three-pointers in Game 1 and James again had a huge game with 31 points, eight rebounds, and six assists as the Cavs won on the Hawks' floor. Smith dedicated the game to his mom, Ida, who'd supported him through his tumultuous life. He'd had suspensions, feuds with coaches, and legal troubles and tragedy. In 2007, he drove an SUV through a stop sign near his home in New Jersey and collided with another car. His close friend Andre Bell, who was in the passenger seat, died from his injuries. Neither Smith nor Bell were wearing seat belts. Smith avoided major injury. He later pleaded guilty to reckless driving and served twenty-four days in jail. It was a crushing and soul-searching time in his life.

After so many challenges and lessons, it felt to Smith like he was finally getting a chance at doing things the right way. James had been a part of it; he'd taken Smith under his wing as he promised, and Smith was flourishing.

"The chance to come to play with LeBron has been a dream come true," Smith said. "I dreamed about this for years."

In another turn, James praised Blatt for the game plan he'd constructed over the previous week to slow down the Hawks' potent offense and three-point weapon Kyle Korver. It wasn't quite on Smith's level, but Blatt had shouldered plenty of negativity, and James, realizing a chance, tried to change the narrative.

"We have a great coaching staff that gives us a game plan," he said. "Throughout these six days, we've been balancing ways we can try to stop what they do."

But the aftermath was again about Irving as he reaggravated his left knee and was forced to the locker room. "The most frustrating part is seeing holes in the defense I'm used to attacking," he said.

Irving was unsettled about playing on the bad foot and knee and now several times had not finished games because of discomfort. But there were hints from within the team that he just needed to toughen up. He'd been told nothing was seriously wrong, and it left the impression that it was simply about playing through the pain.

"It's a combination of pain management and what the physical symptoms are," Blatt said. "It's just a matter of, is he healthy enough to play? Does he feel healthy enough to play? That's all."

"Everyone's pain tolerance is different, but my responsibility is much higher than a lot of guys," James said, seeming to compare his willingness to play through pain to Irving's. "Not only on this team, but a lot of guys in professional sports, and I take it very seriously."

The day of Game 2, Irving and Cavs team doctor Richard Parker took a private plane from Atlanta to Pensacola, Florida, so Irving could be seen by famed orthopedist Dr. James Andrews. Irving continued to be very concerned about his knee, and Andrews reviewed his tests and his case. He recommended Irving stop treating the right foot issue and focus solely on the knee and rehabilitating it. That included rest.

Irving made it back for the game but did not play. The Cavs didn't need him, winning by 12 as James was great yet again with 30 points, nine rebounds, and 11 assists. In the third quarter, Dellavedova was involved in a controversial play. With a loose ball on the court, he dove to corral it and in the process tried to block out Korver. He instead landed on Korver's ankle, causing a bad sprain that ended up forcing Korver to undergo surgery a few days later. Dellavedova and the Cavs saw it as a hustle play with an unfortunate ending; the Hawks saw it as a player diving at the legs of one of their stars.

The Hawks' last stand came in Cleveland in Game 3, but the Cavs won by three in overtime. Irving sat again. Dellavedova was strong relief, scoring 17 points, but again was involved in controversy. Going for a loose ball, he tripped over another player and fell at the knees of Al Horford, another Hawks star. After the Korver play, the Hawks were wary of Dellavedova. Horford responded by dropping an elbow on Dellavedova's head and neck. He was ejected, like Gibson had been in the previous series, for retaliating.

"He went after my legs," Horford said. "If it was on purpose, we don't know. Maybe it wasn't on purpose. But with his track record, I just felt like it was."

By this point, Dellavedova was reaching cultlike status in Cleveland as his play was vital with Irving out. He had excelled as an Australian rules football player as a child, which formed his sensibility about competition. He focused on basketball by the time he was a teenager, eventually earning a scholarship to St. Mary's College near San Francisco, which had established a pipeline of bringing in Australian players. He was a star there, becoming the school's all-time leader in scoring, assists, games, and three-pointers. Undersized and without much athleticism, he went undrafted.

But Mike Brown, who was the Cavs' coach at the time, had gotten to know Dellavedova's game well. Brown's son, Elijah, was a high school star in Orange County, California, and being recruited by St. Mary's. Brown watched a lot of their games and fell in love with Dellavedova. On draft night, several teams called wanting to sign Dellavedova after he wasn't selected. A little bidding war developed, and it came down to the team offering to guarantee him $100,000 to sign. The Cavs were unsure if he could be an NBA player but decided to make the investment. It turned out to be a quality one. His fearless play and willingness to outwork more talented players had kept him in the league, and his ability to learn the NBA game ended up making him needed. And the fans loved his workmanlike nature and his nickname, Delly.

By Game 4 the Cavs had regained the momentum of the second half of the season. They had found a way to survive without Love, mostly thanks to Thompson. When they crushed the Hawks by 30 points to end the sweep and clinch a trip to the Finals, things turned emotional. The group had earned the celebration and some reflection. Their journey had been unprecedented, and of all the dramatic moments, here they were zooming into the Finals with a seven-game win streak.

"I had to be very patient, which I'm not very patient. I'm not a very patient guy, but I knew I had to work on that," said James after scoring 23 points with nine rebounds and seven assists. He was just three assists away from averaging a triple double for the series.

"To be able to sit at one point during the season and see us at 19–20 and watching my team struggle and me sitting out two weeks, they wanted Coach Blatt fired, saying we needed another point guard, will LeBron and Kyrie be able to play together? So many storylines were just happening at that point in time. For us to be sitting at this point today being able to represent the Eastern Conference in the Finals, this is special. It's very special."

After a grinding six months, Blatt was holding another trophy, this one for winning the Eastern Conference. He'd won many before in Europe, and here he was doing it again. As his fans, especially in Israel, pointed out, he must be doing something right.

"I know it's hard for people to understand because they don't really know well my path and my career, but this also is a new situation for me and a new place for me," Blatt said.

"LeBron came home. I left home to come here, and I left a lot of people that I love dearly and a lot of people that I'm close, so close to, in order to pursue a dream. That's a big sacrifice on the part of my family and the place that I'm from. It's special because it's all worthwhile."

Part of the reason for the confidence was Irving, who returned and looked healthier as he scored 16 points in just 22 minutes. The treatment Andrews suggested was working and Irving was hopeful. They had some more time off before the next series and he was hoping it would help.

Their opponent would be the Golden State Warriors, who'd become the favorite after going through the season 67–15 as their point guard Stephen Curry morphed into one of the league's most dominating players in winning the Most Valuable Player Award. They'd only lost three times in three series before reaching the Finals and would have home court advantage.

Even considering all that, the Cavs were feeling confident. They'd smashed the Warriors the last time they'd played. And they had the best record over the last three months of the season. James was playing at a high level. The role players were delivering. Blatt had pieced together a lineup that was working without Love. They figured they'd weathered the worst of the storm.

They hadn't.

Chapter 10

"IT DIDN'T FEEL RIGHT"

Drederick Irving slammed the door to the trainer's room and quickly walked out of the locker room into the hallway. A few minutes later Jeff Wechsler, the agent for Kyrie Irving, entered and reopened the training room door and went in. Family members or agents being in a locker room is unheard of and the training room is one of the most guarded places in professional sports.

This was an extreme situation. Irving had collapsed during overtime of Game 1 of the Finals and limped off the floor. It was his left knee again. This time it was different and Irving knew it. The pain was acute. He'd been trying to drive on the Warriors' Klay Thompson when they banged knees, and he'd dropped to the court as the pain seared around his knee. As he rounded the corner, exiting the tunnel from the court with help from trainer Steve Spiro, he slammed his jersey to the concrete floor in pain and frustration. The left knee, the one he'd been rehabbing and treating with every therapy known to medicine for weeks, was on fire.

The Cavs had gone step for step with the Warriors all night. Coach David Blatt believed his team's best chance was to slow the Warriors and their offensive talents down, and they had done so, with LeBron James controlling the ball and the team's defenders desperately attempting to stay with the Warriors' shooters.

Neither team led by more than three during the fourth quarter, with James and Irving scoring or assisting on every basket. With 30 seconds left and the game tied, Irving leapt to make a fantastic block on Curry from behind. It was probably the finest defensive play of his career. He had looked healthy throughout the game, which was a huge development, as he scored 23 points and moved well.

Regardless of how the game turned out, that portended well for the Cavs' hopes in the series. If James could exert his will and Irving was close to his normal self, the underdogs believed they had a chance. The Cavs ended up getting two chances to win the game at the end of the fourth quarter, with Iman Shumpert's shot at the buzzer just missing as it skidded off the rim.

Then Irving went down and the Cavs fell apart. Curry scored four quick points and Harrison Barnes made a three-pointer, blowing the game open. The Warriors won by eight, Curry finishing with 26. James had 44 points but took 38 shots to get there, missing 20. James had sworn off that type of volume scoring earlier in his career, and playing that way—dominating the ball and finding ways to shoot even if the shots weren't quality—made him sick. But the once deep Cavs had gotten thin and he agreed this was the best chance.

In the training room Dr. Richard Parker manipulated Irving's knee. One of the finest surgeons in the country, Parker didn't find any damage to the ligaments. Just like the MRIs showed, everything was still connected. So why was Irving in so much pain? His father pulled general manager David Griffin aside. Irving had played 44 minutes as he was recovering from knee issues. The Cavs had sent him to the best to be examined and thrown all their resources at caring for him. But Blatt had played him heavy minutes.

In the Cavs' previous six games, Irving had been unable to finish three because of the left knee. Two other games he didn't play at all. He was mystified and, once again, concerned.

"I don't know what I felt but it didn't feel right. I'm in some pain. It was different than what I had been experiencing," he said as he looked down at the throbbing joint. "Your body works in mysterious ways. When something gives out. I don't know. Obviously you can hear in the tone of my voice I'm a little worried."

The next morning Irving went again to get imaging. The scan showed something stunning: He had fractured his left kneecap. He was done for the rest of the series and probably for some of the following season. A flight was arranged and he returned to Cleveland with Parker, who was to perform surgery immediately to repair it.

The team believed it was a direct result of the blow from Thompson and nothing to do with the previous inflammation or the heavy minutes. But there was some question about whether Irving had been overworked, weakening the knee and opening himself up to the injury.

"There were no minute restrictions coming into Game 1. There were no minute restrictions in Game 4 against Atlanta," Blatt said, trying to defend himself. "My take on the injury was that he got kneed in the side of his knee. It was a contact injury, and the result was a fracture of the kneecap."

Either way, the Cavs were now without two of their three best players (Love was still in the early stages of recovery from shoulder surgery), plus down 1–0 in the series. It had been a long, hard season of body blows and recoveries. This had the feeling of a knockout punch.

"It's a huge blow for our team, especially at this stage," James said. "You want to try to be as close to full strength as possible throughout these games, especially when you're going against a worthy opponent like we're facing. So it's a tough situation."

Matthew Dellavedova, who had played nine empty minutes in Game 1, was promoted to starting point guard. Blatt believed the only way to compete was to turn the game ugly and to try to play physical. The Warriors had some guys who didn't mind physical play, talented forward Draymond Green and rugged center Andrew Bogut among them. But the Cavs believed they could be tougher than the Warriors' sweet-shooting guards, Thompson and Curry. Golden State played a free-flowing style under coach Steve Kerr. They wanted to move quickly and be able to create space to do so. It was pleasant to watch and hard to stop when they got going—Curry and Thompson had the ability to go on numbing shooting streaks against which there was really nothing that could be done. So the Cavs would try to take that away by force.

Blatt put together a game plan where he'd ride big men Timofey Mozgov and Tristan Thompson and continue letting James dictate the offense with methodical possessions. In losing Kevin Love and Irving, the Cavs were down two great offensive players. But one upside was their replacements, Dellavedova and Thompson, were strong defensive players and Blatt could leverage that.

It showed up immediately in Game 2, where Dellavedova's dogged defense seemed to ruffle Curry. The Cavs pounded the Warriors on the boards and Thompson got seven offensive rebounds just himself, getting the team invaluable extra chances. The Cavs were abysmal on offense, shooting just 33 percent. James played a grueling style of bully ball, going a horrific 11-of-35 shooting. James went whole seasons without taking 30 shots in a game; now he was averaging nearly 40 in the series. But he drew nine shooting fouls and made 14 free throws, assembling 39 points, 16 rebounds, and 11 assists in one of the most prolific Finals games of his career. The Cavs won, 95–93, in overtime.

Thompson lit the Cavs up with 34 points, but Curry went just 5-of-23 shooting. When Dellavedova was guarding him, Curry was 0-for-8. Blatt used only seven players. When it was over, James slammed the ball to the floor in fatigue and triumph. It was one of the most improbable wins of his career. The series was 1–1.

Dellavedova's improbable rise continued. Several months earlier, Griffin searched the market for a trade for another backup point guard because he wasn't sure Dellavedova could handle the position in a playoff setting. Now he wasn't just surviving, he'd made himself into a vital piece of the Cavs' upset hopes. It had caused him to be a breakout celebrity. As for his demeanor, Dellavedova said he wasn't nervous, he was more concerned about staying hydrated because of all the energy it took to guard Curry.

"Obviously he's a guy that's been counted out his whole life," James said about his Australian teammate. "Probably people have been telling him he's too small, he's not fast enough, can't shoot it enough, can't handle it good enough, and he's beat the odds so many times."

Blatt joked the drama was part of the plan to help wake up fans in Israel where the games were broadcast in the middle of the night. Blatt's success had inspired national pride there. Though he was from Massachusetts, Blatt had lived in Israel for most of his adult life and considered it home. Numerous Israeli media outlets had come to cover the series, and Blatt was giving some interviews in Hebrew. It led to a different dynamic in press conferences, as some of the Israelis were upset Cavs players weren't giving Blatt enough credit for his game plan.

"The funny thing for us in Israel—and LeBron just sat here—we haven't heard the name David Blatt mentioned even one time. And now after becoming the first coach in Cavaliers history to win a game in NBA Finals, how much credit do you think he deserves for this win?" a reporter asked Dellavedova.

"Coach Blatt deserves a lot of credit," Dellavedova said. "We've got a good game plan going into the game. I think he's done a really good job all year. I enjoy playing for him."

Game 3 was a quick turnaround. After having two days between Games 1 and 2, there was just one day before Game 3 and the teams had to travel. For the Cavs, who were depleted, it hit them harder. The game plan was the same: Grind it out and let James shoulder the massive load. Again, amazingly, it worked and the Cavs won another ugly game, 96–91.

James again missed 20 shots but made 10 free throws as he finished with 40 points, 12 rebounds, and eight assists. He had 123 points in the first three games, the most ever in that span in Finals history. Dellavedova did it again, playing the game of his life and scoring a career-high 20 points. In the fourth quarter, he tripped as he was fouled and he flung a shot toward the rim. The ball banked in as he watched, lying on his stomach, setting up a three-point play. If the crowd could have, they'd have stormed the court and carried him out into the streets.

Up 2–1, James held the stat sheet and looked at all his missed shots with a furrowed brow. "I'm not okay with it but I'm so outside the box right now," he said. "This is a totally different challenge. I've never played where two All-Stars were out."

The Cavs being ahead in the series was just a stunning development. Their bruising style seemed to have taken the Warriors, who specialized in speed, flow, and shooting, out of their comfort zone. They'd been rattled and were down 17 points at one point in Game 3.

In the afterglow, however, there was a toll. The effort had completely zapped Dellavedova. He limped into the cold tub inside the locker room after the game to get treatment and virtually his entire body cramped. He couldn't move, calling to teammates and staff for help. They carried him to a training table and trainers started rubbing his muscles, trying to stop the seizing. Doctors started an IV to get him fluids. There was enough concern that he was sent to the hospital to be observed overnight.

Meanwhile Shumpert, whose defensive activity had been important, was in pain in his left shoulder. He'd gotten it jammed reaching for a loose ball, the same shoulder he'd dislocated earlier in the season. He was scheduled for an MRI the following day.

Something else happened too. The Warriors had used the second half to find momentum. Curry was 1-of-6 shooting in the first half against Dellavedova, his slump deepening. But with Dellavedova weakening and Curry finding some sets that could free him, the MVP had an explosive second half as he scored 24 points. The Warriors had scored 36 in the fourth, looking much more like themselves.

As the outside world began to wonder if the Cavs could really pull this upset off, the Israeli media were rallying to credit Blatt for his game plan that was making it possible. They peppered James and Blatt with questions about it. They asked why James didn't always include Blatt in the decision making when Blatt was proving to be a tactician. James, as he'd been for most of the season, was tepid in his replies as he made it clear he was still going to be working independently of Blatt when he saw fit.

"I think our relationship continues to grow every day," he said. "My mind is always working throughout the game. Sometimes I'm able to say it verbally, sometimes I'm just thinking the game and hoping the coaching staff and players and the guys and Coach Blatt know whatever I'm doing, it's for the best of the team. And he's allowing me to do that, and I respect that a lot."

Blatt, as he'd learned to do throughout the season, said he would keep giving James space. "I can't honestly tell you that in every case I know exactly what he's going to do," he said. "I do have a very high level of confidence that he's going to recognize the situation and make the right decision."

In Game 4, Kerr made a lineup change, removing Bogut and

inserting forward Andre Iguodala. The smaller, faster lineup was aimed at breaking the Cavs' stranglehold on the pace. It worked nearly instantly as the Cavs' slower big men weren't able to cover the quicker Warriors. Iguodala especially played well, scoring 22 points. Mozgov took advantage of the smaller defenders and scored 28 points with 10 rebounds, but it was a trade-off the Warriors were willing to live with.

Playing their third game in five days while essentially only using their core six players, the Cavs were physically spent. Dellavedova was not himself, clearly feeling the effects of the previous games. Shumpert was going with one good arm because of a sprained shoulder. Even James slowed down, scoring just 22 points.

Perhaps it was also because in the second quarter James went flying into the first row of photographers after being fouled by Bogut. He banged his head against a camera, opening up a gash, and landed at the feet of Nike executives Lynn Merritt and Ted Curvy. As James bled, Mike Mancias rushing to him with a towel, his close friend Merritt was on national television lambasting the photographer for not moving fast enough. In a metaphor for the night, James ended up needing stitches and the Warriors won, 103–82.

After the game, some of the team's veterans were grumbling in the locker room that they weren't getting a chance, namely Mike Miller and Shawn Marion. With Irving, Love, and Anderson Varejão all done for the season, and veteran centers Brendan Haywood and Kendrick Perkins unusable against the Warriors' small lineups, Blatt didn't have many options on his roster. He was in survival mode.

The Warriors had the edge going home with the series tied. Then their advantage expanded early in Game 5 when Blatt yanked Mozgov from the game. Unable to keep up with the Warriors' speed, Blatt relented and went small to match the Warriors. With a limited choice, he didn't have much of a choice. He'd been checkmated by a deeper team. As soon as Blatt made the substitution five minutes in, Kerr smiled to himself on the sideline and thought, "This is Steph's night."

He was right. With the floor spread with smaller players and Dellavedova and Shumpert limited, the MVP finally broke free. He nailed seven three-pointers and piled up 37 points, the crowd rejoicing in seeing their favorite player return to form.

Frustration with the situation seemed to spill over on the Cavs bench. Marc Stein, who was covering the series for ESPN Radio and was positioned behind the bench, described James's harsh treatment of Blatt during the game.

"I witnessed from right behind the bench, [James] shaking his head vociferously in protest after one play Blatt drew up in the third quarter of Game 5, amounting to the loudest nonverbal scolding you could imagine—which forced Blatt, in front of his whole team, to wipe the board clean and draw up something else," Stein wrote. "James essentially called timeouts and made substitutions. He openly barked at Blatt after decisions he didn't like. He huddled frequently with [assistant coach Ty] Lue, often looking at anyone other than Blatt."

This had been happening off and on for months and everyone around the team knew it. In a way, Blatt had become a sympathetic figure. His team was depleted and his star still fought and undermined him at times. But Blatt's attitude of endless confidence during the season, especially touting his experience level, didn't always inspire understanding. Then again, James was the reason the Cavs were in this position. It was a cruel bargain Blatt had to manage, and do so mostly alone. It was not what he thought he'd signed up for.

As for James's play, he missed 19 more shots, his inefficient scoring continuing to pester him, but he racked up 40 points, 14 rebounds, and 11 assists. In total, it was a tour de force, but it was looking like it wasn't going to be enough.

By this point it had become clear the Warriors had figured out a game plan and the Cavs were probably going to lose in a war of attrition. James had worked so hard and assembled enough numbers that some were suggesting he might win the MVP of the Finals on a losing team, something that hadn't happened for nearly fifty years since Jerry West did it with the Los Angeles Lakers. James didn't entertain such questions, but he did send a message about what he thought the series was proving.

"I still feel confident because I'm the best player in the world," he said, a jab at Curry, who'd finally had an impactful game.

After the game, Blatt was hammered by some for only playing Mozgov five minutes and giving up a size advantage. "Did I make a mistake?" he said. "Listen, when you're coaching a game, you've got to make decisions. I felt that the best chance for us to stay in the game and to have a chance to win was to play it the way we played it."

He was probably correct. With the Warriors' lineup change, playing Mozgov was just as dangerous as trying to match up small. After everything he'd gone through during the season, Blatt was doing some of his finest coaching in the Finals. The outmanned Cavs should've been done, but Blatt's moves had helped them stay alive.

Mozgov was back for Game 6 in Cleveland and he scored 17 points with 12 rebounds. James missed 20 shots again—he missed a record 118 shots over the six games. But once again his efforts were at an all-time elite level, with 32 points, 18 rebounds, and nine assists. Yet the Warriors led by as much as 15 in the second half and finished off winning their first championship since 1975.

James averaged 35.8 points, 13.3 rebounds, and 8.8 assists in the series, the first player ever to lead both teams in all three categories in Finals history. It was better than anything Bill Russell, Wilt Chamberlain, Magic Johnson, Michael Jordan, or Kobe Bryant had ever done. He didn't get the MVP—it went to Iguodala, who scored 25 points in the clinching game. Iguodala had battled James on defense for much of the series and forced many of those missed shots.

For more than an hour after the game, James sat at his locker with a towel over his head. This was his fourth Finals loss and second in a row. He lamented his team didn't have a chance because of injuries, while the Warriors were 100 percent healthy. He was bitter about the circumstances. Outside, Warriors players soaking in champagne stomped down the hall past the Cavs locker room to a room that was set up to have photographs taken with the trophy. In the silence, their howls were audible.

"You question it, especially when you get to this point," James said. "I always look at it, would I rather not make the playoffs or lose in the Finals? I don't know. I don't know. I'm almost starting to be like, I'd rather not even make the playoffs than to lose in the Finals."

James was speaking from a dark place and didn't really mean it. He'd been to five consecutive Finals and now three times had left without the trophy. In these moments he'd forgotten what it was like to win, wallowing in the loss. He'd also forgotten what he'd written eleven months earlier.

"I'm not promising a championship. I know how hard that is to deliver. We're not ready right now. No way. Of course, I want to win next year, but I'm realistic," he had written in his letter when returning to Cleveland. "It will be a long process, much longer than it was in 2010. My patience will get tested. I know that. I'm going into a situation with a young team and a new coach."

It was hard for James now to have the same perspective as when he spoke those words the previous July. Of everything he had been through in his career, the journey of this season had been the hardest. In some ways, it was rewarding. He felt he'd carried the largest burden of his career, having to provide more leadership than ever. Sometimes it had been misplaced and done damage. Even in his twelfth season, he was still learning. This was one of the grandest learning experiences of his life.

He also realized there was a new challenge. After his battles with the Spurs and Thunder, this Warriors team was a new beast to deal with. They were young, the core of the team was signed to contracts, and they had a coach who had reached them. James had dealt with young stars arriving to challenge him, Derrick Rose, Kevin Durant, and Kawhi Leonard among them. He'd found ways to manage them. But Curry, well, Curry was a different sort of challenge. There was a special edge growing there already.

Sitting alone in that chair, fatigued and emotionally gutted, James didn't want to consider the future. If he had been told what would happen the following year, he wouldn't have believed it anyway.

Chapter 11

EXCEEDING AN UNLIMITED BUDGET

The rooftop pool at the five-star Peninsula Hotel in Beverly Hills has twelve private cabanas, each with its own flatscreen, sound system, and telephone for ordering refreshments from the adjacent juice bar. It has long been a popular spot for secretive meetings because of its seclusion and amenities. LeBron James often used the hotel as a Los Angeles base during the summer months. Even after he bought a $21 million six-bedroom mansion in nearby Brentwood in 2015, he frequently returned to the rooftop restaurant and pool.

On a sunny day in late June, less than two weeks after the Cavs' season ended and three days before the start of free agency, James and some friends rented out several of the cabanas for an afternoon of relaxation. James was in town on Nike business and enjoying some rest before starting offseason workouts.

Kevin Love arrived and grabbed a chair from a cabana next door and pulled it over to sit next to James, who was expecting him. The meeting had been arranged and was informal but still important. The loss to the Warriors was still raw and his shoulder was still healing. Several days earlier, before he left Cleveland for the summer, Love had met with David Griffin and they discussed his big free agent decision that was coming up. For nearly a year, Love had professed he never wanted to leave Cleveland and he intended to re-sign long-term. Over and over he was asked about it, and over and over he repeated versions of the same answer: He planned to stay. He had discussed his contract

134 | RETURN OF THE KING

with teammates, and when he talked about options, it was usually about how long a deal to sign, not where he would sign.

Love told Griffin he wanted to have a meeting with James before he made a decision. Griffin wouldn't make a formal offer until after July 1, but it was clear the Cavs were prepared to give Love a maximum contract offer. Numerous teams had coveted Love for years, including the Lakers. There would've been a great deal to consider, especially considering the various little dustups Love had had with James and David Blatt during his transitional season. But his mind was essentially made up.

In the aftermath of Game 1 of the Finals, the night when Kyrie Irving limped out of the arena after a bitter overtime loss, Love sat in a corner with a smirk on his face and a light in his eyes. "I want to be in a moment like that, I've never wanted to be in a game more than that one," he said in an interview with ESPN after the game. He may have already been close in his mind, but seeing, if not touching, a Finals game had convinced him he couldn't go back to a non-contender as he'd lived with for years in Minnesota. He was going to stay.

Even as speculation raged about what teams Love might consider, all he wanted was to have an air-clearing session with James as the final step. When they found out they were going to be in L.A., James invited Love to the Peninsula.

"He wanted to have a sitdown with me and talk about everything," James said. "He wanted to talk about the season, what could happen with the team going forward. I was absolutely open to it. I was one of the people that wanted him there when we made the trade. The fact that he committed to us let me know the type of guy we have."

Love was in a moment NBA players dream about, an unrestricted free agent with huge offers about to come from teams across the league. He was about to bypass all the other options. Before he did, he wanted to get a feel for where James was. Because James too was about to become an unrestricted free agent. Several days after the Finals, he informed the Cavs that he was not picking up his player option and would hit the market. The assumption was he'd re-sign as well. Love, who was also about to pass on a player option, wanted to make sure James was staying and how he felt about their partnership continuing.

"A lot of stuff was very honest, and we came to a really good place and we agreed on a lot of things, so I think that was also a very big deal when you're talking to the best player in the world," Love said. "Truthfully, I expressed this to LeBron, and he'd been through [free agency] a couple of times. Now, I could actually go wherever I want and pick the team I want to play for. But every time I went through the different scenarios, I always came out at the same place, and that was to be in Cleveland and try to win championships. I would be able to really help this team win, and going forward make a very big impact on this team and on this city, trying to bring home a championship or championships."

James and Love parted on good terms. Both had decided, even as they basked in the L.A. sun, that they'd be staying in Cleveland. On July 1, even with teams bombarding his agent to set up pitch meetings, Love agreed to a five-year, $112 million deal to stay with the Cavs. After trading away Andrew Wiggins, who'd subsequently gone on to win Rookie of the Year with the Timberwolves, getting Love to commit long-term to stay was a huge victory for the team. Especially after his first season hardly went to script.

With little fanfare, James let the team know he'd be re-signing and eventually did a one-year deal as he had the season before.

These were the important decisions for the Cavs, although they were in the players' hands and not the team's. But Griffin's work was far from over. The roster was littered with free agents—Iman Shumpert, Tristan Thompson, J. R. Smith, and postseason hero Matthew Dellavedova in addition to James and Love.

The contract extension Kyrie Irving had signed the season before was set to kick in on July 1, more than doubling his salary from $7 million to $14.7 million. Love's new deal raised his salary from $15.7 million to $19.5 million. James's salary went from $20.6 million to $22.9 million. Owner Dan Gilbert was thrilled his stars were locked down and was happy to sign off. Those new star deals added $14 million to the payroll from the year before, and all the other free agents were anxious to get large raises as well.

The previous December, Griffin had prioritized getting Shumpert in a trade with Smith as a throw-in piece. Smith had proved he was more valuable than that. His playoffs were uneven—the suspension and an ill-timed shooting slump in the Finals left a sour taste—but he'd made a generally positive impact. But it was Shumpert, who was younger and seen as a better defender, that the team had prioritized all along. When Griffin and Gilbert mapped out their offseason strategy, they decided to focus on locking down Shumpert over Smith.

In the first moments of free agency, the Portland Trail Blazers agreed to a four-year, $30 million contract with journeyman small forward Al-Farouq Aminu, who'd averaged 10 points and nine rebounds a game the previous season in Dallas while playing for less than a million dollars. It stunned the market and shook the Cavs a little. They'd projected Shumpert on a higher level, and with Aminu setting the market fast, they realized Shumpert was going to be more expensive. Shumpert was a restricted free agent, meaning the Cavs had the right to match any offer. But instead of letting him test the market, they quickly increased their offer. Before the sun set on the first day of free agency, Shumpert had agreed to a four-year, $40 million deal even though he'd averaged just nine points and five rebounds during the playoffs. It represented a $6.3 million raise, kicking Gilbert's payroll additions to more than $20 million for the upcoming season. It also pushed the team into the luxury tax, meaning it would cost millions more.

The huge new outlay had consequences. The team had an option for the following season on Timofey Mozgov. In meetings, members of the front office pondered not picking up the $4.9 million option and looking to negotiate a new, longer contract. But with so much money coming on the books, the team was wary of adding more.

Dellavedova was caught in the same situation. Like Shumpert, he was a restricted free agent. He and his representatives were looking to cash in on his amazing postseason run. They were hoping for a three-year deal for between $3 and $4 million per year. Ultimately the Cavs didn't do the long-term deal and instead got Dellavedova to accept a one-year, $1.2 million deal so he could be a free agent again the next year. It worked out for both as both Mozgov and Dellavedova ended up signing huge free agent contracts a year later in 2016.

It was not so simple with the remaining restricted free agent,

Thompson. He'd proven to be a valuable role player because of his rebounding and defensive abilities. Just twenty-four and a big man, Thompson had plenty of value. He also hadn't missed a game in three and a half seasons, a reliability that was almost unmatched in the league.

Thompson had something that was hard to quantify but relevant in this situation—he was excellent playing alongside James. He was a strong screen setter and could free James with a pick and then roll to the rim to grab offensive rebounds. His quickness for his size made it easier to play smaller and quicker lineups that favored James, because Thompson was effective in switching to smaller players on defense. Finding these sorts of partners was valuable for James, but it wasn't valuable to the entire league, which set the stage for a complex negotiation for Thompson.

In the fall of 2014 as he was about to start his first season with James, Thompson and the Cavs had contract extension talks that failed. On October 31, the deadline for players to extend their contracts, the team offered Thompson a four-year, $50 million deal. He'd averaged 11.7 points and nine rebounds the season before, strong numbers but not star quality. He was represented by Rich Paul and Mark Termini, the same agents who had put together James's deal to return to the Cavs. Paul and Termini had done extensive research and salary-cap projections and they believed Thompson could get more if he waited until he got to the open market the following summer. They advised him to turn down the deal and he did.

That night, Thompson had 16 points and 13 rebounds in a win in Chicago. As Blatt was in the hallway telling people it wasn't really his first career win, Thompson sat at his locker and looked at texts from Paul. Part owner Nate Forbes, who sometimes handled contract talks, had made a final offer, pushing the total to $52 million. Thompson and his agents again said no. The number eventually leaked to the media and there was surprise that Thompson had turned down so much money. As the season went along he was heckled by fans about it, especially when he had an off night. Sometimes even rival players would pester him, often to try to get under his skin at the free throw line.

Thompson then played all 82 games again, and his offensive rebounding in the playoffs plus his ability to guard a variety of positions was vital for Blatt's game plans after the team lost Love to injury. He'd bet on himself and it was looking like it paid off. The turned-down $52 million over four years was forgotten and the Cavs started new five-year offers at more than $70 million. Thompson again said no. Paul and Termini had another number in mind: around $90 million over five years.

The Cavs, with so much money already committed, froze. As they had matching rights, the team knew it could still keep Thompson if another team made such an offer. But other teams, seeing how much the Cavs were spending, believed they would match and none made an offer. By mid-July, talks had broken off and the sides settled into a stalemate.

Other moves happened. Shawn Marion retired and Mike Miller, looking for a bigger role elsewhere, was traded. The Cavs replaced them with Mo Williams, a veteran guard who played with the team from 2008 to 2011, and Richard Jefferson.

A star in his younger days with the New Jersey Nets, Jefferson had transitioned to a valued role player. He'd committed to playing for the Dallas Mavericks, but when LA Clippers star DeAndre Jordan reneged on an agreement to sign there, Jefferson asked Mavs owner Mark Cuban to be let out of his agreement. Cuban obliged and Jefferson turned to Cleveland. After making the Finals his first two seasons in 2002 and 2003, Jefferson had not been back. He hoped James would be his ticket.

"I came to Cleveland for one reason," he said. "To play with LeBron James."

As Thompson waited the Cavs out, J. R. Smith was going through his own restless summer. He opted out of the final year of his contract, which had promised him $6.4 million. As he talked with the Cavs prior to the decision, they'd suggested he opt in. Smith believed he was in for a raise and so he opted out. Then the Cavs gave a big offer to Shumpert and not him. As the days in July passed, Smith watched as numerous other shooting guards got huge contracts. His phone didn't ring.

"The market was going crazy, I mean it was ridiculous," Smith said. "You see so many people getting paid. I started to look at myself in the mirror and was like, 'Damn, am I really what everybody saying I am? Am I really a cancer?' We'd just gotten to the Finals and I'm not trying to toot my horn, but I thought I'd had a major part in that."

Smith had thought he'd proven to teams he was changed man. His friends believed it; that summer he surprised them when he broke up with a girlfriend and proposed to Jewel Harris, whom he'd dated on and off for years and with whom he had a seven-year-old daughter, Demi. Smith missed seeing his daughter regularly when he was traded to Cleveland, and it convinced him to focus on family. This was a compelling narrative of maturation, but teams just remembered him getting suspended for that wicked elbow in the playoffs a few months before.

In early September, Smith accepted a one-year offer from the Cavs for $5 million, a pay cut. Shortly thereafter, he fired his agent. But he really didn't have many options other than trying to prove himself again. At age thirty, he'd gotten tired of it.

A week after signing, Smith flew to Miami, where he joined his Cavs teammates at a three-day minicamp that was put together by James. It had become commonplace for teams to hold informal training sessions in the summer, often in places that doubled as vacation spots for players, like Southern California, Florida, or New York. But this was no vacation. The veteran players who arrived at the University of Miami, where James had set up full use of the facilities, expecting some scrimmaging and shooting while music was blaring, were surprised. There were drills, weight training sessions, and two-a-day workouts. It was organized like a real training camp with Cavs coaches there observing.

On the sidelines doing some very light work was Irving, who had rented a home in Miami to do rehab on his knee after the June surgery. So was Love, still in the midst of rehab on his left shoulder from his May surgery. It was clear that both were quite some time away from being able to play, especially Irving, whose progress was slow.

Thompson wasn't there. Even though James and Thompson were both represented by Paul, James stayed out of the contract dispute other than to make some public comments that the team needed him back. A perception existed that James ran the Cavs front office, fostered after his influence in executing the Wiggins-for-Love trade became known. Gilbert and Griffin chafed at this and so did James and Paul, who was establishing a reputation as an agent independent of James. In all honesty, had James truly been running the Cavs, Blatt likely would've been fired early in the 2014–15 season and Thompson would probably have had a contract on July 1 along with Love and Shumpert.

James was irked at the coverage of his treatment of Blatt during the previous season, accurate or not. In mid-July, he attended a Summer League game in Las Vegas where Blatt was working with some of the team's young players. James walked up to Blatt during the game, embraced him, and sat down beside him in a very public manner. There was a lot of surprise at the moment, including from Blatt, who'd just barely survived months of James's challenges.

So Blatt was back for a second season but Thompson was not. In 2007, two years after Gilbert bought the Cavs, two unsigned restricted free agents skipped all of training camp in contract impasses. Sasha Pavlovic, a role-playing wing, ended up signing just before the start of the season. Anderson Varejão, who was still on the team, ended up not signing until December. Also involved was Termini, who represented Jim Jackson when he held out of the first 54 games of his rookie season with the Dallas Mavericks in 1992 in a contract dispute. These were two sides who weren't afraid to dig in.

A problem for the Cavs was their leverage was limited by injuries. Love was still hurt, Varejão was recovering from his Achilles' surgery the previous year, and in the offseason, Mozgov had knee surgery and was entering camp out of shape and sluggish. After the workouts in Miami, Shumpert went back to his home in Atlanta and snapped a ligament in his wrist while dunking, requiring surgery that would keep him out several months. James's back was also a concern as camp started. And there was the springy and energetic Thompson, who hadn't missed a game in nearly four seasons.

Paul attempted to maneuver in the talks, dropping requests for a five-year deal and instead asking the Cavs for a three-year deal worth $53 million. This offer, at $17.6 million per season, was still higher than the Cavs were willing to go. Another issue was the Cavs wanted to have a team option year or non-guaranteed money at the end of the deal. So while they upped their offer to $80 million over five years, it wasn't all guaranteed. The stalemate extended.

Finally, with just days to go before the start of the regular season, the sides found their common ground. Thompson got a five-year deal for $82 million, all of it guaranteed. It was for $30 million more than he'd turned down 12 months before.

When the numbers were totaled up, Gilbert had green-lit $290 million in guarantees to Love, James, Shumpert, Thompson, and Smith, and that didn't count Irving's new deal, which technically had been signed a year earlier. The Cavs were facing a luxury tax bill of $60 million, the second-highest ever. The promise Gilbert had made to James when they met near Fort Lauderdale in early July 2014 was being kept: The billionaire was going deep into his coffers to pay to put a high-priced team around James.

The night the deal was completed, Gilbert stepped onstage at an event for season ticket holders. He told the crowd the news without mentioning the salary number they'd all been reading on their phones. "I gave David Griffin and Nate Forbes an unlimited budget," he said. "And they exceeded it."

One thing the reassembled Cavs couldn't exceed was expectations. For months as their players healed from surgeries, they quietly—and sometimes not so quietly—complained that their loss to the Warriors had been a matter of bad luck. With the team loaded and its health coming back, Gilbert had put them in a position where they no longer were going to have any excuse.

The Cavs had bristled watching the Warriors celebrate, feeling there was an unfairness they couldn't do anything about. "We ran out of talent," James told *USA Today* in an interview about the loss. "There was a lot of talent sitting in suits. I've been watching basketball for a long time, I'm a historian of the game. I don't know any other team that's gotten to the Finals without two All-Stars."

James's implication was that they'd faced extreme, in his mind historic, obstacles. The Warriors had been fully healthy throughout the season and the playoffs. Not only had they played the injury-riddled Cavs, but some of their other opponents had had significant injuries as well.

Irving took it a step further. "I felt like we would have definitely won an NBA championship if everyone was healthy," he said. "But almost doesn't count."

The concept of luck playing a role upset the Warriors, who felt they'd been the best team from the start of the season. They felt as if some, including the Cavs, were attaching an asterisk to their accomplishment. It was apparent the Warriors were paying attention to the slights, almost keeping track of them. It's sometimes challenging for the defending champions to come back the following season with the same focus. In this case, the veiled shots at their legitimacy provided a fresh layer of motivation to see the Cavs again.

"I apologize for us being healthy. I apologize for us playing who was in front of us. I apologize for all the accolades we received as a team and individually," Steph Curry said. "I'm very, truly sorry, and we'll rectify that situation this year."

Interestingly, the Cavs felt the same way.

Chapter 12

LATE NIGHTS WITH THE WARRIORS

On a Tuesday morning in mid-October, LeBron James was lying on his stomach in an outpatient surgical suite at the Cleveland Clinic, and he was miserable. Not just because a doctor was putting a series of needles in his lower back, but because he also had a developing case of the flu.

For the second time in less than a year, James was getting an anti-inflammatory injection to help ease pain. The previous time, ten months earlier, it had worked wonders as he took two weeks off and had come back like a new man. With two weeks to go before the start of a new season he was having it done again, hoping the effects would last well into the season.

"My rookie year I felt fresh," he said. "I haven't felt fresh since. But I'll get my back right and I'll get stronger."

Things weren't going so well for the Cavs at this point, and James needing time off to recover from the procedure was only part of the issue. Two weeks into the preseason, Kyrie Irving, Kevin Love, Anderson Varejão, Iman Shumpert, and Timofey Mozgov were all in various stages of recovery from surgeries. Then J. R. Smith and Matthew Dellavedova suffered minor injuries. Now James was shut down. Not surprisingly, the team was a mess, showing no rhythm and losing their first five preseason games.

"I'm not having fun right now," David Blatt said after his team lost an exhibition game by 22 points to the Indiana Pacers.

Blatt had come into the season with an optimistic attitude,

proclaiming himself better prepared for this job now that he'd been through a rugged first season. The belief that the team had been loaded up for another chance at a title had briefly buoyed him. The week in Miami for the minicamp had seemed productive too.

"I had a lot to learn. I didn't always realize how much I had to learn about the game here and about the ways of the game here. I'm start-ing the season in a much better place," he said, seeming more out-wardly contrite than in his first season. "I'm certainly more confident in understanding the things that I need to do and the situations that I'm going to face, and that's a good feeling."

James wasn't exactly feeling the same way. Several times during the preseason he and veteran teammate James Jones led players-only discussions. At one, James chided his teammates for their, in his opinion, relaxed attitude. It was understandable in a way; many of the players were on new rich contracts and also still enjoying the success of the previous season. Many others were on the sidelines or in the training room recovering from injuries.

The season opened in Chicago, and there was some good news. James was back and so was Love, who was cleared to return in time to play in one preseason game. Midway through the first quarter at the United Center, everyone's attention turned when President Barack Obama appeared out of the tunnel to take a seat at center court with a friend, businessman Marty Nesbitt. It was not a surprise—the Secret Service had screened everyone in the building. Obama is an NBA fan and Bulls supporter. He had a relationship with James, who cam-paigned for him in both 2008 and 2012 and had visited at the White House several times.

James, though, was not at his best. When he was out of the game, he had to lie on the baseline to stretch out his still-recovering back. He scored 25 points but wasn't himself. Late in the game he drove for what would've been a game-tying basket, but his lift was lacking. Pau Gasol, the Bulls' center, blocked the shot. The Bulls, who'd had their season ended on the same floor by the Cavs five months earlier, eked out a two-point win.

James waved off concerns about his back and his balky jump shot and was more pleased that Love scored 18 points in his return. And seeing Obama. "For the president of the United States to grace open-ing night here in Chicago, it's an honor," he said. "Something I can tell my kids about a long time from now, and to actually be able to have the film. Kids don't believe you sometimes."

The year before, almost to the day, Blatt had taken what could've been an easy public relations victory, both to fans and his players, and tainted it when he dismissed the celebration for his first NBA win. This was different, but, standing in the same hallway, Blatt seemed to do it again when asked about playing in front of the president. "I've been in front of presidents in other parts of the world, actually," he said. "But of the United States, yes, first time."

Like with Blatt's career wins point, again this was accurate. He had a personal relationship with Israeli prime minister Benjamin Netanyahu. In 2013, Russian president Vladimir Putin awarded him a medal for "promotion of peace and cooperation between peoples" after his successful tenure as Russian national team coach. Blatt, very much a man of the world, was used to interacting with world lead-ers. So, no, coaching in front of Obama was not a unique moment for him. But again he passed on a chance at a layup opportunity and made headlines unnecessarily. Despite his hopes that the transition was behind him, he was still learning to navigate the landscape.

The team flew to Memphis for a game the next night. Despite the quick turnaround, they completely crushed a usually strong Grizzlies team by 30 points. After a miserable preseason, it was the first time in months the team felt the taste of a real win. Love had a strong night, scoring 17 points with 13 rebounds.

In the moment, James got excited about Love's performance. He started talking about the meeting the two had the previous summer by the pool in L.A. Then he made some unusually bold statements.

"Kevin is going to be our main focus," James said. "He's going to have a hell of a season. He's going to get back to that All-Star status. He's the focal point of us offensively. I know I can go out and get mine when I need it. But I need Kev to be as aggressive as he was tonight."

Love as a main focus? The player who was routinely forgotten about and sometimes seemed to disappear at the end of games?

Love talked a big game too. "We talked about that I can do more," he said, referring to the pool summit. "I think that he knew that. Since then I think everybody has really stepped up and asked what they can do in their respective roles. From a comfort standpoint, I just feel a lot, a lot better."

For a while, it actually happened. The victory in Memphis was the start of an eight-game win streak that restored the team's swagger. Love had 24 points and 14 rebounds against Miami. In Philadelphia, James became the youngest player to score 25,000 career points, hitting the number on a dunk after a lob from Dellavedova that showed his back was feeling much better. "The man above reached out and touched me on that," he said after barely missing a triple double that night.

Love had 22 points and 19 rebounds and James had 29 points in a win over Indiana. On a key play in the final 30 seconds, James hit Love for a layup to seal the game after a timeout where the play was designed. Blatt credited James for calling the play—always a sensitive topic.

"I suggested that we should run it and Coach allowed me to, allowed us to put it in the works," James said.

It wasn't a big deal but pointed to a larger trend. Whether out of a desire for harmony or a reaction to criticism, James was attempting to be more publicly supportive of Blatt. He'd complained about him for a year and likely wouldn't have objected to Blatt's firing. But he never asked management to make a change. He seemed to have come to a place where he wanted to try to make it work. During their first season together, he at times went out of his way to undermine the coach. This season, at least at the start, he was going out of his way to help.

To those around the team, though, it was still lip service. James still didn't pay Blatt a great deal of respect, even if he was now sometimes polite about it. He still clearly had a connection with other assistants, specifically Tyronn Lue. And it was still Lue who was most likely to challenge James, even if it ruffled him.

The winning streak ended in Milwaukee with a double-overtime loss. With the game tied near the end of regulation, James asked Blatt not to call timeout if the Cavs were able to get a defensive stop. He wanted to catch the Bucks by surprise and go for a game-winner. The Cavs got the stop, and just as James was headed up the floor, the whistle blew for a Cleveland timeout. James fumed, pounding the ball against the court. Only Blatt hadn't called the timeout. Officials mistakenly heard another player on the bench call it. James missed after the stoppage and eventually the team lost.

"We're not a great team right now," James said, frustrated by the loss. "We're a good team, but we have to improve on a lot of things in order for us to get better and play at a high level every night."

His mood worsened at the next stop on the road trip, a five-point loss in Detroit despite 30 points from James. The Cavs were 8–3, a respectable number considering Irving and Shumpert were still out and Mozgov's knee was still bothering him. Mozgov was out of shape and not playing with confidence and several times openly complained that the knee was still hurting—all red flags.

Meanwhile, the Golden State Warriors won that night, improving to 12–0 on the season, with Stephen Curry off to a scorching start as he racked up three-pointers. The Warriors were blowing teams out with regularity, and their new dedication to an ultra-small lineup, which they'd honed in beating the Cavs during the Finals, was proving to be devastating.

Some players didn't watch the league on off nights, but James was obsessed with it. Sometimes he'd keep friends and family waiting outside the locker room after games because he was watching the end of games. On the road, where the visiting locker rooms often didn't have TVs with access to all games, James would sometimes use an app on his phone to pull up live games. He was such a fan of the NBA's phone app that he once complained to the league about its functionality. Changes were quickly made.

Though James had a lucrative sponsorship with Kia and commercials that showed him arriving at games in the company's high-end sedan, he was frequently driven to practices and games in a specially outfitted van that had huge leather seats and tinted windows. It had a strong sound system, which James loved to employ at times, but he would often use the vehicle's giant TV to watch games. At his home in Akron, he had a room outfitted with a matrix of flatscreens, which gave him the ability to watch numerous games at once.

He didn't like admitting he was keeping such a close eye on the

Warriors, to do so would give them a bit of a mental edge. In fact, as the season unfolded he sometimes posted on social media during Warriors games, commenting about shows or movies he was watching as if to imply he didn't care about Golden State. It was all a cover; he cared deeply.

James knew Kobe Bryant was going to retire before Bryant made the official announcement in late November. When James came back after home games or on off nights after his kids went to bed or he was on the road in a hotel, he wanted to watch Bryant play in those West games that started at 10:30 p.m. He wanted to savor Bryant's final days and even take some notes—someday that would be him on the swan song.

But he couldn't help himself. His eyes would wander to the channel with the Warriors game. What were they doing? Often it was blasting another opponent, their drive both impressive and depressing to James. Whether it was their continuity, their talent, or their desire to shut people up about the "lucky" narrative, they were playing together like a philharmonic. Late in those nights James couldn't help but compare, and he didn't like how the Cavs were measuring up.

It spilled out in Detroit after the second consecutive loss. Not just at the way the team was playing, which was sluggish to his mind, but also how they were already lagging behind the team that was on its way to a record regular season.

"We haven't done anything," James complained. "We didn't win anything. We lost. We lost in the Finals. That's enough motivation for myself. I think we need to understand that. We lost in the Finals. We didn't win. And the team that beat us looks more hungry than we are. It shouldn't be that way."

The team went home and avenged the Bucks loss, beating them by 15, with Love having another excellent game, scoring 22 points with 15 rebounds. James had 27 points and played more minutes than he needed to. In the absence of key players, James's minutes were up over the previous year, which was not a trend the organization wanted. There was little choice, however, and matters grew worse when Mo Williams, who'd done a good job as a fill-in starter for Irving at point guard, began to have significant knee pain and skipped the game. During the game Mozgov hurt his shoulder and was headed to the

Cleveland Clinic for an MRI. Mozgov's knee, which Cavs doctors believed was healed, was really holding him back on defense, and now he had a sprained shoulder too.

Despite these challenges, James stuck with his plan to show leadership when it came to Blatt. Regardless of what was happening in the practices and huddles, he projected support. Even with the team not living up to the standard he was hoping for, he paid Blatt an unexpected strong compliment after the Bucks win. "He does his job as great as any coach can do in this league," he said.

Blatt's experience coaching James had been a roller coaster. He'd taken a lot of blows, both direct and indirect, and it was exhausting at times to manage. Blatt's friends and coaching allies were continually surprised at how he dealt with James. The fire from his European days was missing. He had never been afraid to put a player in his place before. But with James, Blatt was consistently on his heels. He tried not to let this show; part of his personality was to always present an all-knowing attitude. That trait had its virtues in the ruthless environment of an NBA head coach. In this case, he knew to take the James compliment and return it.

"It's pretty easy to team up with a guy like that and it's also, it's refreshing to come every day and to know that you're about the same things with your best guy," Blatt said. "LeBron is that. He's a leader, he's a great player, and he wants to win. You can't ask for more than that from any player, particularly your star player."

Neither of them were being truthful about how they felt about the other. But the quotes looked good on the screen and it minimized distraction. Evidence of the true reality came during the next game. The Cavs were pounding the Atlanta Hawks on their home floor, but James was still irritated by some of his teammates' erratic play.

With the Cavs up by 26 points in the third quarter, James became enraged after the team committed a turnover. He got so angry that he walked off the court and sat on the bench, taking himself out of the game. Blatt didn't know what was happening. James's backup, Richard Jefferson, scrambled to get his warmups off to get in the game. The referees were not pleased and they gave James a technical foul. Blatt lightly admonished him, saying he was out of line, which he was.

"I blew a gasket," James explained.

As the Warriors continued to rip teams to pieces on their way to a record 24–0 start, James's anger with how the wounded Cavs compared continued to expand. The Wednesday before Thanksgiving, the Cavs lost in Toronto to fall to 3–4 on the road. Dellavedova was dealing with an injury, Williams's knee was aching, and Irving was still rehabbing, not close to playing. But James was still furious.

The team wasn't flying after the game. They were staying in Toronto and having a team Thanksgiving meal before going to Charlotte the next day. James and Jones again called a players-only meeting.

"We got to have a bunker mentality when you go on the road!" James bellowed. "You've got to understand it's you guys versus everyone else, versus the fans, versus the opposing group. Adversity is going to happen. It's all mind-set. It comes from within. It's either you got it or you don't."

The team responded with a quality win in Charlotte as both James and Love had double doubles. They came home and beat the Brooklyn Nets the next night, James scoring 26 points and nailing an impressive hook shot over the Nets' giant center, Brook Lopez, with two seconds left to win. But the team did not play well as a whole.

It carried over as they lost their next three games. Washington Wizards star point guard John Wall crushed them, scoring 35 points in a win. Then the team lost in overtime in New Orleans. James was playing great but still playing with anger. He had 37 points in New Orleans and scored 23 of them in the fourth quarter alone, with basically no one else shooting. After his earlier comments about Love being the "focal point of the offense," the big man took just nine shots in the Wizards loss and was a phantom against New Orleans. When asked why he felt like he needed to shoot so much, James snapped, "Who else was going to do it?"

James no longer cared about the injuries, his disillusion growing. Blatt seemed unable to do anything about it. Love remained inconsistent, as did James's trust in him. The Cavs front office, especially general manager David Griffin, was taking worrisome notice. The team wasn't playing great, but James's dour mood was a real concern.

"It's only one guy in the world, ever, where everything will be all right when he comes back, and that's Jesus Christ," James said, get-ting unusually biblical as he waved off the notion that things would be better when the team was healthier. "Other than that, you can't bank on nobody being okay."

The overtime game delayed departure. The Cavs' charter didn't leave Louis Armstrong Airport until after midnight, and by the time the Airbus 319 jet pulled into the private air terminal that James used to call home in Miami, it was very late on the East Coast. The team didn't get into their hotel downtown until after 3 a.m. With all of that in mind, the Cavs decided to deactivate James for the game against his former team the next night so he could rest.

The Heat took the gift and smashed the Cavs by 15 points, meaning the Cavs were now 5–6 over their previous 11 games. Love's slump continued, he made 2-of-11 shots. The crowd chided James as he sat on the bench in a suit, chanting "LeBron is tired" over and over. James held up his hand and extended his ring finger, an attempt to remind fans he'd led the Heat to two rings while he was there.

When the team got back to Cleveland, Mozgov and Williams went to doctors. Mozgov was concerned about his knee, and, as he was playing in the final year of his contract, he was worried how much money it was costing him. He got a second opinion, which again told him it was healthy. Williams got an MRI on his left knee, which continued to ache.

The team needed something uplifting. It happened when they came together to execute a comeback win against the Blazers, James scoring 14 of his 33 points in the fourth quarter. Then there was a boost when Shumpert made his season debut after missing 21 games and contributed as the Cavs blasted the Magic by 40 points.

The team flew to Boston in better spirits for what promised to be a charged game. It was the first meeting since the intense playoff series the season before where cheap shots resulted in injuries, suspensions, and bad blood. Kelly Olynyk had formally apologized to Love for the play that dislocated Love's shoulder. But Smith never said a word to Jae Crowder, who'd suffered a sprained knee after Smith dropped him with an elbow in the same game. The Celtics forward made it known he was expecting Smith to do so in person.

"Yeah, he might want to wait on that. He can't hold his breath for it," Smith said. "I'll give it to him sooner or later...It's pretty ballsy, though, to ask for an apology from another man."

Meanwhile, the Cavs had another strong performance as they won by 12 points, perhaps their best road victory of the season to that point. That was all forgotten, though, after what happened during the game.

For years, the Celtics have taken a moment during each home game to honor a citizen from the community. Called "Heroes Among Us," the event often highlights the work of police officers and firefighters who have saved lives, plus those who work to improve the city. On this night the Celtics were honoring sixteen-year-old Aaron Miller, who was born with cerebral palsy that affected his right side. Despite the challenge, Miller had excelled and become a golfer and basketball player. As his story was being told during a timeout, James's eyes floated up to the scoreboard to watch.

Miller stood with a smile on his face, wearing a Celtics jersey, as the crowd stood to applaud him. James got up and found himself running over to the boy. When he reached him he extended his hand, but Aaron's right hand was limited. So James grabbed him by the head and shoulders. Aaron's eyes opened wide and he screamed, "Oh my God!" As James turned, Aaron said something else: "Look at my shoes!"

James looked. They were James's signature Nike model. It was a version that didn't have laces but a strap instead. Part of the design was for people like Aaron who had difficulties tying laces. James was moved seeing how it had helped this challenged young basketball player. Aaron was so excited by the moment he instinctively hugged his mother, who was standing with him.

"I designed those shoes for kids with conditions where they're not able to tie their own shoestrings, and he had a pair on," James said. "When I saw that, when I saw his story, I felt like I was a part of him."

After the game, James returned to see Aaron, who had been given courtside seats. When James arrived he was only in his socks. He'd taken off and signed his shoes from the game and handed them to Aaron.

"He congratulated me," Aaron told the *Boston Globe*, "and said, 'You deserve it. You're an inspiration to all of us.'"

The excitement that night wasn't over. The team flew home, arriving just before 2 a.m. When Shumpert got to his home he found his fiancée, well-known singer Teyana Taylor, in distress. She was eight months pregnant and suddenly in labor. Shumpert called 911. As he was being transferred to an EMT, Taylor gave birth to the couple's first daughter, whom they named Iman but nicknamed "Junie." Shumpert delivered her while listening to instructions as an ambulance was dispatched, including using a cord from a pair of headphones to tie off the umbilical cord. Both mother and daughter were okay.

"She did two pushes and the baby came out," Shumpert said. "That was enough excitement for anybody. I'm good for the year. Junie just wanted me to catch her, that's all. I've got the best hands in the business."

The drama kept going and the Cavs kept winning. They had their biggest victory of the season, beating the Oklahoma City Thunder by four at home. The Thunder stars—Kevin Durant, Russell Westbrook, and Serge Ibaka—all played well, combining for 75 points. But the Cavs were just better. James had a huge game, with 33 points, nine rebounds, and 11 assists. Thompson was earning his contract as he grabbed 11 offensive rebounds. For the first time in a while, the Cavs were showing some championship-level form as Irving neared his return.

But with five minutes to play, James was chasing a loose ball out of bounds when he crashed into the first row of seats, where pro golfer Jason Day, a Cavs fan who had won the PGA Championship a few months earlier, was sitting with his wife, Ellie, as a guest of the team. He had just done a promotion hitting foam balls into the crowd.

James always took great care to avoid running into spectators and often took the worst of it. The season before, he had hurt his knee jumping over the first row in Miami trying to avoid fans. But this time he couldn't and he wiped several people out, including Ellie Day, who banged her head against a barrier. Paramedics were called and Ellie was taken off in a stretcher with a neck brace after being strapped to a backboard. She turned out to be okay after a night in the hospital, and James was relieved.

Three days later, Irving was cleared to play. He missed the first 24 games of the season—and the last five games of the Finals—recovering from the broken kneecap. He returned slowly, playing 24 minutes in a blowout victory over Philadelphia. He looked okay, scoring 12 points.

But he wasn't 100 percent. The next game he showed rust, going just 1-of-6 against the Knicks. He was already a little frustrated, and he took the rare step of coming back out to the floor to practice after the game as workers were cleaning the arena, another example of him mimicking Kobe Bryant. But the Cavs won again and were riding a six-game win streak as they prepared to leave for the West Coast.

On Christmas Eve, the team boarded their plane for a long flight to California. It was the marquee Christmas matchup on the schedule, a rematch with the Warriors, who were sitting at sparkling 26–1 waiting for the Cavs, who were 19–7. For the first time since Christmas Eve the year before, the day when they learned that Anderson Varejão had torn his Achilles', the team was fully healthy. Just in time for a huge game.

With health and the win streak, there was finally a feeling of stability within the team. Now that they were settled and whole, they believed everything would calm down. After everything they'd been through, they should've known better.

Chapter 13

"THEATER OF THE ABSURD"

Christmas is a massive day on the NBA calendar. The season is technically about seven weeks old, but with football winding down and most of America gathered with family, it has become the league's time to reintroduce itself to casual fans. A lot of planning goes into the matchups and there are special uniforms, special shoes, and even special commercials to take marketing advantage of the profile. For a player, being involved in a Christmas game is an honor even as it puts a strain on families.

The Cavs had a brutal trip around the holiday, four games in five nights across the West. Still, they were amped for their rematch with the Warriors in Oakland. The Warriors were undefeated at home, not having lost there since the Cavs won Game 2 in the Finals. This time the Cavs were healthy—no complaints about the Warriors not having to deal with Kyrie Irving or Kevin Love—and they expected to play their style. What happened was a little surprising.

Whether it was specifically David Blatt's game plan or not, the Cavs fell right back into their Finals mode. They went slow and big, trying to bruise the quick and slick Warriors. Like it was June again, Blatt slashed his rotation and benched Richard Jefferson, who had been performing well as LeBron James's backup, and he cut Mo Williams's playing time. Irving and Love played terribly. They combined to go 0-of-11 from three-point range. It was an ugly slugfest, even Steph Curry looked off as he missed 9 of his 15 shots.

It was hardly a showcase for the league's two best teams. The slowdown pace kept the game close, but the Warriors ended up winning by six, 89–83. It was by far Golden State's lowest-scoring game—the Warriors had scored more than 115 points 15 times already. It broke a stretch of 47 straight home games where they scored at least 100 points. And yet they walked out with a 27–1 record.

What followed was another throwback to the previous year: attacks on the Cavs' coach. Blatt had not articulated his game plan effectively to the players, and they were upset at how things unfolded.

"It's going to take some time to get back into rhythm, and all of us, not just the players, but everyone, to get back in rhythm," James said, breaking his string of Blatt support with a thinly veiled shot.

"Surprising," Jefferson said about not playing. "Just because it was one of those games you look forward to as a player. I hadn't played on Christmas Day in twelve years. Now thirteen years."

"There's not been a lot of communication right now," said Anderson Varejão, who had been in and out of the lineup. "Just waiting to see what is going to happen."

There were a number of reasons the Cavs lost, but there was no missing that the players were put off by Blatt's approach and how they hadn't been included. Blatt was in a challenging spot. He'd just gotten his whole team healthy and had to transition to having more players. He didn't make his choices clear to the team, though, and it triggered blowback.

"The key thing in any relationship on any good team with any staff, with any group, is communication," Jefferson said.

The next night the team played in Portland, and they were in a sour mood. Irving was not cleared to play on back-to-back days yet, so he sat and the lineup changed again. From the opening moment, the team looked like it wasn't collectively interested in being there. It may not have been a direct boycott aimed at Blatt, but it was a negative response.

From his seat in the stands, team general manager David Griffin was alarmed. It was stunning how down his team was playing. He was already concerned that they were too uptight, that there was a missing enjoyment that accompanied their success. The Warriors always had fun when they played. The Cavs did not, even when they won sometimes, a tone that was often spearheaded by James. Griffin had been tracking this for some time, but it manifested itself that night.

The Blazers had a great shooting night, drilling a bunch of three-pointers in the opening minutes, but the Cavs looked to just quit at the challenge. The score was a shocking 34–12 after the first quarter and finished 105–76.

"For the first eight weeks we had built chemistry, we knew who was playing, we knew who wasn't playing," James said. "We have no rhythm. We have some guys who don't know if they're going to play, or if they aren't going to play, and it's hurting our rhythm a little bit."

That was diplomatic. Many on the team were fuming. Blatt knew there were issues, and he discussed it with Griffin. After a day off to cool down, he called a team meeting the morning of a game in Phoenix and tried to refocus the team.

"In tough times you've got to show a little bit of leadership and lift your troops," Blatt told Cleveland.com about the meeting. "That was the whole purpose of it, to fire them up a little bit and lift them a little bit. They certainly this year have been doing their part, and I had to step in and do something myself."

The Suns were a weak team and it was a messy game, though the Cavs played better than in Portland. They probably couldn't have played worse. Irving returned and scored 22 points, making a late three-pointer that carried the Cavs to a four-point win. That relieved some pressure, but the team's body language was off. James played most of the game with a scowl and barked at teammates when they made mistakes. The problem was, he was making mistakes too. In a sign of where his head was at, he took just 10 shots and had just 14 points. The unrest was centered on Blatt, James's previous game plan to be supportive having been suspended.

With James setting the mood, the locker room was tense even following a win. The look on James's face was telling. He was like a coiled snake, sending out strong warnings to stay away.

"Guys, we won the game," James Jones said. "That should be the only thing that matters."

During the road trip and for much of the season, Griffin was in the locker room to witness it. He was deeply concerned by what he was seeing and what he was feeling. Never before in his twenty-four years in the league had he sensed such bubbling anger after a victory. This was a win, breaking a losing streak, and all he saw was a dispirited group. He also witnessed who the players were leaning on. It wasn't Blatt, it was Ty Lue.

The team went to Denver for the final game of the trip. The next morning, NBA.com released a story examining shooting numbers across the league and determined James was having the worst jump-shooting season of any contributing player. It pointed out he was shooting a miserable 28.5 percent outside the paint. His jumper indeed had looked off, and his three-point percentage had badly slipped. His form had suffered—he had a bad habit of leaning on his jumpers, which he'd battled his whole career—and the early-season back issues had thrown off his rhythm. But no one realized how bad it had gotten until the numbers went public.

After reading the article, James didn't wait for the bus but instead took a car over to the arena early to get extra shooting in. "I saw it," was all he would say.

Irving again had to sit because of the back-to-back, yo-yoing Blatt's options again. It didn't make much of a difference. James again was in a bad mood, and it was carrying over to the floor. The Cavs led the game throughout and James had an answer for the shooting numbers, nailing a series of jumpers on his way to 34 points. The Cavs led from the start and picked up a win to end the road trip. Watching the game casually, that's all that would've been apparent.

James was relieved by the performance, not so much because the team won but because he hadn't flown off the handle to the media the night before in Phoenix when he was simmering with rage. Much of it, though perhaps not all, was aimed at Blatt.

"Thank God we play in the NBA, with a game the next day, and not the NFL," James said. "Because if it was the NFL, I would have went off and let the quotes fester for a week."

Not watching the game casually was Griffin. A Phoenix native, he'd stayed in Arizona to spend time with family instead of going to Denver. As he watched, he grew more dejected as it played out. He saw James was dogging it. Over and over, Griffin watched as James didn't run back on defense, a half-quit showing Griffin knew was damaging. James set the example and the tone. Griffin later had his staff watch the film and count. Nine. Nine times it happened, James not getting back on defense.

Griffin hung his head, his family members realizing something was wrong. His team was up by 11 at the half—why did he look sick to his stomach? He'd pondered it for some time and he'd tried to put it off. But in that moment Griffin came to the conclusion that he was going to have to fire David Blatt.

The Cavs were in first place in the East. The team was in the midst of transition as players returned from injury. James was hardly an ally, but he'd come to accept Blatt was his coach. Blatt was in the middle of a three-year contract and the Cavs were already paying off fired coach Mike Brown for the next three years. Exactly a year before, as the New Year's holiday arrived, Griffin had defended the coach when calls within the organization to fire Blatt arose, because he didn't believe he'd been given a fair chance. Now he was feeling the opposite way. He'd just never seen a team that was more comfortable in dealing with adversity than it was with success. He believed Blatt, purposely or not, was a root cause.

After winning in Denver, the team took three days off, which is unusual during the season. Even with extended breaks between games, typically teams practice. But after being away for Christmas, everyone needed a break. James didn't take the team charter back to Cleveland. Instead a private plane was waiting, and he flew to Aspen, where he celebrated his thirty-first birthday and the New Year with his wife, mother, and some friends. Other players went on brief trips and generally unplugged.

When the team reconvened for practice on New Year's Day, Griffin sat in on the team's film session, and it was he who got on James about his actions in Denver. Not getting back on defense and his general attitude was a problem, and Griffin called him out on it. That the GM was making the comments in the film session and not the coach was indicative of the dynamic that had existed between James and Blatt. For Blatt, this was a survival technique; he often had to try to set his agenda around James. This was untenable, but it was both of their faults: James for his frequent unwillingness to trust Blatt, but also Blatt for not setting a tone that all players would be held accountable.

The team whipped the Magic by 25 in their first game of 2016 as James's hot shooting continued, including four three-pointers. During the break he'd watched film of his shooting and analyzed how it had changed since he was in Miami, where he developed an excellent shooting touch. He made adjustments.

They followed it up with a 22-point beating of Toronto, the team in second place in the East. Irving looked fantastic, racking up 25 points and displaying his full array of spin moves, crossovers, and speed changes that really showed his knee was improving. He did it against Raptors point guard Kyle Lowry, who had 23 points.

After the game the locker room was looser. As James was about to leave, Blatt came out of his office wearing only a towel and asked to meet with James. This was unusual—coaches had their own dressing area and didn't walk through the locker room undressed like players. James was surprised, part amused and part annoyed.

"Coach," he said. "I can't talk to you like this."

James did go into Blatt's office. After a short talk he came out. "That man was naked," he said as he left the room. It was a bizarre, though mostly lighthearted moment. It was also clear from its tenor that neither Blatt nor James knew that upstairs a decision to change coaches was under discussion.

Griffin had gone to ownership and told them what he wanted to do. A year before, it was owner Dan Gilbert who was thinking a change had to be made and Griffin asking for more time. Now the roles were reversed, and Gilbert was surprised by Griffin's intention. The team was about to leave on a six-game road trip and making a move during such a trip was unwise.

"At first Nate [Forbes] and I weren't sure. But there was no doubt in Griff's mind we had to do it," Gilbert said. "He had conviction about it."

The team, though, kept winning. They made it five in a row in Washington, with James and Irving having classic performances. James scored 34 and Irving put up 32, outplaying Wizards star John Wall, who had 20 points. Wall had created a little stir a few days before the game when he openly complained that Irving was ahead of him in All-Star voting despite missing most of the season, calling it "a joke."

The Wizards ran with it and made an actual joke. During a timeout in the second half, the videoboard showed a prepackaged skit where fans wearing Irving jerseys were asked which player was getting their All-Star vote, Irving or Wall. Naturally, they said Wall, and the point was made. But the Cavs players were watching. Irving was a demon down the stretch, scoring 19 points in the fourth quarter after seeing the video.

"We didn't like it as a team," J. R. Smith said. "We didn't like it at all."

"I saw it for sure," James said.

"I really have no comment," Irving said.

With the schedule soft, the Cavs' streak rolled on. They won in Minnesota and Philadelphia, two of the worst teams in the league, with ease. James had 37 points in Philly, making 15 of 22 shots as the shooting numbers continued to rise. The winning streak hit eight in Dallas as first Love and then Irving made clutch three-pointers in overtime.

James's mood improved with the team, and himself, playing better. He even got back to saying kind words about Blatt, again making it clear that he was out of the loop of what was being considered in the front office. They were qualified comments, but they were positive.

"I think every game is another learning experience for Coach Blatt," James told ESPN in an interview about the state of the team. "There's coaches with more tenure in our league, obviously, and there's guys with a better résumé than he has. But one thing he tries to do is just put us in a position to win and then it's up to us... In sports, kind of the coaches always get the worst of it."

Blatt remained hopeful that the two would develop a relationship, but he, too, was guarded. He'd seen James's mood swings before, one day patting him on the back and the next savaging him either to his face or behind his back. He kept hoping they could find some trust between each other. At the core, that didn't really exist, and Blatt knew it.

"I think it's him and everyone else in the program recognizing that we were very, very close," Blatt said. "Perhaps the next step is that confidence in one another and that trust in one another."

There really was no next step—there were few steps left between the Cavs and Blatt. He just didn't know it.

The winning streak came to an end in San Antonio, where the Spurs were undefeated at home and it showed. They overcame a 12-point Cavs lead to beat them. Irving was outplayed by Tony Parker, and James struggled to score at times on defensive ace Kawhi Leonard.

That night, Blatt made another one of his PR missteps. The L.A. Clippers' DeAndre Jordan had gotten sick, breaking his streak of 360 consecutive games played. That meant the Cavs' iron man, Tristan Thompson, took over the streak for most consecutive games played, as he was playing in his 325th straight game.

Blatt was asked about it. This, again, was a layup moment. The reporters needed a positive comment for their stories and patting Thompson on the head was easy. Blatt dismissed it.

"He didn't break a record. He's the current," Blatt said. "I'm leading the league in field goal percentage. I haven't missed a shot this year."

No, it wasn't the record. A.C. Green has the record with 1,192 straight games. It wasn't even the team record. But Thompson was proud, talking about playing through ankle sprains and food poisoning. Blatt shrugged. Another misread, another miffed player, another moment when Griffin was left scratching his head.

The Cavs won by 14 the next night in Houston to finish the trip at 5–1. After he'd sometimes struggled to maintain positivity even after victories, James expressed his confidence in where the team was headed. He didn't worry about a close loss in San Antonio. For a moment he'd even been willing to take his team off the Golden State standard. James said he believed the Cavs were good enough to beat any team in the league in a playoff series.

He said it with a purpose. The Cavs were getting two days off and then hosting the Warriors. James felt they were ready. Irving was healthier than he'd been at Christmas. This long road trip had gone well. There was momentum and James's comments would add to the motivation—at least he'd hoped.

The day before the game, Curry needled the Cavs when he said he was looking forward to coming back to the visitors' locker room at Quicken Loans Arena. "Walking in that locker room, it'll be good memories," he said. "Hopefully, it still smells a little bit like champagne."

The Cavs would've been fortunate had Curry stopped with trash talk. No, he and his teammates walked in with their 37–4 record not smelling champagne—they were smelling blood. The Cavs might have had some confidence after winning nine of their previous 10 games, but their new rival had something on another level than confidence. They were running so hot and so smooth that they'd taken the game to an art form, their array of passes becoming a blur until they found an open man. Curry was making shots from everywhere with ease, some of them nearing 40 feet from the hoop. Draymond Green was becoming a Swiss Army knife, able to deploy different talents at different times, all of them useful. Klay Thompson's quick release and tremendous size made him a brutal assignment.

The Warriors unleashed their full power at the Cavs, wanting to make a lasting statement on the terms of their relative standing. They embarrassed their hosts, crushing them, 132–98, with Curry shooting and shimmy-shaking his way to 35 points.

At one point the Warriors got up 43 points, the most James had trailed in the 1,227 games of his NBA career. It was probably the most he'd been behind in any game in his life. It was beyond demoralizing. The Cavs had—rightly, they believed—clung to a belief that the Warriors couldn't beat them when at full strength. This humbling night proved they were dead wrong.

It was a miserable game for Love. Already he'd predictably seen his role diminish since Irving came back, his scoring average dropping to 12.4 points a game from 17.6. He scored only three points and was exposed several times on defense, leading to highlights filling social media and questions arising about his fitness to play against the Warriors' lineup.

Smith showed his dark side again, tackling Warriors forward Harrison Barnes and being ejected for the flagrant foul.

In the fourth quarter the game was decided and the starters were pulled. With the game in hand, Warriors interim coach Luke Walton, filling in for coach Steve Kerr because of an illness, sat down. Blatt didn't have the option. Sitting in his seat on the bench was James, chewing on Lue's ear and venting. This was very public, but the reality was it was just symbolic. James said nice things sometimes, but he'd long since effectively walled off Blatt and made Lue his most meaningful contact on the coaching staff.

Afterward, Blatt tried to shoulder some blame, saying he didn't have the team ready. It was deeper than that. The Cavs weren't equipped to handle what the Warriors, on their way to setting a regular-season win record, were throwing at them. Naturally after such a setback, Blatt was in line to be reviewed, and that happened. But it was not about a coach—one team was just way ahead of the other.

"Tonight was an example of how far we've got to go to get to a championship level," James said.

"They definitely played like the champions," Irving said. "They came in and just kicked our ass."

When asked about the state of the team, Love gave a strange answer. "It's going to take a lot of guys looking themselves in the mirror, and it all starts with our leader over there," he said, gesturing to James's locker. Was Love, after a horrible personal performance, pointing at James as a culprit?

James certainly thought so. The next day, he called a team meeting so things could be aired out.

Love said his point was misconstrued. "All I meant was that LeBron is our leader and we follow him at the end of the day," he said. "We all got to be better for each other, him, our fans, our organization, each and every player on this team, our coaches."

James talked to Love personally about the quote and cleared the air after the misstep. "We talked about it," he said. "I take the man at his word."

There were other discussions going on, though, between Gilbert and Griffin. The Blatt issue had been in the air for a few weeks. Gilbert still wasn't sure it was the right call. He'd fired plenty of coaches over the previous ten years. And he had been talked out of firing more. In this case, he was conflicted. But he decided that he'd support his general manager and clear the way for the firing. This wasn't always the case for Gilbert. He'd acted on his own before regardless of his GM's wishes. But this time it was going to be on Griffin's shoulders and the results would be on them as well. Gilbert gave his blessing.

"It was all Griff and it took a lot of balls," Gilbert said. "I told him, 'Griff, they're going to kill us. We're leading the East and we're going to fire our coach in the middle of the year.' Here's what it came down to: In my gut, heart and soul, can we win the NBA championship with this coach? He's a good man, he's a good human being, but can these players rally around him? The answer we had to realize was likely not. We had Ty there. If we didn't have Ty, I don't think we could do it."

The team had a back-to-back coming in Brooklyn, then a home game with the Clippers. After that, when there was an off day, Blatt would be let go.

The team won in Brooklyn, Love bouncing back with 17 points and 18 rebounds. Then they had a nice three-point home victory over the Clippers, one of the West's best teams. Love was strong again with 18 points and 16 rebounds, as James delivered 22 points and 12 assists. It seemed like a stabilizing win. It was not.

Blatt had no idea it was coming. He again admonished the media for criticism and praised his team for their ability to battle through adversity.

"I hear a lot of far-reaching conclusions and personally I don't like it," he said. "But there's nothing I can do about it. I think this team has done pretty well dealing with the adversity that we've had. I think this team is in pretty good position, although people choose to over-look that, which I don't think is fair.

"It's about my team. It's about my guys and I don't like it. I don't like it at all," he said, his confidence rising after the win. "This wasn't promised to us. Nobody gave us that. We had to work for it and they've been working hard and doing a good job overall, a really good job."

In many people's eyes it was a good job. It was the exact halfway point of the season and the team was 30–11 and in first place. A few more wins and Blatt would clinch being named the East coach for the All-Star game in Toronto two weeks later.

The next morning, a Friday, Griffin asked to talk to Blatt. Because of the back-to-back the previous two days, the team had been given the day off and the practice facility was mostly empty. Griffin told Blatt he was being let go.

Blatt was stunned. His coaches were shocked. His peers in the league were angry. The nation of Israel would later become outraged.

Griffin called Lue, who wasn't yet at work. Like Blatt, Lue was blindsided. He didn't agree with the decision. Lue had wanted this job eighteen months earlier. At one point he thought he had it. He ended up in the unorthodox position of being the lead assistant to a man who beat him for the job. Griffin had leaned toward Lue at the time, but he accepted the Blatt choice. After seeing Lue work up close, Griffin was convinced he was going to be a good head coach.

Griffin saw Lue connected with players, some of whom used to be his peers when he played in the league. But he was more impressed Lue was not afraid to hold players accountable. It was an historic decision, firing a coach in first place at midseason, but Griffin was doing it because he also believed in Lue, not because he thought Blatt had failed. He told Lue he would not be interim coach—he wanted him to be the new permanent head coach. He offered him a contract extension and a raise.

Lue was concerned how it looked, like he might've undermined Blatt to get the job. He didn't sign the contract, because he didn't want to make it seem like he'd been negotiating. But he did accept the job.

Blatt had been given a difficult hand when he showed up his first day in 2014, weeks before James had signed and Love was traded for. He'd made mistakes, perhaps the largest being not recognizing just how big a change coaching in the NBA would be from his European roots. It was blatant he saw the two as somewhat parallel, and it was just as obvious that was an error in judgment. People in the NBA, players in the NBA, don't see it equally, and Blatt learned the hard way.

"When I came to the NBA I was under the impression that this was going to be a breeze," he said before starting his second season. "I've been coaching for twenty years at the highest level in Europe. I coached in the national team environment, coached professional teams, coached EuroLeague teams. I thought I knew basketball and I thought I knew how to coach. Which, in my mind, I did. But I realized that when I came over here it was a very, very different game with a whole new set of problems and a whole slew of things to deal with inside and outside of the game."

Ultimately, he never was able to bridge that gap. He may never have won James over. When Blatt wasn't able to hold James accountable, he gave up any hope of finding any real footing. Griffin believed Lue could perform better in that role.

"I think it was clear to everyone what was going on," Gilbert said. "LeBron wants to be challenged and that's hard because he can be intimidating. David just wasn't able to connect."

Griffin asked the team leaders to gather the team for a meeting at 3:30 that afternoon. They were scattered, none of them expecting to have to come in that day. When they got together the word was out, but they still weren't totally sure what happened. They joked that they were getting called in to be told Love had been traded because those rumors raged after Love's poor game against the Warriors.

There was an assumption by outsiders James was involved with the move, because of his well-known issues with Blatt. He also had a connection with Lue, which dated to James's teenage years when Lue was in the league. But Griffin didn't tell James prior to the firing. He didn't feel the need to ask. James's actions had made his feelings on the matter plain.

This would become a point of contention for those evaluating the unusual coaching change. Common sense dictated James, the center of the franchise, would be involved in such a major transaction. Some could never be convinced that he wasn't consulted. But Griffin, Gilbert, and James swear it not to be true.

James didn't perform the coup de grâce—that was Griffin. James did do damage along the way. Both of these statements can be true. And both men could end up being correct in their assessment of Blatt's job performance.

For decades, star players have played a role in coaching changes. For decades, star players have been blamed for forcing coaches out regardless of the truth. Often there's little room for nuance in understanding what happened. None of that will change in the future. James knew the score.

"Like it or love it or hate it, we got to respect it," he said. "I can't get caught up and worried about what other people are thinking. I stopped doing that a long time ago in my career."

After the team meeting, Lue and James had a private conversation. "I told him, 'I got to hold you accountable. It starts with you first. And if I can hold you accountable in front of the team and doing the right things, then everybody else has got to fall in line, fall in place.'"

James may not have admitted it publicly, but he'd longed at times to play for a former player. His first head coach, Paul Silas, was a former player, but there was a more than forty-year age gap. It was like a grandfather-grandson relationship, especially given how protective Silas was of the young James at the time. After that it was ten years of tacticians, former video coordinators like Brown and Erik Spoelstra, grinders who grew up in the league but never played. Blatt was from, it felt to James, another world. Even when he was playing for the Olympic team it was under Mike Krzyzewski, a legend, but not a player. James had connected to former players turned coaches like Doc Rivers, going against him for years. Lue was a Rivers disciple, having coached with him in Boston and L.A.

"We've been friends since I was seventeen years old, but at the end of the day, he's still the coach and I'm underneath him," James said about Lue. "He will coach me and push me, and I'll listen to everything he has to say and go from there. Don't try to make it a story of why me and Coach Lue are so tight. I think it's a lot of coaches and players that's close in this league. It just happened to be me."

And that was happening for the first time in James's career.

Griffin called a news conference to explain the decision. Gilbert was not there, which was right. This was Griffin's decision and he intended to take full ownership of it.

"David spent the last year and a half under incredible scrutiny, he was doing it without his family, and he was working to mold a group of individuals that are incredibly willful," Griffin said. "That's not easy and I understand that. Decisions like these tend to make themselves. Every decision is made with an answer to the following question: Does it put us in the best position to deliver championships? I go to bed every night thinking about that question."

Griffin talked about the lack of connection he felt within the team.

He talked about how the players weren't showing buy-in to the coach. He explained it wasn't based on the win-loss record—how could it be?—it was about the bigger picture.

"Are our hearts, minds, and souls in what we're doing? Are we really trying to achieve something as a unit?" Griffin said he asked himself. "We need to build a collective spirit. Halfway through this season we have failed. Each step forward has been followed by two steps back. Pretty good is not what we're here for. We're pretty good right now. That's not what we're in the business to be."

Then he insisted no player had anything directly to do with the decision, saying, "I'm not taking a poll, my job is to lead a franchise. I didn't ask anyone's opinion. I'm in the locker room. I know what it's supposed to feel like."

There were opinions, though. There had been heavy coaching turnover across the NBA over the previous two years and the league's coaches felt like they were under attack.

"I'm embarrassed for our league that something like this could happen," Dallas coach Rick Carlisle said. "It's just bizarre. It just leaves you with a bit of an empty feeling because Blatt's a great guy and he did a great job there."

"He had the most scrutinized job that you could possibly have," said Rivers, who a day earlier had seen his team vanquished by Blatt's Cavs. "I think the reward for coaching LeBron is you get scrutinized. It's hard. They have a great record, the best in the East, and you get fired for it."

"Back in my day, you used to have to at least lose games before you got fired," Orlando coach Scott Skiles said.

"That one, to me, elevated all of the coach firings totally into the theater of the absurd," said Pistons coach Stan Van Gundy. "It was insane."

After his team became the latest to take a 30-point beating at the hands of Golden State, the Spurs' legendary coach, Gregg Popovich, took aim at Griffin. "I'm just glad my general manager wasn't in the locker room, because it might have gotten me fired," Popovich said, mocking Griffin's comment that his observations in the locker room led him to the Blatt firing.

Twenty years earlier Popovich had been a general manager when he fired his coach, Bob Hill, and put himself in the job. So it was ironic that Popovich would hit Griffin, but it was just part of a growing chorus.

Already with a massive payroll and huge expectations, the Blatt firing had upped the ante for both James and Griffin. History was going to judge them on this. They were both aware of it.

And they were also aware that when sudden changes happened to teams, whether it was a coaching move or a major trade, sometimes things got worse before they got better.

Chapter 14

"THAT'S WHAT THE COACH WANTS"

Kyrie Irving was gulping for air, his chest burning so badly from exertion that he fouled Jimmy Butler, the Chicago Bulls' All-Star guard, out of fatigue so he could get out of the game. When he got to the bench, Kevin Love was already sitting there with the same symptoms.

A few seconds later there was LeBron James slumping onto a chair near him, chest heaving and asking for the water bottle. There were five minutes left in the first quarter; why were all of the Cavs stars on the bench?

"We're not in good enough shape right now to play the way I want to play," Ty Lue said, explaining why his players were gassed moments into his first game as coach.

Lue's first forty-eight hours on the job were forceful. He was a popular teammate and coach, and congratulatory messages from friends and acquaintances poured in when his promotion became public. In the hours after taking the job he received 716 text messages.

"It was a good day for me," Lue said. "And a bad day for Blatt."

Amid the stress of the changeover, Lue was concerned about the perception that he'd undercut Blatt to get the job. It's natural for there to be speculation when an assistant replaces a head coach. In Lue's situation, it was unavoidable despite all parties denying it. Lue had been preparing himself to be a head coach, and there were times during Blatt's tenure when he must've wondered about his boss's job security. But on this move he'd been in the dark.

"I know how loyal I was to Coach Blatt and the people that know me understand that," Lue told Cleveland.com. "I have no control over what people think. I have a job to do and I'm going to do my best."

Lue didn't even get to hold a full practice before his first game, but he used his new authority anyway. He said he wouldn't be doing things differently from Blatt but he planned to do them better. One of his first moves was to tell the players they were going back to a traditional approach when it came to pregame introductions.

For months, the Cavs players did not run out and high-five teammates when the starting lineups were called. With the scoreboard flashing elaborate videos and fire shooting from giant swords in the ceiling, the team had adopted an approach where they huddled together. It was James who came up with the concept; he wanted to promote focus before tip-off. Blatt agreed—this was the sort of thing he would not challenge James on anyway—and it became policy. In an effort to lighten the mood, Lue said that policy was finished, at least for home games.

"When they call your name, run out, be introduced," Lue told the players.

"That's what the coach wants, that's what we do," James said. "There's no fighting. No ifs, ands, or buts."

It may have seemed trivial, but from the start, Lue was setting a tone that he would be issuing some edicts. The concept of calling his players, many of whom were proud of their world-class athlete status, out of shape on day one was a little more complex but took guts.

Lue wanted to play more uptempo. He didn't like that the Cavs ranked as the third-slowest team in the league in possessions per game under Blatt. He intended to hit the accelerator and called players out by name who couldn't keep up.

The Bulls trounced the Cavs in Lue's first game, beating them 96–83. The result was secondary to Lue's objective of changing attitude and focus.

Two days later, James put a shirtless photo on social media following a 7 a.m. workout in his home weight room as he stood next to his personalized golden lion Nike logo emblazoned on the padded floor. He was clearly in top physical condition, which was the point he was making in his own way after Lue had implied his players were out of shape.

"I don't think I'm in bad shape at all, just need to get in better shape for what we want to do," he said. "I'm not that far off. I can get there in less than a week."

Lue had other pieces of business. He hired a past colleague, Mike Longabardi, to join his coaching staff. Lue had previously been in charge of the Cavs defense, with Blatt, such as it was, in charge of the offense. He wanted to take over the offense, and he brought Long-abardi in to handle his old role. Part of what Lue wanted was to engage Irving more. Lue thought he sometimes worried too much about his role in the offense and did not focus enough on pure aggression. A year after James had chided Irving for not passing enough, Lue said to worry about attacking first and passing second.

The team won the next two games, slaying league weaklings Minnesota and Phoenix. The victories assured the team would have the East's best record going into the All-Star break, and therefore Lue would be the All-Star coach. It was unprecedented and awkward, a coach who'd been in charge for three games being declared an All-Star. Lue suggested Blatt be allowed to come back and coach the game in Toronto, fully knowing there was no way that would happen.

Other than James and Lue, though, there would be no other Cavs who would make it. The Raptors' Kyle Lowry passed Irving in votes, getting in as a starter. And the league's coaches passed over Love for the second straight year. He answered by putting up 29 points with five three-pointers in a win over Detroit as Irving added 28 and James 20. It was the first time all season the three each scored over 20 in a game. The pace was growing, as Lue wanted, and the scoring was going up.

The questions to the players started pouring in, asking them to compare Lue and Blatt. For the most part, they avoided direct comparisons. However, James dropped hints, repeatedly praising Lue and adopting a submissive role.

"Coach gets on us in film sessions."

"Coach Lue is the captain of the ship. We've got to do whatever he barks out."

"It's great to have a leader like Coach Lue."

Then again, he had given Blatt lip service at times too. James had taken some criticism from fans and media after Blatt's exit. The term "coach killer" was used, which James found insulting. While his feelings toward Blatt were mostly out in the open by then, plenty drew their own conclusions. The coach killer tag ate at James because he felt just the opposite. He felt that throughout his career he'd uplifted coaches. He'd helped them win awards, helped them get raises, helped them get other jobs. His first high school coach, Keith Dambrot, got a college job and then was a successful head coach at the University of Akron. James had been pulling coaches up since he was sixteen. In short, he felt he was worth any sort of challenges that may have come with him.

More important, James and the team appeared to be responding to the changes Lue was pushing, and the distractions involving the coach had been eliminated.

A big moment came when the Cavs whipped the San Antonio Spurs, 117–103. The Spurs came with the league's best defense and the Cavs ran them out of the gym. It was the first victory against one of the top teams from the West, a flaw that had been gnawing at the team. Once again Irving, Love, and James all topped 20 points. The next night they won in Indiana with four players scoring 19 or more points.

Over the previous two seasons, though, it had become apparent the Cavs were rarely able to hold on to positive vibes. General manager David Griffin had developed a saying, partly out of despair, that the Cavs hated prosperity and loved adversity.

So right after Lue looked like he was getting some traction and the changes were paying off with a five-game win streak, the team dumped back-to-back games in Charlotte and at home to Boston. The loss to the Celtics was harsh: They managed to blow a four-point lead in the final seven seconds after an ill-timed foul and a defensive breakdown let the Celtics construct a stunning five-point possession.

With the offense in overdrive, the team's defense started to rapidly decline. That had been a calling card and had carried them in the postseason the year before. Lue's proficiency in running that aspect had been one of the things that had impressed both the players and the front office. Now that he'd given it up and preached speed and scoring, attention to detail on defense was predictably slipping.

"Right now, we're still kind of running old stuff and new stuff and trying to combine it and it's kind of messing the guys' heads up," Lue said. "That's on me, that's my fault."

James's positive vibes came to an end after the Boston loss. After scoring 30 points, he was so frustrated that he immediately reported to the weight room for an unusual postgame workout in an effort to get his anger out.

The Cavs won the next three games, with their offense continuing to zoom. They beat the Pelicans by 15, with Irving scoring 29 as Lue continued to urge aggression. Smith made six three-pointers in that win and six more in the next game as they smashed the Sacramento Kings by 20. Irving had 32 in that one, hitting five three-pointers of his own after he entered the game shooting a career-worst 25 percent on them.

In the final game before All-Star Weekend, the Cavs put up 120 points on the Los Angeles Lakers and Irving was terrific again, scoring a season-high 35. Lue's pushing helped, but Irving's knee getting healthier was a factor.

James and Kobe Bryant had been connected for the previous decade as the faces of the NBA, but the real relationship was between Irving and Bryant. They had become friendly. Bryant isn't really friends with many, especially competitors, and it gave Irving tremendous pride to play so well against him as he went through the final season of his twenty-year career.

Irving knew that in Bryant's final game against his hero, Michael Jordan, he'd scored 55 points. The Cavs and Lakers were to play once more, but Irving wanted to deliver such a game to guarantee a memory. Bryant didn't play very well with a bad knee and shoulder, scoring 17 points. For Irving, it was a dream.

"Going against your mentor, one of the guys that you want to prove something to every time you go out and play, there was definitely some added incentive going in there," Irving said.

"He has a killer mentality," Bryant said of Irving. "He can shoot the long ball. His midrange game is excellent. And he can finish at the rim. He has all the tools there. The way he played tonight, he can do this pretty much every night."

The team broke for All-Star Weekend, a plane waiting to take James and the coaching staff to Toronto after the victory, with other players having their own flight plans to Mexico and the Caribbean. Irving went to Los Angeles to spend Valentine's Day with his girlfriend, the singer Kehlani Parrish.

There would be no vacation for Griffin, who was engaged in trade talks with several teams. He was trying to find a way to add some more shooting, as he felt it was going to be vital to have versatility in the upcoming playoffs.

He also was on the lookout for another big man. Timofey Mozgov had been in and out of the starting lineup all season. He had moments, but his knee wasn't fully healthy and it affected his confidence. A year before, the Cavs had traded two first-round picks for him, and he'd been a key piece in their playoff run. But as he headed toward free agency, the Cavs were having a tough time seeing him as a long-term answer.

The issue for Griffin was making a move without adding to the payroll. The Cavs were sitting at about $110 million in salaries, and that would come with luxury tax charges approaching $70 million for going so far over the salary cap.

The player Griffin wanted was Channing Frye, a good-shooting big man who played for the Orlando Magic. The Cavs had seen Frye as a great fit alongside James as far back as 2009 when they chased him in free agency. In 2014, Griffin went after him again, but both times Frye took better offers. He was now having a down season, averaging just five points, and the Magic had made him available. But his salary was $8 million and Orlando didn't want to take back long-term salary in a deal. The Los Angeles Clippers were also in the bidding and felt like they might be able to get him.

Several things fell into place in the last twenty-four hours before the trade deadline. The Clippers couldn't close the deal with Orlando and moved on to a different trade. Griffin then found a way to make the deal work financially as he got the Portland Trail Blazers to trade for Anderson Varejão, taking $10 million off the team's books and making room for Frye in a three-team deal. It cost the Cavs a first-round pick, their 2018 selection, and they had to trade a popular player who'd been with the team for twelve seasons. But Griffin got his desired shooting big man, and in the transaction the Cavs were able to save about $10 million in salary and taxes.

"That was a very difficult phone call to have," Griffin said. "There's very little I've enjoyed less in my professional career than letting Andy know he was traded."

Varejão was crushed. And it got worse when the Blazers immediately cut him—they'd only done the trade to get the first-round pick. The NBA is a business. So Varejão responded with his own business move and signed with the Warriors, his old team's central rival.

The first game after the deal was against the Bulls. Now, several weeks into Lue's regime, the performance was more stable and honed. James tossed in 25 and Love added 15 points and 14 rebounds as they beat the Bulls for the first time all season.

Two days later they went to Oklahoma City on a Saturday afternoon, arriving in the early evening ahead of their nationally televised Sunday afternoon game against the Thunder. As with the Spurs game two weeks prior, this was a test. They'd been putting together wins, but real progress was choppy.

After dinner, players headed back to the Skirvin Hotel, a grand old building three blocks from the arena where all visiting teams stay. It has a reputation for being haunted. Over the years players have reported hearing strange noises, including crying babies in the middle of the night. When Wesley Johnson was playing for the Phoenix Suns he awoke one morning to find his bathroom door closed and his bathtub inexplicably filled with water.

At 3 a.m. Irving woke up in his room with an itching feeling on his body. It wasn't a ghost. He flipped on the light and saw bedbugs crawling around his sheets and pillow.

"Just imagine how freaked out you'd be if you saw friggin' five big bedbugs just sitting on your pillow," Irving said. "I woke up itching, and I'm just looking around and I'm like, 'Are you serious right now?' I was so tired at that point."

Irving yanked off his clothes and tried to sleep on the couch in his room. He abandoned most of the clothes he had in the room and left shaken. Midway through the first quarter the next afternoon, he told the trainers he was feeling ill. He went to the locker room and was done for the game. The critters seemed to have gotten into his head.

"I was freaked out, then I started feeling nauseous," he said.

Hilton, which runs the Skirvin, admitted what Irving knew—that management had found the bugs in the room. The hotel offered a formal apology.

While Irving was trying to keep it together, the team didn't seem all that affected by his departure. They smashed the Thunder by 23. The enigma that was Love did it again. Sometimes when James or Irving missed a game, Love became ineffective. Other times he took advantage of the extra shots and space. This game was the latter—he had one of the best performances of the season, with 29 points and 11 rebounds. In one of the pinnacle moments of the season for the team, they played terrifically in all facets and looked every bit the championship contender they were in vanquishing a high-quality opponent on the road.

In typical fashion, they then went back home the next day and lost momentum by losing to the Detroit Pistons, though Irving was over his bedbug-induced anxiety and scored 30 points. Just when it looked like they had gained some acceleration with the Bulls and Thunder wins, they unexpectedly slid into a dark period.

A visit to Toronto, the team with the second-best record in the East, went poorly when the Cavs blew a nine-point lead with five minutes to play. Lowry was sensational and repeatedly burned Irving as he scored a career-high 43 points, including the game-winner at the buzzer. He'd played against Irving many times, and Irving had plenty of victories on his belt from the rivalry, but this one was lopsided. Irving had just 10 points and one assist.

"He had a hell of a game," James said. "But that's what All-Stars do."

That could've been just a compliment. Or it could've been one of James's little digs in referencing how Lowry had beaten out Irving for an All-Star spot. Lowry got it because of a huge Canadian voting push to have one of their players start the game, which was being played in Toronto. Irving wasn't voted in by the coaches because he had missed so much time with injury. Irving had been an All-Star twice before; his status wasn't in question. Nonetheless, it felt like a bit of a jab after he had been so outplayed.

Whatever it was, it was a tremor before a passive-aggressive James storm was about to arrive.

James skipped the next game. He'd been worn down a little and took the night off in Washington. The underachieving Wizards drilled the Cavs, getting up by as many as 29 points against a lifeless defense. James was so frustrated he left the bench with five minutes to go and was off to the bus within minutes of the end of the game.

Lue yanked all his frontline players except for Irving, whom for some reason he played until the bitter end. Irving ended up scoring 28 points, but he was in the game either as some form of punishment or because it reached a point where he didn't want to come out.

Against the Pacers, the team was headed for a third straight loss at home but rallied in the fourth quarter to win. "When our backs are against the wall, that's when we tend to play harder," Lue said. "It's annoying."

At this juncture, annoyance was growing around the team. A report appeared in the media that Irving had grown unhappy in Cleveland playing alongside James. In truth, many of James's teammates got unhappy with him at times. Love and Irving had their bouts with it the season before for sure. But Love and Irving also knew they'd never seen the playoffs before they got on the same team with James. There were rewards to dealing with occasional downsides.

Irving, however, didn't exactly kill the story when the chance arose after the win over the Pacers. "There's nothing to really address," he said. "Obviously there's going to be some misunderstandings, it's part of being on a team."

The team had three days off and some decompression was needed. Lue told the players they'd have two straight days with no practice. James and his wife got away and flew to Miami. The time was his to use. It was warm in Florida and cold in Cleveland. But he allowed his dinner and workouts with Dwyane Wade to make it onto social media, letting the world know of his midseason side trip.

Then, while in Miami, he sent out a cryptic tweet that read, "It's

OK to know you've made a mistake. Cause we all do it at times. Just be ready to live with whatever comes with it and be with...those who will protect you at all cost."

Just like the year before with his tweets about Love, many assumed this was directed at a teammate. With the Irving events, some concluded it was aimed at him. James denied it was for anyone on his team and brushed off people who wondered why he'd go hang out with Wade in the middle of the season. "I don't care," he said dismissively.

Then it was back to Twitter with another pointed comment with an uncertain target: "Can't replace being around great friends that reciprocate the same energy back to you in all facets of life."

Again assumptions were made that he was saying he liked being with Wade more than with his own teammates. Again, James didn't explain himself. That he was scheduled to become a free agent in the summer fed some unwanted speculation.

On a video that Richard Jefferson took and put on social media, James mocked the media and the overheated analysis. As he was eating a banana, James pretended he was a reporter asking him, "Why are you eating a banana, LeBron? Does that mean you're going to slip on a banana peel out of Cleveland?"

Then again, James had left in free agency twice before in his career. The idea wasn't exactly ludicrous and his behavior was a challenge to read.

There were more important things going on. While the team was on hiatus, the front office was working hard to land Joe Johnson, the veteran shooting guard who secured his release from the Brooklyn Nets and was now a free agent. The Cavs put on a strong recruiting process, believing he could help as a role player off the bench and that he would want to come compete for a title. James made several recruiting pitches; the two knew each other from Team USA.

But Johnson rejected the Cavs and instead signed in Miami, visiting the Heat at the same time James was there on his mini-vacation.

As they seemed to do in such times, the Cavs pivoted. They came back from their break with two excellent wins, getting retribution on the Wizards by winning by 25 points and then making up for the ugly loss to the Celtics by beating them by 17.

And, on cue, they backed that up with a miserable loss to the Memphis Grizzlies. Missing five of their top seven players because of injury, the Grizzlies only had eight players in uniform. Tony Allen, the team's veteran defensive specialist, came away with 26 points, the most he'd scored in more than five years.

"We didn't respect them," James said. "I can sit up here and say that we're a team that's ready to start the playoffs tomorrow, but we're not."

The team rebounded by winning three of four on a western road trip. They won in Sacramento, putting up 120 points as Irving had 30 and James 25. The team spent four days in Los Angeles, where James played his final game against Bryant.

The two stars never had much of a relationship when they were both in their prime. They played together on the 2008 Olympic team, but there was a distance between them even as teammates, which Bryant preferred anyway. Between 2007 and 2016, either Bryant or James would be in every Finals, but they never played against each other. The nearest miss was in 2009 when James's Cavs lost to the Magic in the conference finals. That left a hole in their rivalry.

In 2010 after the Lakers had won back-to-back titles, Bryant needled James when he signed with the Miami Heat. Just after the announcement, he sent James a text: "Go ahead and get another MVP, if you want. And find the city you want to live in. But we're going to win the championship. Don't worry about it."

James won two MVPs and two titles in Miami. Bryant was done winning as the later stages of his career were wrecked with injuries. But he had his five rings to lord over James. As Bryant mellowed in his final two years in the league, the barrier between the two started to come down. Searching for a way to overcome the injuries to pull off the upset in the 2015 Finals, James communicated with Bryant. Never in his career had James been an advice-seeker. But he was willing to listen to Kobe.

Because of injuries and circumstance, Bryant and James only played each other 22 times even though they were in the league for 13 seasons together. James polished off his 16th win against Bryant with 24 points. Bryant gave a final strong performance against James, making 11 of 16 shots and scoring 26 points.

"We're two sportsmen and we love the lights," James said. "We get up for the best moments, and for us to give the fans and give our beautiful sport one last opportunity to watch us both on the same floor and give them a show. It was great."

As he left the James rivalry behind, Bryant had a few words of wisdom to impart. "You have to be true to who you are and authentic," he said, "and I think every team should have that lightning rod because the happy-go-lucky stuff doesn't work, I don't care what anybody says. You have to have that inner conflict, you have to have that person that's really driving these things. From the Cavs' perspective, it's hard for me to tell from afar who should be that person. LeBron's not that person. He brings people together, that's what he does naturally and he's phenomenal at it, but you have to have somebody else that's going to create that tension. Maybe it's Kyrie."

Bryant was half right. Some more inner conflict was coming. But it wasn't from Irving, it was from James. And it left his new coach and his general manager irate.

Chapter 15

MEETING AT TRUMP'S

On a Monday morning, as the Cavs finished a game-day walk-through preparing for the Denver Nuggets, Ty Lue asked LeBron James to come in for a meeting. Lue was unhappy and was going to address it.

The team spent the previous weekend in Florida, first beating the Orlando Magic but then getting crushed by the Miami Heat. In Miami on Saturday night, the entire team had laid an egg. The Heat were playing well despite losing star Chris Bosh for the season and were a potential playoff opponent.

This losing of focus was a bad habit. Losing happens, but losing with an absence of effort is a plague in the NBA. Coaches treat it like a mold: It has to be killed before it spreads. But none of that was what Lue wanted to talk to James about.

At halftime in Miami, James went to the center of the floor and spent several minutes talking to friend Dwyane Wade. They covered their mouths with their warmups so they couldn't be overheard, but whatever they were saying was funny, because James was laughing. At the time, the Cavs were down 21 points.

Lue is all for fraternization with friends; he was one of the most connected guys in the league. One of the things that awed David Griffin about Lue in his first season was seeing players from opposing teams come up to see him before games. Before, not during. Lue thought James's actions set a bad example. He wanted it stamped out.

"I just told him we can't have that, being down like we were and him being the leader," Lue told Cleveland.com about the meeting.

"Just me being a competitor, I didn't like it. We had a long talk about it. It was good. He understood, he apologized."

This was a time when it was fair to judge the difference between David Blatt and Lue. Blatt avoided confrontations with James, something James eventually started to take advantage of. Lue was not afraid to seek them out. It had already been happening in film sessions and huddles. Lue had told players, including James, to shut up during timeouts. James still held tremendous influence, and Lue made him a partner in some decisions. But James was not going to go largely unchecked by the coach anymore.

Lue thought his chat did its job. That day James opened his Twitter account and unfollowed the Cavs official account. A few days later he would explain this was the beginning of him focusing in a run-up to the playoffs. He had a routine of blocking out distractions during the postseason. And he was starting early this year, perhaps his discussion with Lue being a factor.

Once again, however, without context the move seemed strange, another coded social media message. He unfollowed other accounts as well, but with more than 25 million followers, nothing he did on the platform went unnoticed.

That he went out and led the team to a win over the Nuggets that night, putting up a triple double that clinched the Central Division title, seemed to be less important to many fans who were perplexed or even alarmed by the move. James became annoyed the focus was on social media and not his play and refused to talk about it.

The next day, Bleacher Report released a long-planned story about James and friend Carmelo Anthony. James had done an interview for the piece six weeks earlier. In it, he talked about how someday he'd love to play on the same team as Anthony and his other close NBA friends, Chris Paul and Wade. This group had begun calling itself "The Brotherhood." Their families were close and they vacationed together the previous summer, chartering a yacht and sailing out into the Atlantic for a week off the Bahamas.

"It would definitely be cool if it happened, but we don't know how realistic it could be to have us four," James said in the interview. "If you got an opportunity to work with three of your best friends, no matter what, it's not even about sports, it's about being around guys that you don't even have to say nothing, you automatically know. We just have that type of history. Can it happen? I don't know if it can even happen, but it would be cool."

It was a hypothetical and only a small part of the story. It was also an old interview. But that's not how the public consumed it. Or James's teammates. What they saw was this progression: James visits Wade in Miami, James chats Wade up during a blowout loss, James unfollows Cavs, James talks about wanting to play with his close friends a few months before becoming a free agent again.

With all the issues the Cavs were having getting themselves together on the court, this was unneeded turbulence. Griffin was especially upset. He'd stuck his neck out by firing a coach on a first-place team because he was concerned about the togetherness of the team, and James was not helping matters.

Griffin wasn't delusional. He knew even with these hiccups, James was one of the most valuable players in the history of the league. If the trade-off was occasional issues because of meaningless blips in the news cycle, that's a deal he was thrilled to make. But Griffin also stressed during the coaching change that accountability in the organization was paramount. He had to back up his words or his credibility was at stake. So after seeing the story, he asked to meet with James.

It wasn't just Lue and Griffin who were wondering what James was up to. His close friends were puzzled too. James typically saw all angles—awareness and foresight are two of his greatest traits. The same ability that allows him to see passing lanes or predict chances to grab steals carried off the floor. He was highly aware of what his words and actions could do. He'd become an expert at leveraging this gift, whether it was to generate business opportunities, motivate teammates, or sublimely tweak rivals. He didn't like it, but James knew all this activity had the potential to cause problems.

"He was off his rocker for a little while," James's friend and business partner Maverick Carter told *Sports Illustrated*. "He's a perfectionist. He likes everything perfect, and he knew this team could be better."

Whether it was the talk with Lue, the talk with Griffin, or the urging of those in his inner circle, James did respond. There would be no more self-inflicted controversies from him for the rest of the season. "It wasn't going well, and I had to look in the mirror," he told *SI*. "I had to reset, recalibrate and get out of that little funk I was in."

A few days later the team went to New York City for a three-day stay, where they'd play both the Nets and Knicks. At the first stop, in Brooklyn, they had yet another inexplicable performance. The Nets, one of the worst teams in the league, won by nine. The Cavs were miserable in the fourth quarter, with Kyrie Irving and Kevin Love missing all their shots. They were 10 games away from starting the playoffs, healthy, and loaded with talent. The Golden State Warriors, their chief rivals, were a few days away from locking up their 70th win and the Cavs were still having huge breakdowns.

Lue had seen enough. The next day there was no practice, but a film session was scheduled. Film became the least important thing. The team was staying at the Trump SoHo, a high-rise tower with floor-to-ceiling windows overlooking lower Manhattan. But no one in the ballroom was looking out them. Lue took control of the room and unleashed a profanity-laced challenge to his players.

He targeted his three stars. He said they had to trust each other, they had to set a standard of knowing what each of them were going to bring every night. Not some nights. Every one. He said they had to police each other. If one guy didn't do his job, they were responsible for calling them out. Lue especially went after Love and his habit of fading away when teammates weren't including him. He told Love he was a great player and should demand his teammates, especially James and Irving, respect him and include him.

It was not the type of discussion that would usually happen in late March, but nothing about this season had been typical. Lue had made it clear on his team there was no golden child, everyone was open to being called out just as everyone could be praised. Even if it were the stars. Then he yielded the floor and the players had their say. It became a giant therapy session.

"To change culture, you can't treat everyone the same way," Lue said. "Sitting down and getting on the same page of understanding what they need from each other on a nightly basis and understanding that they have to trust each other and also trust the team. We had that talk in front of everyone and everyone kind of gave their opinion and kind of talked about what they expected and what we needed to do better. I think from that day on, we kind of took off and we became a better team."

It wasn't just the players; Lue had looked inward. The team's defense had regressed since he took over. His new assistant, Mike Longabardi, had highly detailed scouting reports and game plans. On paper it was impressive. But on the fly, the team wasn't executing. They'd been the sixth-best defensive team in the league under Lue. Since Longabardi became the defensive coordinator, they'd dropped to 13th. Lue admitted he'd overreached and made a mistake. He tossed out the complex defensive coverages and went back to a more basic approach, and he would again oversee the defense within the game.

The next day, the Cavs whipped the Knicks at Madison Square Garden. James had another triple double and Love looked refreshed, scoring 28 points with 12 rebounds. It kicked off a hot streak for Love—he'd average 19 points and shoot 46 percent on three-pointers over the last 10 games of the regular season. His confidence, it seemed to the team, spawned from the meeting where Lue had given him a tough-love pep talk. It wasn't just Love. In the coming weeks, Lue would refer to that gathering being a turning point in the team's mind-set. Whether it was the words or the calendar—the playoffs were almost there—the Cavs' days of aimless performances were at an end.

But there was still distraction. It was Irving's turn. During the season, he'd publicly been dating a popular young R&B singer, Kehlani Parrish. Both of them had huge fan bases among teens and young adults, and their relationship played out on social media and the gossip sites. In March they broke up. Kehlani began dating an ex-boyfriend, Canadian recording artist Jahron Brathwaite, who performed under the name PartyNextDoor. After several days of attention where she was accused of cheating on Irving, Kehlani attempted suicide. The resulting drama of the supposed love triangle forced Irving to address the situation.

It was a stressful time for Irving, who was privately still dealing with the relationship ending. Then it became public. That Kehlani was from Oakland and a Warriors fan—she had recorded a song celebrating the team's victory over Irving's Cavs the previous summer—only added fuel to the hecklers who were descending into Irving's real and digital life.

"I've been through a ton of adversity in my life," Irving said. "There's nothing anything or anyone can say that I can't get through. I've been through enough already in my short twenty-four years that most people can say for their whole entire lives."

That may have been what he was telling himself, but his game suffered. After his personal life became a headline generator, he went into a weeklong slump. Compounding matters, he was under the weather.

He rebounded with a clutch overtime three-pointer in Atlanta and the Cavs beat the Hawks in a game that felt like a playoff matchup. It was crucial for them keeping their lead on the Raptors for the top seed in the East. James had 29 points in the win, but Irving's 20 and his big basket seemed to help improve his mood.

"Everything surrounding our team is just crazy," Irving said. "To think that we're still in first place and we're still the team to beat, honestly."

Irving created more attention by calling the Cavs the team to beat with the Warriors setting records. At least this reaction was to basketball, though, and that was a relief even if Lue tried to temper enthusiasm a bit. But Irving was correct; the team had weathered a remarkable number of distractions. They still were erratic at times, and that was worrisome looking forward, but in general they showed resiliency.

Something else was happening behind the scenes: They were becoming closer as a team. The catalyst for it was unexpected, new pickup Channing Frye. He was helping on the floor. Four times in his first month with the team he made four or more three-pointers in the exact role Griffin had envisioned. And his sunny disposition and daily joy started rubbing off on his teammates.

"I get excited for everything," Frye said. "That's just who I am. I get excited when we get into these nice hotels and I see how many different soaps we have to choose from."

It's Frye's nature, but it also is the result of a life-altering situation he experienced several years earlier, in which a heart ailment not only put his career in peril but also threatened his life. He ended up missing an entire season. After his recovery, his outlook on his career took a turn. Some players say they're just happy to be in the NBA. Frye truly meant it.

His positively and, frankly, his naiveté, ended up being a bonus. He'd played in all four corners of the league, from New York to Portland to Phoenix to Orlando, but was blown away by the amenities provided for the players in Cleveland. He was especially impressed with the made-to-order breakfast options at the team facility. That he could have a chef whip up a fresh burrito with a whole wheat tortilla, egg whites, goat cheese, and chicken sausage left him in awe. And then there was the French toast.

"When I first saw the spread, I was like, 'Free burritos before shootaround? Are you [kidding] me? This is the best!'" Frye wrote in an essay for *The Players' Tribune*. "Life moves so fast in the NBA, sometimes we players don't appreciate the little things. Let's enjoy this wonderful French toast. Made-to-order omelets. Let's eat these breakfast burritos. Let's get some wins and let's make history."

Frye arrived after the Blatt drama, after the early spats between the stars, after the contract stalemates. He was a fresh face in every regard, and with his close friend and former college teammate Richard Jefferson, he was generating smiles throughout the team.

Frye was unaware, for example, of the cliques. James had his closer friends—J.R. Smith, James Jones, and Tristan Thompson mostly—and other players had regular dinner partners and conversationalists on flights and bus rides. Once Frye got everyone's cell phone numbers, he started sending group texts to numerous guys looking to set up dinners or have conversations about games that were happening on TV.

"All of a sudden I was just on a text chain with LeBron, Kev, and Champ [Jones's nickname]. You're just like, 'Chan, why did you include us?'" Jefferson said. "He's like, 'I don't know, you guys are the ones I wanted to talk to.' All of a sudden the four of us are texting through a game."

"You have this seven-foot professional goofball that walks in and everything changes. Channing doesn't know anything about the supposed locker room dynamic. Channing doesn't know anything. He's an adult kid. And he's going to send stupid jokes and now we're all sending stupid jokes to one another and he's kind of breaking down barriers. And when you inject that energy of a guy that just wants to be friends with everybody, wants to laugh with everybody, you all realize how good it can be."

The Cavs rested some players as the season wound down, causing them to lose a game or two. Irving had a minor ankle issue. Iman Shumpert missed a game with a sore knee. James took several games off, the team trying to keep him as fresh as possible for the playoff run. But they did enough to stay out ahead of the Raptors.

On the second-to-last night of the season, they clinched home court advantage throughout the Eastern Conference playoffs, winning their 57th game in beating the Hawks again. James was magnificent with 34 points, and Irving's legs looked strong. He nailed five three-pointers to rack up 35 points. Irving had gotten himself in tremendous physical condition, especially considering he missed so much of the season. He was never out of shape early in his career, but he wasn't in the sort of condition that he could've been. His regimented recovery from the knee surgery and Lue's mandated conditioning efforts had worked. Irving was ripped and looking strong.

Meanwhile, for all his unusual behavior, James had put together a dominating finish to the season. He was named Eastern Conference Player of the Month for February, March, and April. Stephen Curry was about to win the first-ever unanimous MVP award as the Warriors were about to win their 73rd game. But under the radar, at least as under the radar as James could get, he may have been the league's best player over the finishing kick.

After Lue's admonishment about the halftime antics with Wade in Miami, James's focus was noticeably improved. He averaged 28.4 points, eight rebounds, and 8.5 assists, and shot 51 percent on three-pointers and 63 percent overall for the rest of the season. He had gotten to a point in his career where he slowly built during the year, aiming to ramp up for the playoffs. Maybe he'd have played his best and most focused basketball over the final two months with Blatt as the coach too. Or maybe Lue's style of challenging him was really making a difference. The Cavs front office believed it was the latter.

Combined with Love's improved play after his cursing session with Lue, the team was feeling rather good about itself. Not everyone agreed. They'd had so many bad losses and so many times they'd looked like they'd arrived only to fall back. It was hard to believe they'd really turned a corner.

Lue, a realist, knew what he saw. With James playing this well and him feeling his team coming closer together and getting into shape, he could see it. "I hope LeBron can keep it up," he said. "If he plays like this, man, we're going to be tough to beat."

Chapter 16

LIL' KEV

Stan Van Gundy was irked. It was in the midst of a playoff game, the first one for the Detroit Pistons in seven years, and there was a microphone in his face for the standard in-game interview that has become a regular part of nationally televised games. The heavily favored Cavs were ahead by just two points after the first quarter.

"A couple calls have upset our guys," Van Gundy complained to Lisa Salters of ESPN. "They've got to understand, LeBron's LeBron. They're not going to call offensive fouls on him. He gets to do whatever he wants. They've got to understand that."

Over the years, a parade of underdogs had applied an array of tactics to deal with James in playoff series. They'd tried to beat him up, swarm him, leave him isolated, bait him into fights, and so on. Van Gundy revealed his strategy early: He was going to try to goad officials into calling fouls on James.

Van Gundy had beaten James as an underdog before, in the 2009 conference finals when he coached the Orlando Magic. James was brilliant in that series, averaging 38.5 points, eight rebounds, and eight assists before losing in six games. He had done it with a benign tumor that had developed in his jaw area, which was removed in an intricate four-hour surgery two days after the series ended. Van Gundy's strategy of shutting down James's teammates had worked in that series, and he was working on another move seven years later.

The league dinged Van Gundy with a $25,000 fine for the comment. But it was only the beginning of the Pistons trying to get under

James's skin. Despite being the No. 8 seed, Detroit felt the Cavs might be vulnerable. They'd had a worse record under Ty Lue (27–14) than the fired David Blatt (30–11) as their defense sagged after the change. Also, the Pistons believed the Cavs' best players, James and Kyrie Irving, could be goaded into taking three-pointers, and that was exactly what the Pistons wanted. James shot 31 percent during the season on threes, his lowest percentage since his rookie season, as he'd fallen into a bad habit of losing balance on long shots. Irving, his legs not quite as strong as usual after he returned from knee surgery, had hit 32 percent on threes, the worst season of his career.

What the Pistons didn't consider was Irving's rigorous conditioning during the second half of the season had gotten him into the best shape of his career. Over the final five games of the regular season, his three-point shooting had jumped to 42 percent.

So Detroit backed off and dared the stars to shoot. With James, their defenders gave him space and waited back in position, hoping he'd either take a long shot or run over them for offensive fouls. The Cavs won Game 1, but by just five points. Irving took advantage of all the space the Pistons were giving him and drilled five three-pointers to finish with 31 points. Kevin Love made four three-pointers and had 28. James had 22 points and 11 rebounds.

But the Pistons were undeterred, especially rookie Stanley Johnson. He'd first played against James two summers before. While James was having meetings and considering his jump to Cleveland during his Nike camp in Las Vegas, he played in a pickup game with Johnson on the other side. About to start at the University of Arizona, Johnson was aggressive and rough with James and certainly unafraid, trash-talking the legend at his own camp.

Johnson played several minutes of effective defense on James in Game 1 and then made himself the center of attention afterward. "We think, we know, we can win the series," he said. "Honestly, LeBron's a physical guy. But if he wants to try and grab me and throw me to the floor, and you call a foul on me, I just don't understand that. I've never had a person grab my jersey and try to throw me to the floor."

Between Van Gundy and Johnson, the Pistons' strategy was transparent. "I'm not having an individual matchup with Stan or an individual matchup with Stanley or any other Stan they can possess," James said with a dismissive shrug. There had been a litany of antagonists in his playoff past, including DeShawn Stevenson of the Washington Wizards and Lance Stephenson of the Indiana Pacers, both journeyman guards who attempted unorthodox playoff tactics with James. Stephenson had famously tried blowing in James's ear during playoff games.

A few minutes into Game 2, the Pistons were up nine and Johnson was part of the hot start. James then sent a message as the two passed on the floor, leaning into Johnson and purposely bumping him. A literal brushback.

"I'm definitely in his head, that's for sure," Johnson said. "I don't know what you take from that. I don't take anything from it but a cheap shot, a cheap-ass bump."

Problem was, Johnson's act didn't work. James made seven of nine shots that night when Johnson was guarding him. He was even making three-pointers, shaking his head as the Pistons gave him space. He ended with 27 points. J. R. Smith made seven three-pointers, Irving added four more, and the Cavs ended up winning by 17.

The Pistons' strategy wasn't working, but Johnson doubled down. "He jabbers, he moves his mouth sometimes," he said. "Their whole team does, kind of like their little cheerleaders on the bench. They're always saying something like they're actually in the game. They might as well just be in the stands, in my opinion."

After the game, Van Gundy dismissed a coaching move by Lue that had proven quite effective. Lue jostled his lineup to make James essentially the point guard of the second unit, while making sure Love and Irving played together while James was resting. In the past, Lue and Blatt had always tried to keep James and Love together, with Irving being out there with the second unit. It was a small but impactful change that ended up being one of Lue's finest strategy moves in the entire postseason. But like Johnson had run his mouth with James, Van Gundy mocked Lue.

"That's really smart coaching. It is. That's really smart coaching, to put LeBron on the floor," Van Gundy said. "I give him a lot of credit for that adjustment, if that's what you want to call it."

Meanwhile, Van Gundy's game plan of daring the Cavs to shoot threes was not working. They made 20 of them.

The Cavs ended up sweeping the series after taking Games 3 and 4 in Detroit. Love, James, and Irving all scored over 20 points in Game 3, in which the Pistons moved on to roughhousing James. During the second quarter, Pistons center Andre Drummond elbowed James in the neck. He was not disciplined by the league, part of a trend of the NBA allowing rough play as Boston Celtics guard Isaiah Thomas avoided suspension after hitting Atlanta Hawks guard Dennis Schröder in the head in another series.

"Initially I was surprised," said James, who believed for years that the NBA let opponents get away with hard fouls on him even as the opponents insisted it was he who got favorable whistles. "But then I thought who he did it to and I wasn't surprised."

Game 4 was decided by two points and the Pistons were furious over calls at the end. Irving had 31 points, finishing off a masterpiece of a series. He hit four three-pointers, shooting 47 percent for the four games. He led the Cavs in scoring at 27.5 points, just the second time in 34 career playoff series that James didn't lead his team in scoring.

When it was over, Irving shouted "Bye-bye!" to courtside fans who'd been heckling him. James walked off the floor without shaking any Pistons players' hands. Forgetting about their opponents, Cavs players began praising Lue for his game plans and in-game moves in the series, including a late out-of-bounds play in Game 3 that freed Irving for a clinching three-pointer with less than two seconds on the shot clock.

"We definitely recognize it and understand that it's his first challenge, and he succeeded as well as any coach could," James said. "He physically, mentally, and spiritually prepared us every single night."

"For him, his first playoffs, he's been great," Tristan Thompson said. "We were like, 'Man, you can just see it on the court.' His poise. It's his first time, and a lot of guys might be nervous or shaking or come to timeouts and not know what to say. But T-Lue, he was fearless."

Thompson and James seemed genuine in their comments, but it also again felt like the statements were coded. Players often noticed Blatt's discomfort in huddles and sometimes losing track of everything from who was in the game to the number of timeouts. As if the point hadn't been hammered home enough, the Cavs players kept piling on with how much they liked playing for their new coach.

The drive to the airport and the loading of equipment in the cargo hold takes longer than the actual twenty-five-minute flight between Detroit and Cleveland. But in that span, something happened that would become a galvanizing moment. As he waited for the flight to leave, Richard Jefferson started flipping through a magazine that was in the seatback pocket. He came across an ad for a Tommy Bahama tropical shirt, and the model had a striking resemblance to Love, right down to the length of the beard.

Love had a mixed history when it came to bonding with teammates, even with his dry, likable sense of humor. He also had done some modeling for clothing lines, something teammates were quite aware of. Jefferson was the class clown and, united with Channing Frye, he was constantly on the lookout for ways to lighten the mood.

Jefferson roared with laughter at the ad and immediately tore it out and began passing it around the plane. With the euphoria of having just won a series, the team was in a good mood. Teammates took turns putting the photo in front of their faces and doing impressions of Love. They nicknamed the model "Lil' Kev."

Over the next several days, Jefferson started bringing the page to team functions. He arrived at Love's house to pick him up for a team dinner several days later with Lil' Kev in the front seat and Frye relegated to the back. It was a dose of camaraderie that was particularly useful in the playoffs, and it helped bring Love out of his shell, something team staffers marveled at as he truly embraced the ongoing prank.

The team had plenty of time for antics, as they had to wait eight days between playoff games. They got the Hawks in the second round in a rematch of the previous season's conference finals. In that span something more interesting than Lil' Kev happened. Warriors star Stephen Curry slipped in a pool of sweat in a playoff game in Houston, causing him to fall and sprain his knee, knocking him out for several weeks.

The Warriors won the series, but after what seemed like no adversity for two years, it was the first time they faced some uncertainty.

The Cavs, who had faded into the background a little as the Warriors assembled a record 73-win season, took notice.

The Cavs didn't seem to have much concern for the Hawks. They swept that series too, running their playoff win streak to eight. The hot three-point shooting from the Pistons series didn't just carry over, it became a central part of the game plan as the usually stout Atlanta defense was unable to keep up with the Cavs' perimeter players.

Lue once again made a strong coaching move, deploying lineups with Love and Frye playing together. Though that lineup was defensively suspect, the Hawks were unable to handle the array of long-range options.

The Cavs won Game 2 by 25 points and hit a playoff record 25 three-pointers, with the starting lineup combining for 18 of them. Smith made seven by himself. The box score looked like something from another league. The team made nine more three-point baskets than two-point baskets. It continued in Game 3 as they made 20 more threes, this time Frye hitting seven in one of the finest games of his career.

"We didn't prepare for Love and Frye playing together," Hawks center Al Horford said. "They took advantage."

After seeing the Warriors dismantle the league with three-point shooting, the Cavs were now doing it better than their rivals. The addition of Frye made a difference, but Irving and James emerging from long slumps was just as important. As the bench celebrated each make, Lue stood stoically as his plans for an open, uptempo offense blossomed in front of him.

Game 4 was closer, the Cavs winning by a single point, with James making the game-winning basket and the game-winning defensive play in the final minute. It was Love's turn that night: He nailed eight three-pointers with his teammates shouting about Lil' Kev the whole way. By this point the tattered ad had been laminated for protection and was traveling with the team like a mascot.

The Hawks lamented a few calls, including a suspect goaltend on Paul Millsap, but after 16 more three-pointers it was clear the better team had moved on. The Cavs set a slate of new records for their shooting, the 77 three-pointers they hit in the four games being perhaps the most jaw-dropping.

After the game, there was a buffet set up outside the team locker room. Players heading to the bus stopped by the table to get a meal to take with them. As Love worked his way down the line, a call echoed down the concrete hall from a group of his teammates: "Don't forget to make a plate for Lil' Kev!"

"You can't tell me that Lil' Kev didn't matter during the playoffs," Jefferson said. "It's so random. Think about something as random as Lil' Kev. Thirty, forty years from now, someone will show a picture of that and there will be fans that will be like, 'Oh, that's Lil' Kev.' It was an excellent tool. It gave the fans something that they really enjoyed. I'll stand by the fact that it put our team in a different light. It showed how much fun we were having. It showed that we had something unique. Something all our own."

The team had to wait nine days for its next opponent, as it took the Toronto Raptors seven games to win their second-round series with the Miami Heat. In that time the Cavs practiced, but their passion was more on the growing Lil' Kev phenomenon.

The Cavs marketing department had developed a slogan and a campaign for the playoffs weeks in advance: "All In." This was a poker reference that owner Dan Gilbert, who also owned several casinos, including one in Cleveland, always liked. Shoving all the chips into the middle, as Gilbert did with his $160 million payroll, was a reasonable way to term it. It was on huge banners on the exterior of the arena, on signage around the interior, and printed on tens of thousands of T-shirts. But as far as the team was concerned, Lil' Kev was the rallying cry for their postseason run.

In the days that passed, as the Cavs killed time, the meme grew. Players started wearing T-shirts with the face of the unsuspecting model from the Tommy Bahama ad. Masks were made. And players ordered up the gaudy shirt the ad was pitching and began wearing it.

There was something else, too, that the team was doing to build camaraderie, but it remained a secret. Late in the regular season, James Jones approached the Cavs owners with an idea for the playoffs. He wanted the team to have a symbol, a motivation, to use during the playoffs. After discussion, the idea was hatched for a puzzle of sixteen pieces, all in gold, one for each win that would be needed to gain the title. When fully assembled, the puzzle would form the Larry O'Brien Trophy. After each victory, a different Cavs player would set a golden piece in place, the trophy slowly being put together. Then it would be hidden away in a special case and would travel everywhere with the team during the postseason.

"We needed something to bring us together," Jones said. "Every guy was a piece. We assembled this team. So we had to assemble the puzzle."

The Raptors arrived in Cleveland fatigued and wounded. Their starting center, Jonas Valanciunas, was out with an injury and they only had one day to recover after eliminating the Heat. They had also been shaken by watching the film of the Cavs hitting all those three-pointers against Atlanta and entered with a quickly tossed-together game plan to try to slow them down.

It did work and it didn't. The Cavs only made seven three-pointers in Game 1, but they made 28 baskets in the paint and crushed Toronto by 31 points. James and Irving combined to make 22 of 30 shots. Kyle Lowry, the Raptors' stout point guard, a major concern for Cleveland, scored only eight points.

Game 2 was nearly as lopsided. The Cavs won by 19 points as James, Irving, and Love combined for 65 points. Smith, who arrived with a sports coat over his Lil' Kev shirt, made three three-pointers. Lowry managed just 10 points and walked off the bench to the locker room before the end of the first half in frustration. It was a decision that got him roasted by the Toronto media, especially after he said he'd needed to leave the floor to "relax his mind."

Hall of Famer Kareem Abdul-Jabbar attended the game and stopped by the Cavs locker room. He waited for James, and when the Cavs star arrived they embraced.

"How do you feel?" Abdul-Jabbar asked James after congratulating him on the win.

At that point the Cavs were 10–0 in the postseason, had won the first two games of the conference finals by a combined 50 points, and James had played just two games in the previous twelve days. He'd had a triple double that night in just 33 minutes. Meanwhile, Curry was just limping back from his knee injury as the Warriors had to fight their way through the second round and had fallen behind the Oklahoma City Thunder in the Western finals.

"I feel great," James said.

For the better part of two years, the Cavs had gotten used to a near-constant state of drama. Whether it was with each other, with their coach, or with injuries, there had rarely been any period of successful calm. Now, finally, there was. They were playing brilliantly, they were healthy, they were generally in a good place with their coach, and, thanks to Frye and Jefferson, they'd never been looser as a group.

They took the short flight to Toronto and posed for pictures together on the sunny tarmac as Canadian customs officials searched their baggage for contraband, a little home-country advantage as the visiting team got some extra scrutiny. At that point, even airport delays couldn't spoil their mood.

They finally tasted a little adversity in Game 3 when the Raptors rallied back to win by 15 points. Irving and Love played miserably, combining to shoot 4-of-28. James was hit flush in the jaw by Thompson by accident. He assumed it was one of the Raptors who hit him, and when he tumbled to the court some thought he was exaggerating for effect.

"I'm not trying to sell a call. I got hit with an elbow," James growled on the matter. "Sell a call for what? There was no call there to be sold. That's it. I was going to say something else to you, but I'm going to leave it alone."

Late in the game, Raptors backup center Bismack Biyombo leveled James with a flagrant foul, wrapping his arm around his neck on a drive and pulling him to the court. The crowd cheered Biyombo, who was making his presence felt as he played in place of Valanciunas, and James hopped up to confront him. In the final 15 seconds, end-of-bench Cavs player Dahntay Jones entered the game and hit Biyombo in the groin with a closed fist, dropping the Congolese big man to the ground.

Jones was suspended by the league for the next game. James, recognizing Jones had leveled the blow as a defense to him, offered to pay his fine. It was an interesting gesture that only added to the spice that was suddenly injected into the series. However, Jones's salary for the entire year had been just $8,800 because he'd signed on the last day of the season. By the calculation used for suspension fines, he was only docked $80. James made $210,000 per game.

Raptors coach Dwane Casey, unsatisfied with the victory, attacked the referees because the Cavs had shot 27 more free throws over the first three games. "Bismack is getting fouled so much. He's not getting the calls," Casey said. "He's getting hit. There's one play where they almost have a brawl. He gets killed on that play ... Some of those fouls are unbelievable."

The league fined Casey $25,000. The Raptors then didn't go to the foul line for the entire first half of Game 4. It didn't hurt. Lowry finally arrived and scored 35 points as he repeatedly bested the Cavs' perimeter defense. DeMar DeRozan, his backcourt mate, scored 32 and the Raptors won by six points. They'd evened the series at 2–2, and for the first time it looked like the Cavs had some weaknesses.

Love played poorly again, shooting 4-of-14. He was 5-of-23 in the two games in Toronto, and Lue benched him in the fourth quarter.

In the locker room, Love's teammates noticed he was down. This, in reality, was where all the bonding would matter. For all the jokes and the T-shirts, that was where the relationships would truly be tested. Sure enough, the first two to be at his side were Frye and Jefferson. Lil' Kev was not the topic.

"Channing basically told me no one's immune to the NBA playoffs. These things happen. You have to keep fighting through it. In order for us to win, he said I need to be aggressive," Love said. "I give him credit for staying on me and staying vocal."

Jefferson kept the mood light. The Raptors' playoff slogan was "We the North," a communal reference to Toronto's geographic location. As Jefferson left the building he made a proclamation: "We the South will be fine."

Before Game 5, Lue also approached Love for a chat. Weeks earlier, when Lue held that emotional meeting in New York City, he'd appealed to Love's ego in telling him he was a star and should start acting like it. This time he was more encouraging and he urged Love to stay involved and look to shoot his way out of the slump. The team had learned Love by then, and they knew he was prone to getting down on himself. They'd found a way to bring him out of his shell with the comedy of his alter ego.

It worked. Love exploded in the next game, making his first six shots. He scored 19 points in the first half and 25 for the game as the Cavs smashed Toronto by 38 points to take back the series lead. James, Irving, and Love together put up 71 points, one of the classic three-pronged attacks that the foundation of the team was built on.

"I've been a part of some really adverse situations, and I just didn't believe that this was one of them," James said. "From the very moment that we lost Game 4, I was just very calm about the whole situation."

This was a kind way of saying that despite what had happened in Toronto, he wasn't really worried about the Raptors. He proved to be correct when the Cavs ended the series two days later with a 26-point win back in Toronto. James was strong, scoring 33 points with 11 rebounds. Irving had 30 of his own and Love 20 as the Cavs' might showed through.

It was the 25th consecutive series that James personally had been part of a road win, breaking an obscure and seemingly untouchable Michael Jordan record. He was off to the Finals for the sixth time in a row and the seventh time in his career. Yet he celebrated after the victory like few times he had in his career, embracing teammates and clutching them by the shoulders in gratification.

"I didn't appreciate last year, myself personally, getting to the Finals," James said. "Just so much was going on in my mind, knowing that Kevin was out for the rest of the season and knowing that Kyrie was dealing with injuries all the way from the first round. I just didn't appreciate it. It's definitely a different feeling. Having these guys right here at full strength, having our team at full strength and the way I feel personally, I appreciate this moment, to be able to be part of it and to be there once again."

As he'd told Abdul-Jabbar the week before, he was feeling great. There was no champagne in the locker room; the team hadn't wanted to go all out in the celebration. So the team showered each other with what they had: water. Lots and lots of water. As they bounced around, they picked up the buckets of ice supposed to be used to soak their knees and feet and instead started throwing them around the room.

The visiting locker room at the Air Canada Centre has rubber floors—it's primarily designed as a hockey dressing room—and the water turned the room into a slippery lake.

The Cavs were going back to the Finals, and if they could avoid any falls on the wet floor, they'd be going healthy this time.

Smith took possession of the trophy the team had won that night and he didn't want to let it go. But he needed a shower, and so he kissed it and set it on top of his locker for safety.

"I'll be right back," he said, addressing the silver ball. "I'm going to get your golden sister next."

Chapter 17

"FOLLOW MY LEAD"

After dinner on the evening of June 3, LeBron James came back to his hotel suite at the Four Seasons in downtown San Francisco with his small group of friends that he kept close during the playoffs. The room looked over Yerba Buena Gardens, but the focus was on the room's 50-inch flatscreen.

Earlier that day, Muhammad Ali had passed away and the entire nation was engaged in remembrance. James had an affinity for Ali as a child, but his respect for him had grown dramatically as he got older and felt a kinship with him as he went through a similar experience of becoming a global sports celebrity. James came to understand that Ali had been a pioneer for someone like him. They would eventually meet as Ali attended several games James played in Phoenix, where Ali lived.

Ali also held a special place in the heart of Lynn Merritt, the Nike vice president who oversaw James's partnership with the corporate giant. Merritt was a role model for James, and he sometimes played the part of father figure. He'd been by his side throughout his highs and lows during his entire career. Not only had they done hundreds of millions in deals together, but Merritt was an adviser on some of the biggest moves James made. Merritt was always around James, flying in from his home in Portland for hundreds of games during the seasons. He'd ride to and from playoff games with James, acting as a sounding board or just a support system. In the playoffs, he was ubiquitous.

Merritt is from Louisville, Kentucky, where he grew up in an underprivileged section of town near where Ali was raised. As Ali rose to prominence and worldwide fame, Merritt watched as a young man trying to advance in the world himself. He felt a connection to Ali—both had gotten out of Louisville and made it. Though he took efforts to stay out of the spotlight, Merritt was one of the most powerful people in basketball. He is a kingmaker. Before his relationship with James, he acted as Ken Griffey Jr.'s main connection to the company.

Merritt would never admit it out loud, but the Finals rematch between the Warriors and the Cavs took on special meaning. The Warriors had rallied from being down 3–1 to the Oklahoma City Thunder to win three straight and get back to defend their title. In Game 6, they trailed by eight points going into the fourth quarter in OKC and Klay Thompson bailed them out with a breathtaking shooting performance, scoring 19 points with five three-pointers in the fourth quarter. Then Stephen Curry shot them into the Finals by making seven three-pointers and scoring 36 in Game 7 in Oakland while he was still recovering from the knee injury earlier in the playoffs.

Curry was fast becoming the most popular player in the league. James, who finished third in MVP voting behind Curry and the San Antonio Spurs' Kawhi Leonard, conceded Curry deserved the award but pointed out, "I think sometimes the word 'valuable' or best player of the year, you can have different results. When you talk about most 'valuable' then you can have a different conversation."

The conversation James wanted to have but couldn't was that he didn't see any player who could touch his value. The Cavs were the worst team in the NBA the four years he was gone, and when he came back were in the Finals twice. Kyrie Irving and Kevin Love were great players but never played in the playoffs before joining James. Though they had injuries, the Miami Heat cratered and missed the playoffs the year after James left them following four straight Finals appearances. That, James believed, is value.

Beyond that, Curry was a deeper rival. In 2013, Nike had passed on matching Curry after a lucrative offer from competitor Under Armour. Nike hadn't prioritized Curry, whose early career was marred by ankle injuries, and they had a deep roster with James, Kobe Bryant, and Kevin Durant among many others, including Irving. Curry had gone on to an explosive three seasons where his sweet-shooting ability, attractive baby face, and beautiful family had made him a marketing superstar. Young kids adored him and Under Armour had mirrored that rise as they continued to emerge as a thorn in Nike's side.

So for Merritt this was more than just supporting James. It was, in many ways, Nike versus Under Armour at the highest-profile level. It was James and Irving, two players with their own Nike lines, against UA's signature man. Yet Merritt knew the task for James and the Cavs was going to be extreme. The Warriors had staggered a little in the postseason, but they were almost unbeatable at home and they had momentum after beating the Thunder three straight.

When he came to San Francisco for the start of the Finals, Merritt brought with him a DVD of Ali's famous "Thrilla in Manila" fight, the 1975 bout between Ali and Joe Frazier that was regarded as one of the greatest fights of all time. Ali and Frazier were bitter rivals and this fight settled their rivalry, the third fight after each had beaten each other once. Merritt got the disc and slipped it in for James to watch.

The room quickly got emotional as the forty-year-old footage played, not just as they watched the fighters work—Frazier smashing Ali with two vicious left hooks that sent him to the ropes and then Ali coming back with a series of bruising blows that ended up forcing Frazier's corner to stop the fight after the 14th round—but at Ali's accomplishments in his life that had just ended.

"It was just an unbelievable pound-for-pound slugfest, just two greats just seizing the opportunity and seizing the moment to be in it and do what they love to do," James said.

"He paved the way for guys like myself, I understood that he is the greatest of all time, and he was the greatest of all time because of what he did outside of the ring. Obviously, we knew how great of a boxer he was, but I think that was only 20 percent of what made him as great as he was. What he stood for, I mean, it's a guy who basically had to give up a belt and relish everything that he had done because of what he believed in and ended up in jail because of his beliefs. It's a guy who stood up for so many different things throughout the times where it was so difficult for African Americans to even walk in the streets."

Within a few months, James donated $2.5 million for an Ali exhibit at the Smithsonian National Museum of African American History and Culture in Washington. His production company also made a deal with HBO to make a documentary about Ali's life.

The Cavs had lost Game 1 to the Warriors, 104–89. It was a missed opportunity. Curry and Thompson, the Warriors' two great weapons, had not played well. Curry missed 11 of his 15 shots and Thompson made just one three-pointer. But the Warriors bench, led by lanky and talented backup guard Shaun Livingston's 20 points, had felled the Cavs.

The Cavs were briefly ahead in the third quarter, leading Warriors coach Steve Kerr to angrily smash a clipboard on the bench in a rare outburst. But they didn't have enough down the stretch, a feeling that was all too much like the previous season. J. R. Smith, whose contributions were needed, burned off the outer layer of skin on his right hand diving for a ball in the first quarter and was in so much discomfort he didn't shoot for the rest of the game.

This was all on James's and Merritt's minds as they finished the night and finished the fight. They talked about what was ahead of James, down 0–1 in the Finals to the Warriors again. They knew he was going to need something special to pull this off. He was going to need a few heroic performances to beat Golden State. A few Ali-esque moments. Maybe three, they thought.

But one didn't come the next day. Some within the Warriors privately felt beating the Thunder—a team that had given them problems throughout the season—was the tallest mountain they needed to climb. It would be hard to argue that: The bookies and the computers agreed they were heavy favorites coming into the series, and it only appeared to confirm that when they totally smashed the Cavs, 110–77, in Game 2.

It was the seventh consecutive time they'd beaten the Cavs, dating to the previous Finals, and the third time by double digits in the four meetings that season. Draymond Green, a player the Cavs struggled to defend, scored 28 points. Again neither Thompson nor Curry got red hot, although combined with Green the All-Star trio had 13 three-pointers, and Golden State still won easily. The 48 total points they'd outscored the Cavs by set a record for widest margin for the first two games in Finals history.

With the confidence flowing, the Warriors couldn't help themselves as they started to brag about their destined place in history.

"I don't really look at are you the best team of all time, are we the best team of all time? Because I think it's all subjective. To say we're better than the Showtime Lakers, how can you say that? We never played them," Green said before Thompson cut him off.

"We are better than the Showtime Lakers," said Thompson with confidence. His father, Mychael, won two titles with the Showtime Lakers in the 1980s.

Green then compared the Warriors to the 1995–96 Bulls, the team whose regular-season win streak the Warriors beat that season. "Like saying we're better than the Bulls, it's like we'll never play them. It's two completely different eras. So I don't really get off on the are you the best team of all times."

Regardless of the argument, that Green and Thompson were openly indulging it midway through a series was a window into their feelings. They were confident they were a few days away from finishing off a title and taking their place among the all-time greats.

The Cavs could've been miffed at the perceived slight, but they had bigger issues. They'd been embarrassed. A year of talking about getting a chance at the Warriors with their full team and things being different—well, there was a difference: They were getting beat worse. As the team was getting ready to pack up and head home, assistant coach Phil Handy asked Lue if he could address the team.

Handy is a development specialist. He works with players individually on skills before and after practices and games. He was a holdover from Byron Scott's staff in Cleveland, now two coaches ago. Irving and Handy had a close relationship, mostly from all their workouts together. He was rarely vocal. During games he sat behind the bench and didn't take part in much in-game strategy. But he was an Oakland native and he was furious that the team had been crushed in his hometown.

Handy unleashed a stream of expletives admonishing the team for lackluster play. He couldn't believe they'd allowed themselves to get whipped in such a vitally important game. The players were taken aback; most of them had never seen this side of Handy. It wouldn't help defending the three-pointer, but it was a new voice rattling the situation to get them thinking.

Love didn't hear it. He was already gone from the locker room, feeling nauseous and disoriented. Late in the first half, the Warriors' Harrison Barnes caught him with an elbow. Love dropped to the ground and clutched his head. Lue called a timeout, but Love stayed in the game and finished the half. A few moments later, he made a three-pointer. He went to the locker room with his teammates.

"I didn't even know what happened, but at halftime he showed no symptoms," Lue said. "He didn't talk about it."

Early in the third quarter, though, Love started to get woozy and couldn't run in a straight line. He was quickly pulled from the game and diagnosed with a concussion. It left his ability to play again in the series in doubt because he had to enter the league's concussion protocol, which meant his return time was undetermined and based on an independent doctor's review.

It was just another problem. So was Irving. He was subpar in Games 1 and 2, shooting just 12-of-36 and repeatedly getting beaten on the defensive end. The Warriors deployed defensive strategies aimed at isolating Irving, switching on pick-and-rolls to limit his ability to attack. The result was some of Irving's bad habits returning, specifically his tendency to hold the ball and not pass. He didn't have an assist until the fourth quarter of Game 2, opening up some old wounds.

Irving was polarizing in this way. His greatness as a player who could create his own shot was unquestioned, but his reliance on it sometimes irritated his teammates. It had gotten under James's skin in the first games they'd played together. When he was playing this way, his defensive issues felt more pronounced. Even with all the fine performances he turned in along the way to the Finals, the magnifying glass of June made it harder on him.

Before the series, a think tank made up of Harvard students called the Harvard College Sports Analysis Collective released a paper titled "A Modest Proposal: Bench Kyrie Irving." The argument was his offense, as great as the highlights looked, wasn't statistically worth his ball hogging and his lack of defense. By its nature it was overly academic and meant to be shocking, but it did represent a way of thinking that Irving wasn't always a positive influence.

James, frustrated by the losses, didn't mention Irving by name but did make it clear he didn't think everyone was on the same page. He even seemed to indirectly hint at what the Harvard analysts suggested, that Irving might need to be benched at times against Golden State.

"If guys are out there not following the game plan, then Coach has to sub them out, and other guys have to come in and do what he wants to do," James said. "If guys aren't competing then Coach Lue can make a decision at that point."

Lue didn't go to Harvard; he went to Nebraska. And while he studied the numbers and could quote detailed analytics off the top of his head when needed, he was also a former player who took part in Finals games. He understood the pressure and he understood the need for support. He had been in Irving's corner since those early days in 2014, when he helped convince him to sign a contract extension based on promises and trust, even though James wasn't in the picture and the Cavs had done nothing but lose.

Lue did go to Irving to talk. But he didn't tell him to pass more. He told him to attack more. He wanted Irving to shoot, he didn't care if he didn't pass. He just didn't want Irving to wait 15 seconds before making the decision. Lue told Irving to block out the noise and to be himself, and that was not a guy who was frozen with indecision. Perhaps he couldn't shut down Curry on defense—no one in the world could on some nights. But Lue told Irving no one on the Warriors could stop him either.

"No one can stop you one-on-one when you have the ball," Lue told him.

Game 3 was back in Cleveland and was vitally important to the Cavs. The doctors didn't clear Love to play. He was angry when he found out the morning of the game, believing he was symptom free. But he hadn't met all the requirements and it wasn't in the team's hands. The Cavs would have to play without him.

Lue decided to insert Richard Jefferson in his place, to play with an ultra-small lineup to attempt to match the Warriors' versatility. As the crowd roared just before tip-off, James gathered the team outside the locker room.

"Look at the man in front of you!" James said. "Do your job. Follow my lead and do your job!"

Whether it was Handy's speech, Lue's pep talk with Irving, the skin growing back on Smith's hand, or the comfort of being at home, the Cavs looked like a different team. They looked like the team that had won their first 10 playoff games.

James played loose and with force, putting up 32 points, 11 rebounds, and six assists. Irving was back to playing with speed and making quick decisions, forcing the Warriors to their heels as he racked up 30 points. Smith made five three-pointers. Jefferson played well in place of Love, leading some to wonder if the lineup switch should remain permanent. Lue dusted off Timofey Mozgov, who'd barely played after the trade to get Channing Frye, and Mozgov leveled Klay Thompson with a screen, kneeing him in the thigh. Thompson hobbled to the locker room and later called it a dirty play.

Curry had another meek showing and failed to score 20 points for the third straight game, the first time that happened in his playoff career. Now it was his turn to face questions as he appeared to lack acceleration and ability to get open that had been a cornerstone of his MVP season. Just how much his wounded knee was bothering him became an issue.

In the second half after a whistle had stopped play, Curry grabbed the ball and went to harmlessly lay it in the basket as the officials reported the foul. James saw it and leapt in the way, reaching up and blocking the practice shot.

"I didn't want him to see the ball go in," James said. "Whether it's after the whistle or not."

The Cavs ended up winning by 30, the most lopsided loss the Warriors had absorbed all season. It had been a year since the Cavs tasted a win over Golden State, and it was cathartic, even if they still trailed in the series and remained a heavy underdog.

"They came out and played like a team with a sense of desperation, like their season was on the line," Green said. "We came out and played like everything was peaches and cream."

Love came out of the locker room to greet his teammates in the hallway as they arrived after the final horn. They embraced him— he'd felt sick that he couldn't play in what was the biggest game of the season. When they got inside, Love was handed a piece of the puzzle and honored by placing the thirteenth golden peg into its place.

Just three spots were left to be filled.

Chapter 18

3-1 LEAD

Y̶ou're a bitch."

The words from Draymond Green froze LeBron James. Green had said far worse to James over the course of the Finals, and James had used worse language himself to Green and his teammates. But as the Chicago Bulls' Joakim Noah had learned by surprise a year earlier, that was a trigger word for James in the heat of a game.

"I'm a father of three and a man," James said back to Green in the midst of live play, the ball in Andre Iguodala's hands just a few feet away.

"You're still a bitch," Green spat back.

Within seconds, Green and James were tangled with each other. Danny Crawford, one of the NBA's most veteran and respected officials, stepped in and called a foul on each man, hoping to defuse the situation.

"I'm all cool with competition. I'm all fine with that, but some of the words that came out of his mouth were overboard," James said. "I felt like at that point in time it was a little bit outside of basketball."

There were three minutes left in Game 4 and it was essentially decided. The Warriors had stormed back, Steph Curry looking like his MVP self and nailing eight three-pointers on his way to 38 points as he repeatedly silenced the Cleveland crowd. The Warriors were up 10 and about to go up 3–1 in the series heading home, their second consecutive title over the Cavs in a death grip.

But something had just happened that would change the course of the series, something that would become one of the more contro-versial plays in NBA history. It happened so fast that Crawford had missed it, even though it was right in front of him. James was more obsessed with Green's choice of words. Green thought he was acting in self-defense.

James and Green had started out shoving as Green set a pick for Curry. Green pushed James and then James pushed back, Green fall-ing over in an effort to get officials to call a foul. The act miffed James, although he was often guilty of such flopping antics himself. Then he stepped over the top of Green.

This is where opinions diverge. James said he was trying to get back into the play and that was the fastest route. Green and his team-mates believed James was stepping over him in a demeaning way. Though Warriors players were more coarse in their description, they felt James was almost being primal in dragging his lower body over Green's head. Green's response was also as old as time—he swung his arm up and hit James between the legs.

The entire ordeal took only a second in real time. But Green had been disciplined by the league earlier in the playoffs for kicking Thun-der center Steven Adams in the groin on a play the Thunder howled as suspension-worthy while Green insisted it was only the result of body momentum. He'd also tripped a Thunder player and appeared to intentionally strike Adams with a blow to his injured hand. The result was a list of warning penalties by the league.

James was in the middle of an uneven performance. As usual, his statistics were sensational—25 points, 13 rebounds, nine assists, two steals, and three blocks. But he committed seven turnovers, which was crushing against the Warriors' high-speed attack. Worse, he and Irving were in their isolation mode again. Irving had 34 points, which was good, but when they played independent of each other instead of together it worked to the Warriors' advantage, because the Cavs became easier to defend as a whole. James and Irving took 33 of the team's 38 shots in the second half and the Warriors outscored them by 16 points. Love came back from the concussion and Lue brought him off the bench. But he wasn't able to be a difference-maker.

James was frustrated at the officials. He was convinced the Warriors were getting away with roughhousing him. He played 46 minutes and only ended up drawing two shooting fouls. And of course, there was the scoreboard, which read 108–97 at the end.

The Cavs locker room was silent. James sat at his locker, his knees in ice, and quietly picked at a plate of chicken and rice. He was on the verge of falling to 2–5 in his career in the Finals, a number that he knew could be used to horsewhip his legacy for the rest of his life. He was playing at a high level, just as he'd done the previous two Finals that he also lost. As he picked at his meal, a reporter walked up to him with a cell phone. On it was the footage of his run-in with Green. In slow motion, Green's swing into his groin was plain to see. James watched it once, twice, and then a third time before handing the phone back.

"Yeah," he said, "but they won't do anything."

In an office next door, the parties weren't so calm. David Griffin and Ty Lue were in a debate about whether to make the officiating an issue in the postgame press conference. Commenting on officiating during the playoffs is as old as the postseason itself and there's a reason teams do it. Though it almost always triggers a fine from the league—two of the Cavs' opponents had already been slapped with one in the playoffs—it also sometimes works. Griffin and Lue, down 3–1, decided there was nothing left to lose.

"LeBron never gets calls," Lue said. "I mean, he attacks. He's one of the guys that attacks the paint every single play. And he doesn't get a fair whistle all the time because of his strength and because of his power and guys bounce off of him. But those are still fouls, and we weren't able to get them."

"It's been like that all year," James said. "I'm getting hit, but the refs are not seeing it that way."

Pressed further, he cut off the topic: "I'm going to save my 25K, okay?"

James, who is immensely wealthy, is sometimes funny about money. He owns a fleet of cars from classics to Ferraris to high-end luxury cars to a specially outfitted van. He flies liberally on private jets. But after getting to know Warren Buffett in 2006—he even spent a day with him at Buffett's headquarters in Omaha—he took

Buffett's advice to save seriously. He went through a phase where he didn't even want to pay a copay to see a doctor who was outside the network of the Cavs' insurance plan. He didn't like to have the feeling he was wasting money.

The next day, Lue got hit with a $25,000 fine. James did not.

Lue had another message beyond the officiating. The situation was dire. No team had ever come back from being down 3–1 in the Finals. It had happened 33 times in history and only three teams had ever even forced a Game 7, and that hadn't happened for half a century. The Warriors hadn't lost three games in a row in nearly three years. Two of the final three games would be in Oakland, where the Warriors were 50–3 that season and 98–6 over the previous two seasons.

"If you don't think we can win, don't get on the plane," Lue told his team before they left for the night. "We've got to come back anyway, so we might as well come back and play Game 6."

Late in the night, after James had gone home and stewed about the outcome of the game with his wife, he pulled out his phone and opened the Cavs' group text and composed a message.

"No matter how we got to this point, we're here now," James wrote. "We have to go to Golden State for Game 5 and we have to come home anyway. So why not come home and play a Game 6. Let it go, play hard, be focused, follow my lead, and I'll make sure you get home for a Game 6."

The next morning, just a few hours later, James was the first person in to work at the team practice facility. The outlook was indeed bleak, but he was not giving up.

James wasn't the only one with such a feeling. The more Griffin thought about it, the more he grew amused. It got to the point where he was laughing to himself. Of course the team was down 3–1, he thought, they had to be down. His team never did anything the easy way. It was always about coming to the brink of disaster. This wasn't a crisis, Griffin decided, not at all. This was his team playing their game.

Maybe Griffin was punch-drunk from stress and pressure. He'd built a wildly expensive roster and if it failed again he'd get a big dose of blame. He was the one who had fired David Blatt, who had put together a game plan that had pushed the Warriors in the Finals the year before with way less firepower than they had now.

But Griffin didn't see it that way at all. In his twenty-plus seasons working in the NBA, he'd rarely felt a clarity like this. And he felt he had to share it. With his emotions flowing, he composed an email that he didn't just send to the team and coaches, he sent it to the entire company—the sales department, the marketing department, the vice presidents, the secretaries, the security guards.

"Griff called me and said, 'I'm going to send an email to the entire company, how do I do it?' And I said, 'Why, what the hell are you doing?'" said Tad Carper, the Cavs senior vice president of communications. "At that point his intensity level was like somebody who'd had this awakening."

Griffin sent the email. It read:

Family-

If you are like me, and sadly for all of you, many of you are more like me than you'd care to admit, you felt a little like a bomb went off late into last night and maybe even this morning. Needless to say, we are all disappointed that we didn't hold serve at home. However, I have a few thoughts to share with you that I think might make the wait for our Game 5 victory in Oakland and our ultimate triumph in an epic Game 7 a little more reality than dream.

Consider the two seasons we have spent together and think about all these things that make us HISTORICALLY SPECIAL.

We enter LAST SEASON the prohibitive Vegas favorite to win the NBA Title.

Our starting center tears his Achilles, 26 games into the season.

Our MVP focal point misses 2 weeks with a back injury.

We become the first team in NBA history to enter as NBA Title favorites to start a season with a losing record thru 39 games (actually went 19–20).

We trade one player for 3, get our MVP back and go an NBA best 32–7 over the next 39 games. During this stretch we ranked

1st in the NBA in winning percentage (.821), first in scoring differential (10.6) and first in three-pointers made per game (11.8).

We sweep our first round opponent and in Game 4, lose our starting power forward for the remainder of the playoffs and most of the next 6 months.

We win the next round against Chicago despite starting down 2–1 while our starting point guard is battling knee issues. He only plays 12 minutes in the Game 6 win.

We win one game because our assistant coaches save our head coach from calling a time out we didn't actually have. That would have resulted in a technical foul and the ball to Chicago in a tie game. Never seen that before either.

We then sweep a 60-win team and the No. 1 seed in the East while Kyrie misses games 2–3 with the knee issue. WE MOVE ON TO THE NBA FINALS.

LeBron and James Jones appear in their 5th straight NBA Finals.

We drop G1 and lose Kyrie for the remainder of the playoffs. We are now down two All-Stars. So what do we do...

We win the next 2 games to take a 2–1 lead over this same Warriors team.

Our new starting point guard, Delly, has to be taken to the hospital on a stretcher after the G3 win because we can't hydrate him fast enough to combat his muscles that are shutting down from exhaustion.

The Warriors discover their best line-up as a desperation move to save their finals, because we had beaten the piss out of them physically.

Wounded and battered, we eventually succumb but everyone is ready to run it back healthy.

OFFSEASON

Everyone returns, we keep the band intact, a group that went 34–3 in the last 37 games that LeBron, Kevin and Kyrie all play in.

Ownership spends the 2nd most money in NBA history to achieve this.

THIS SEASON

We start training camp without Kevin Love, Kyrie Irving and Iman Shumpert. All of whom are rehabbing from surgery.

We lead the NBA's Eastern Conference literally wire to wire.

We are the #1 seed in the EAST.

We sweep the first and second rounds of the NBA Playoffs.

We are the first team in EASTERN CONFERENCE HISTORY to start the Playoffs 10–0.

Coach Lue becomes the first Head Coach in NBA history to start his career 10–0 in the post season, passing Pat Riley who was 9–0.

We win our 17th straight Eastern Conference game in the Conference Finals, becoming the first team in CONFERENCE HISTORY to do that.

We finish off Toronto in 6 games, winning Game 5 by a FRANCHISE POST SEASON RECORD 38 points.

LeBron and James Jones make their 6th straight NBA Finals appearances. AN NBA RECORD for anyone not a Bill Russell Celtic.

Along the way, we set NBA PLAYOFF records for most consecutive games with 12 or more three-pointers (8). NBA RECORD 77 three-pointers in 4 game sweep of Atlanta. We are the FIRST TEAM IN NBA HISTORY to make 15 three-pointers in 4 straight games. AND, we set the ALL-TIME NBA RECORD for threes in a game with 25 in Game 2 vs. the Hawks.

We enter the NBA FINALS with the LARGEST SCORING DIFFERENTIAL in EASTERN CONFERENCE HISTORY (+177pts).

We win Game 3 by 30 points over a 73-win team. Becoming the first team in NBA FINALS HISTORY to win by 30 after losing by 30 the game prior.

So, what does all this mean? It means more than you have ever dared to imagine, but no more than we have always done. NO TEAM IN NBA HISTORY has ever come back from down 3–1 in the NBA Finals. Rather than asking you the cliché: "Why not us?" I would like to offer the following:

WE HAVE SEEN NBA HISTORY IN THE MAKING EVERYDAY HERE. It's not "why not us?" It's "What the [expletive] else would we do?" We love it harder. We love it RECORD-SETTING. You know in your hearts and in your minds we have been the NBA DRAMA KINGS since we came together. I bet you can, and I'd love for you to add to this HISTORICAL DATABASE. What else speaks to you about the RECORD-SETTING insanity that has been YOUR CLEVELAND CAVALIERS!

Let me be the first to tell you, NBA HISTORY HAS BEEN WAIT-ING ON US. No one has done this, because WE have never been here before. We will become the first, because that is all we have ever known how to do.

NBA HISTORY HAS CHOSEN US. Don't run, don't be afraid. Don't be discouraged. WE WILL SEIZE OUR RIGHTFUL PLACE IN THAT HISTORY!

Griffin printed out copies and put one in every player's locker to make sure they saw it when they arrived for practice.

"That was some letter," owner Dan Gilbert said. "I was like 'you believe we can win three in a row, two games at Golden State? They've lost like two home games in two years.' He believed. That rallied us."

Gilbert is obsessed with surrounding himself with optimism. He uses it as a foundational principle for building his businesses and hiring people. As a result, his Cavs organization is stocked with people who think this way. But Griffin, a lifelong grinder, isn't really one of them. He's self-deprecating with a good sense of humor, but not a sunny optimist. He's much more of a realist, which serves him well as a basketball executive. But he does have a belief in destiny.

When Griffin had a recurrence of cancer it was natural to look at it as terrible luck, but Griffin looked at it as fate. Had he not come to the Cavs, he likely wouldn't have been treated at the Cleveland Clinic, one of the finest cancer hospitals in the world. The doctors there healed him and allowed him to keep working. He did truly believe in the concept of things happening for a reason. He saw that in the Cavs team, even if many of Gilbert's employees thought he might have lost it when they read the email.

There was, however, a reason for hope coming. After reviewing the film, the NBA decided that Green had committed a flagrant foul when hitting James between the legs on that play. The league declared, "Green made unnecessary contact with a retaliatory swipe of his hand to the groin." The act alone carried a fine and, had it been called during the game, would've resulted in two free throws plus possession. But it was the third flagrant foul Green had been assessed in the playoffs. He'd body-slammed the Houston Rockets' Michael Beasley, plus the kick to Adams's groin. The three together triggered an automatic suspension for the next game. And so with that, Green was suspended for Game 5.

The Warriors were incensed and their fans were equally furious and began a wave of backlash against the decision. It was challenging for the public to understand Green wasn't suspended only for the quick swipe at James alone but as the culmination of a series of fouls. Shortly after the Cavs had been complaining about officiating, it was now the Warriors side claiming they'd been wronged. Even the Thunder fans were upset—Green's foul on Adams had been more egregious and didn't result in suspension. Technically the NBA punished Green worse for the Adams kick, a flagrant-2 foul, than for Green's act on James, a flagrant-1. But the nuance was lost in the heat of the reaction.

Meanwhile, the Warriors were angry that James hadn't gotten any punishment for his act of stepping over Green. And they mocked him for being offended that Green called him a "bitch" in the wake of the move.

"I don't know how the man feels, but obviously people have feelings and people's feelings get hurt even if they're called a bad word," Klay Thompson said. "I guess his feelings just got hurt."

Thompson said it minutes after learning Green had been suspended, and his disgust was palpable. What the Warriors said about James privately among each other was clearly much worse.

"I'm not going to comment on what Klay said, because I know where it can go," James said. "It's so hard to take the high road. I've been doing it for thirteen years. It's so hard to continue to do it, and I'm going to do it again."

It did not end there. It quickly spilled onto social media. Marreese

Speights, a Warriors backup forward, tweeted a picture of a baby's bottle, a clear reference to James's complaining. Then Ayesha Curry, who had become perhaps the highest-profile spouse in the NBA, wrote on her Twitter account, "High road. Invisible bridge used to step over said person when open floor is available to the left and right."

Again, it wasn't hard to imagine what was being said in the Curry household about James, especially with the feeling a championship was just hours away.

The next afternoon, Lue was antsy in his hotel room before it was time to leave for the game. He didn't want to watch ESPN and hear about the series, so he turned on the History Channel and watched a documentary about the Civil War. He couldn't help connecting what he was watching to his team's job that night. It was in his head as he addressed the team before they took the floor.

"That happened from 1861 to 1865 and we lost a lot of great men," he told them. "But the thing that stood out to me was they were just showing how they lined up and they were preparing for war and the guys on the front line, they knew they were going to die, but they were willing to die for the guys behind them and they were willing to die and sacrifice for their country. When you're on that front line, you got to be prepared and ready to die. Everybody tonight in this locker room has to be prepared and ready to stand on the front line."

Lue was rolling. "My grandpa taught me a quote a long time ago that everybody can't walk in the streets, that's why they made sidewalks," he barked to the team. "And we got to be the tougher team tonight. We've got to show our toughness."

He closed with this: "The two most important days of your life is when you were born and when you discover the reason why you were born. And I think we were born to be champions. We got a tough road to conquer, but we can do it. We're down 3–1 but we got to have the mind-set that when we go into this game tonight, we're going to win."

"Mark Twain," Love said after hearing the line.

It was from Twain, but Lue didn't even know it. He was grabbing at every piece of nineteenth-century motivation he could think of. Players appreciated his sense of calmness; he was always under control on the sidelines and in huddles. It was something he learned playing for Phil Jackson with the Lakers. But behind the scenes, Lue wasn't afraid to get emotional, as he showed that day at the Trump SoHo late in the season and as he would show several times in Oakland in the coming days.

The crowd that night was peppered with signs supporting Green. Warriors owner Joe Lacob arrived at his courtside seat in a Green jersey, an obvious protest aimed at the NBA officials in the building. Green was barred from the arena but wanted to be close by—if the Warriors won there was to be a party. So he attended the Oakland A's game being played next door at O.co Coliseum against the Texas Rangers. He rented a suite so he could watch the game, and if the Warriors won, there was a tunnel connecting the stadium and Oracle Arena that he could use to be on the floor in minutes. Warriors general manager Bob Myers joined Green in the suite, as did Marshawn Lynch, an Oakland native.

Hidden in a corner of the arena was staging and graffiti guns for a trophy presentation, which arena officials had practiced that afternoon. Champagne was secretly in a back room being iced and hundreds of Warriors family and friends were there with a party planned after a win. The Warriors were ready.

The Cavs were not. Lue made a strategy change, making James the primary ball handler. This had been a seesaw game since the first days of Irving and James playing together back in the fall of 2014. They'd come a long way, but sometimes things worked better when James just played point guard. It worked again as the change helped free James's and Irving's flow. That and they played with newfound determination.

Without Green, their best defender, the Warriors weren't able to cover as much ground, and James and Irving repeatedly beat them with drives. James had been averaging 21 shots a game in the series, but he took 18 just in the first half of Game 5. He was not going to go down without a fight. Also, his jumper, which had been on hiatus for much of the season, returned, and he drilled two three-pointers. He had 25 points at halftime and Irving had 18 of his own.

But Golden State still looked like too much as Thompson, backing up his words aimed at James, was even better. Known for his ability to go on white-hot shooting streaks, Thompson was doing it again as he nailed six three-pointers and scored 26 points. The game was tied.

Less than two minutes into the second half, J. R. Smith drove to the basket and collided with Warriors center Andrew Bogut. Smith fell into Bogut's left knee and Bogut collapsed, rolling on the ground in pain. The arena went silent. Myers got up from the suite with Green next door and ran to the arena. Bogut wasn't much of a scorer and had been benched the year before in the Finals, but he was vitally important as a defender. Without Green, losing Bogut was a huge blow. As Bogut was carried to the locker room it became clear he had a significant injury and would be lost for the series. The Warriors had gotten used to perfect health. But with Curry still not 100 percent on his knee and Green and Bogut gone, they were in unfamiliar territory.

The game changed with the mood, the Cavs quickly opened an 11-point lead as James and Irving kept pounding away on the Warriors' diminished defense. Thompson finished with 37 points and Curry with 25, but they were subdued in the second half, combining to go 1-of-9 on three-pointers. The Cavs were never in danger again, and cruised to a 15-point win. James and Irving both finished with 41 points, combining to make nine three-pointers.

James added 16 rebounds, seven assists, three steals, and three blocks. It was the first time in Finals history teammates had scored 40 points in the same game. It was also the beginning of a fulfillment of two prophecies: that James and Irving could become a historic tandem, and what Lynn Merritt and James had talked about a week earlier, that James would need to conjure some heroic games. This was a heroic game.

Seeing it reminded Lue of a playoff game when he was an assistant coach with the Boston Celtics in 2012. Trying to close out the Miami Heat at home, the Celtics were crushed by James's 45 points in what had been the finest game of James's career. This one might've been even better.

With his Boston days on his mind, Lue made a demand in the locker room. Everyone was asked to fork over $100 to him—the players, the coaches, the support staff, the front office members, and even the owners who were there. Cash was produced, those who didn't have it borrowed from others. When the gathering was over, there was $5,300 that Lue stuffed into an envelope.

"They were all like, 'Where is the money going?'" Lue said.

Lue took the cash and walked into the coach's office and got up on the desk. He slid a ceiling panel aside in the dank old building and stuffed the cash inside.

"We're going to come back, get our money, and get our trophy for Game 7," he said.

It was something Celtics coach Doc Rivers had done back in 2009 after his team lost badly on Christmas Day to the Lakers. Believing the Lakers would make the Finals, Rivers challenged his team to return to L.A. six months later to get their money back. They did, upsetting James's Cavs on the way, although the Lakers beat them in the Finals.

History was still against the Cavs. They had pulled to within 3–2, but Green would be back and the Warriors were still confident, believing the James and Irving explosion had been tied to not having their best defensive player. Golden State won Game 6 in Cleveland to win the title the year before, and they were ready to do so again. They rented out a Morton's Steakhouse for their postgame celebration, as they had the year before, and dozens of friends and family flew with the Warriors to Cleveland to prepare for the celebration.

As tip-off approached, the bus carrying the Warriors family to the arena got stuck in traffic. Then, on its way into the underground parking lot where players and families enter, there was another traffic jam. Ayesha Curry was on the delayed bus and believed it was the Cavs keeping them from getting into the building. She tweeted, "10 mins til game time and the whole team's families are sitting here on a bus. They won't let us in yet. Interesting tactic though."

It was the start of a very frustrating night for both of the Currys. The Cavs' momentum traveled with them from the West Coast. James was a demon, his legs looking fresh and the strategy of him working at point guard continuing to tear apart the Warriors' defensive schemes, even with Green back. In the first quarter alone, James scored nine points and handed out four assists that led to nine more.

The Cavs were up 20 after 12 minutes and the Warriors started to show some fatigue, a result of their thinner bench without Bogut and perhaps the carryover from playing a grueling seven-game series in the conference finals. During a stretch in the second half, James scored 18 consecutive points as his aggression and speed were too much. He scored 41 points again, with eight rebounds, 11 assists, four steals, and three blocks.

One of the blocks was on Curry in the fourth quarter. James blocked Curry five times in the Finals, not counting the menacing deadball block in Game 3. On this one James trailed him and didn't buy a pump fake before swatting it out of bounds. He looked down at the much smaller Curry afterward and fired off a stream of curse words meant to further extenuate the act of dominance. James was putting together a performance for the ages, and he didn't pass up the chance to rub it in against his top rival both in basketball and business. It was somewhat hypocritical, since it was James who had been offended by Green's trash talk, but it was clear he didn't care.

Curry scored 30 points, but it was a miserable night for him. He was called for several questionable fouls. With four minutes left he was called for his disqualifying sixth foul on James on a play that looked harmless. Curry was incensed—rightly so as the foul was not even borderline—and he became so enraged that he took out his mouthpiece and threw it in anger. The plastic smashed Andrew Forbes, the son of Cavs co-owner Nate Forbes, in the chin at his courtside seat.

Throwing an object into the crowd is an automatic ejection, and Curry was sent to the locker room, which was meaningless since he'd already fouled out. All he did was miss the end of the eventual 115–101 final. He was later fined $25,000 by the league for the act.

"I'm happy he threw his mouthpiece," Warriors coach Steve Kerr said. "He had every right to be upset. He's the MVP of the league. He gets six fouls called on him, three of them were absolutely ridiculous."

That got Kerr fined $25,000, the third coach in four series to be fined for complaining about calls against the Cavs. The Warriors, though, felt like there was something against them. First the Green suspension and now the tight officiating on Curry. It seemed like Lue's complaints worked, so why shouldn't Kerr try to see what $25,000 would buy him in Game 7, which was now going to happen?

"I've lost all respect sorry this is absolutely rigged for money...or ratings not sure which. I won't be silent. Just saw it live (sorry)," Ayesha Curry tweeted after the game.

It was a touchstone comment for Warriors fans, who felt as if there was a conspiracy after the Green suspension. Her targets seemed off, though, since the league's payment from TV was fixed no matter how long the series went. The extra game did mean a lot more money, between $15 and $20 million—but for the Game 7 host Warriors for ticket and arena revenue. She was right about the ratings; they were soaring.

She later deleted the tweet and apologized, saying she'd gotten upset because security in the arena had racially profiled her father. It turned out Ayesha's father resembled a man whom NBA security was on the lookout for after he had successfully used fake credentials to access arenas. After he was questioned and his credentials checked, it was ironed out.

None of it ruffled the Cavs, who behind James had started to believe it was possible.

"This is the highest level of basketball I've ever played in my life," said Irving, who scored 23 points. "I know that Game 7 will be the hardest thing ever."

Everything had gone against them the year before and they could feel the karma of it turning. And they could feel James, who was backing up his words and setting a lead for his organization to follow.

"Not many people in the history of sports has said, 'Everyone get on my back: City, state, team, organization, get on my back and I'm going to carry you. If we win or fail, I'll take the blame, but I'm going to lead you,'" Jefferson said as he marveled at James's accomplishments. "He is doing this for his teammates. He is doing this for everyone."

Chapter 19

THE BLOCK. THE SHOT. THE STOP.

The day before Game 7, a van pulled up to the Cavs' hotel and a group piled in. This had been arranged by Ty Lue, and he was joined by two of his assistant coaches, James Posey and Mike Longabardi. Rich Paul, LeBron James's agent, came after he heard about the trip, curious about the destination. So did Lue's good friend Chauncey Billups, who was in town covering the series as an analyst for ESPN, along with a couple of team staffers and Lue's cousin "Doodles."

The van headed north, crossing the Golden Gate Bridge on one of those sunny and clear days where the bay sparkles and San Francisco becomes one of the most picturesque places in the world. They took Route 101, passing Sausalito and into Marin County and all its chic towns with bay views and high-end shopping promenades. They exited the highway and rolled up to a heavily guarded gate at the front of San Quentin State Prison.

It had been a day of tension. There was a light practice in Oakland at the Warriors' facility, which sits on top of a parking deck attached to a downtown hotel. There was the fulfillment of media obligations. The worldwide press was salivating because the storylines were delicious. It was either going to be the completion of the greatest season in league history if the Warriors won, or it was going to be the greatest comeback in Finals history.

Lue wanted to get away and out of the city. Between Games 1 and 2 of the series, he had taken a mental break by going over to Alcatraz for a few hours. He wasn't in the mood for tourist activities now. Instead there would be a field trip, an unusual and unexpected one for any person, much less a man about to coach Game 7 of the NBA Finals.

One of Lue's financial advisers had a connection to San Quentin's warden. It was not going to be a perfunctory tour of the oldest prison in the state of California, consistently home to the largest death row annual count in the country.

After the crew showed their IDs and heard the prison door shut with a thud behind them, a member of the traveling party noticed a sign that read "Inbounds." This caught his eye, of course, because it is a common basketball term. When he asked a guard for an explanation for the sign, he was informed, "Now you are officially part of the prison."

As the group made its way through the premises, they found it to be unsettlingly quiet for a place that housed some 4,000 inmates.

"Where's everybody at?" Lue asked.

"Right now they're being counted," responded a guard.

"What do they do when they're done being counted?" Lue replied.

"They come out here," said the guard.

"Out here where?" Lue asked again.

"With us," the guard said.

The group did the math. There were seven or eight of them with one security guard, and thousands of prisoners—many of them convicted of heinous crimes such as kidnapping, rape, and murder—were about to be released into the yard where they were taking their tour. And here they thought the most dangerous thing they'd face all weekend was defending Steph Curry in the open court.

At that moment, a siren went off signifying the count was finished and the prisoners were free to roam from their cells.

The fear the group felt from the seemingly dicey situation quickly subsided. As they were recognized by the prisoners, the feeling turned from sinister to banter. Warriors fans in the yard talked trash. Cavs fans shouted out support. Lakers fans cheered the former backup point guard for the purple and gold, and Lue, naturally, heard about the iconic moment when Allen Iverson stepped over him during the 2001 Finals. Billups's credentials as "Mr. Big Shot" from his championship days with the Detroit Pistons were called out as some prisoners boasted about their jumpers being more accurate.

Here Lue was, in the midst of some of the most hardened criminals on the face of the earth, and the game of basketball—just like it had always been—was his guiding compass.

He thought about the obvious difference between his lot in life and theirs and couldn't help but marvel at the moment being shared. It brought to mind a familiar refrain: Sports bring everybody together. No matter the race, religion, economic background, or in this case, *freedom*, sports provide a common language to speak, a common distraction from life's complications.

Lue came to the prison looking for an escape from the pressure surrounding the winner-take-all Game 7 and was reminded that the Finals—just a series of basketball games, after all—were serving as an escape for so many others bound to a bleak existence in jail.

Once the trash talk died down, Lue, Billups, and the rest of the group were thanked repeatedly for paying a visit. Talking hoops was therapeutic, the prisoners said. Their mere presence brightened their day, they added.

When the trip ended and the group made the ride back to San Francisco, Lue's mind was back on Game 7, but the dire consequences attached to it all didn't seem quite so significant.

Much like he had done before Game 5, Lue addressed the team the next day, but this time his message wasn't shaped by Mark Twain or the History Channel. It was straight out of San Quentin.

"This could have been any one of us," he told the Cavs in his pregame speech. "The warden said 80 percent of the guys in there may not have ever committed another crime, but just one bad night, one bad car ride, one bad fight or whatever and you could be in there. And from the environments we come from, it could have been any one of us.

"You're riding with a friend, and he's got drugs on him. Or you get in an accident and panic and it's a hit-and-run. Or anything. So we got to take advantage of our opportunities in life. We are in a special place that can bring people together. Don't take it for granted."

By the time tip-off came, the Warriors starting lineup perfectly illustrated Lue's point about just how precarious these chances could be. In at center was Festus Ezeli, Andrew Bogut's backup, for his first start of the postseason.

Steve Kerr went small in Game 6 without Bogut and started Draymond Green at center. It didn't work and Golden State was blown out of the building. A change wasn't surprising, nor was it surprising to see the Cavs score the first points of the game on a dump-off pass in the lane from Kyrie Irving to Tristan Thompson, with Thompson powering right through Ezeli's chest to give Cleveland a 2–0 lead.

For a series that had been decided by an average margin of victory of 19.7 points for the winning team in Games 1–6, Game 7 finally, mercifully, had the feeling early on that it was going to be a tight one worth watching. And people watched. The game had an average viewership of 30.8 million, making it one of the most watched in the history of the sport. By the fourth quarter, more than 40 million Americans were watching, with millions more around the world tuning in at various times of the day.

When Harrison Barnes and Draymond Green hit back-to-back 3s to take an 8–4 lead—a duo that scored a combined eight points in Game 6—Oracle started to shake. But rather than capitalize on that momentum, Klay Thompson airballed a transition three, Ezeli was blocked at the rim, and Kevin Love scored a layup after missing a couple of point-blank attempts and getting his own rebound, drawing the score to 8–6 and allowing the Cavs to settle back into the game.

By the end of the first quarter, the Cavs were up 23–22. Cleveland was pounding the Warriors on the glass, 16–8, and owning the inside, outscoring Golden State 16–4 in the paint. Meanwhile, the Warriors went 5-for-11 from three while the Cavs were 0-for-4 from deep. Cleveland got back into the series by playing the same uptempo pace as Golden State and just doing it better, but Game 7 was regressing back along the NBA's traditional East Coast–West Coast contrasting styles.

The second quarter was a disaster for the Cavs. As if making up for his Game 5 suspension all at once, Green exploded for 15 points. He made one three-pointer and another, screaming and waving his arms in part defiance and part joy. James wasn't guarding him close enough, looking to help Cav defenders elsewhere; he was sluggish and perhaps a bit disrespectful of Green's range. Green hit two more three-pointers, now four in a row. Green, who'd been the goat for a few days, threw his shoulders back and shook his head as he sniffed the hero role.

The Cavs couldn't match it. Their legs looked shaky and they missed nine of the 10 three-pointers they put up in the quarter. They only hung on with toughness, extra rebounds, and James and Irving bullying points near the basket and at the foul line. So it was still a one-point game with a little more than three minutes remaining before the half.

The script was easy to follow for most fans and analysts alike watching it play out. However, there was something Lue saw on the court that was bothering him more than the open shots his team was missing. Late in the second quarter, James came to the bench and Lue approached him.

"What's wrong with your body language?" Lue asked. "You got to pick your body language up."

James demurred. "I'm good. I'm in a good place."

"Well, your body language is not showing that," Lue shot back.

"Coach, I'm good," James insisted.

Lue was going to leave it at that, but James's inconsistent play continued. It didn't matter to Lue that James was either leading or tied with a teammate for the lead in points, rebounds, assists, steals, and blocks up to that point in the game. Lue, a former teammate of Michael Jordan and Kobe Bryant, knew there was more he could give.

In the final timeout before halftime, Lue went back to challenging James, only this time it was in front of the entire team.

"Bron, you got to be better!" he implored. "If we're going to win, you got to be better."

James, again, was incredulous. "What you talking about?" he said. "What are you talking about?"

"You got to be better!" Lue repeated.

"What do you want me to do?" James asked, clearly perturbed.

"I want you to guard Draymond, I want you to shoot your open shots, I want you to be aggressive and stop turning the ball over," Lue rattled off. "Is there anything else?"

The speech didn't take. At least at first. James coughed up his fourth turnover of the half—Golden State as a team only had five— that led to a Leandro Barbosa three and the Warriors' biggest lead of the game, up 47–40 with 2:08 remaining.

James added to his first-half output a badly missed pull-up three that came on an isolation possession before the buzzer sounded. Cleveland trailed 49–42.

There were 24 minutes separating either the greatest comeback in Finals history or simply more soul-crushing disappointment for both the city of Cleveland and for James personally. James's third consecutive Finals defeat was very much in play.

When his team got to the locker room, Lue went in on James once again. It was James, by averaging 41 points, 12 rebounds, nine assists, 3.5 steals, and three blocks in Games 5 and 6, who had gotten the Cavs this far. It would have to be James to take them all the way.

"Bron, you got to be better," Lue said. "You can get mad if you want. You can smack your lips, whatever you want to do, but you got to be better. You're the leader of this team, you got to be better."

Next he turned to Kyrie Irving, who was tied up with Stephen Curry with nine points apiece. "And Kyrie, I want you to be aggressive, but you got to take better shots," Lue said. "I don't mind your shots but you got to take better shots. Be aggressive!"

Lue kept his words short and retreated to the coach's office, giving the players time to ready themselves.

James was fuming. One of the team's security guards, who worked with James in both Miami and Cleveland, later told Lue that he had never seen anyone speak to James like that before.

First, James found Damon Jones, his former teammate during his first stint with the Cavs, who had joined the team as a special assistant for the playoffs after spending the year working with their D-League affiliate, the Canton Charge.

"D-Jones, your boy is on some bullshit!" James said.

"Who are you talking about?" Jones asked. "What's going on?"

"Man, T-Lue, he should never question me," James said. "All the effort I give?"

Jones is more than just a former teammate of James's. He is a friend. But he didn't blindly take his friend's side.

"Listen, I haven't been here all year, but everything I read, I see on TV, you talk about how 'Coach Lue is our leader, he's so poised, he gives us confidence, we believe in him,'" Jones said. "That's all I've seen all year about how much you believe in him and how much you trust him.

"So, why not trust him now?"

James was stumped.

"Fuck you, man," he said. "You right, you right...Fuck you."

Still, he needed further affirmation, so he went to another Jones— James Jones—who has been around him forever, making the last six trips to the Finals with him side by side as a teammate in both Miami and Cleveland.

"Man, I can't believe T-Lue would say that," James began.

"LeBron, is he lying?" James Jones asked.

"No, man, but..." James's voice trailed off.

"Well, there's your answer," James Jones said.

LeBron James had heard enough.

"Fuck y'all!" he said and made his way out of the locker room, back through the tunnel, and onto the court to prep for the biggest half of basketball of his life.

The third quarter started much the way the second quarter ended. As big as this opportunity was for the Cleveland side of things, the Warriors were playing at home where they went 39–2 during the regular season. And even if Curry looked a level below his unanimous-MVP status, they still had Klay Thompson, the guy who got the Warriors to the Finals in the first place with 41 points in Game 6 of the Western Conference finals against the Oklahoma City Thunder as Golden State was on its way to its own comeback from a 3–1 series deficit.

The Cavs quickly cut the Warriors' lead to three, but Thompson scored five straight points on a long pull-up three and a fadeaway jumper over Love to increase the cushion back to eight. With Curry slogging through yet another off shooting night—on his way to failing to connect on better than 40 percent of his shot attempts for the fourth time in the series—Thompson seemed like he would be able to carry the added weight.

The scoreboard read 54–46 in favor of the Warriors after the flurry. In the bowels of the arena in a hidden corner, a bin of champagne bottles now on ice with reams of plastic and tarps that would be used to seal the lockers and floors to protect the winning locker room from damage waited for guidance. It was positioned between the locker rooms, and at this point it looked like it was headed down the carpeted hallway toward the home team and not the bland concrete path to the visitors' room.

But in the next 100 seconds, the score was suddenly tied thanks to Irving and the man his teammates called "Swish."

J. R. Smith, the Cleveland wildcard, had been maligned for wilting on the Finals stage a year ago. With the stakes at their highest, he got the Cavs back in it, canning threes on consecutive possessions. Irving added a layup, blowing by the much slower Ezeli.

Whether it was Lue's halftime speech that did it this time around or not, the Cavs were a different team when staring at elimination. James came out in the third quarter after Lue's direct challenge and put up five assists against zero turnovers. After getting a green light from his coach,, Irving scored 12 third quarter points—more than Curry's and Thompson's 10 points combined in the period. The Cavs regained control of the game, building a seven-point margin of their own before the Warriors rallied to take back the lead heading into the fourth quarter, 76–75.

At this point, the magnitude spiked tenfold. This wasn't just the culmination of a long season or twelve months building toward a Finals rematch. Because of the stakes and the size of the audience, what was happening in these minutes was career-defining. These would be the events that would adorn walls, run endlessly on highlight shows, and, perhaps, create nightmares.

With so much intensity, pressure, and even fatigue, separation between the teams was impossible. The Cavs and Warriors traded baskets as the seconds, and then minutes, ticked off the clock. Golden State pushed ahead by four just past the halfway point of the period, but James responded with six straight points. The Warriors immediately tied it with a Thompson basket.

Through nearly 333 minutes played in the Finals, the cumulative score between Cleveland and Golden State was 699 to 699. The first to 700 would end up winning it all. And getting there was exhausting and excruciating.

For the next two and half minutes, tense and tired offense met resolute defense. Nine shots went up between the two teams and nine shots went awry. LeBron missed three times, falling into the isolation that is a signature of high-pressure moments. But Curry missed too, as did Thompson, Green, and Iguodala. There were no timeouts called. Back and forth they went, the building tensing each time a shot went into the air.

In Cleveland, more than 15,000 were watching inside Quicken Loans Arena, squeezing into seats around the construction of the stage for the Republican National Convention. Outside, thousands more watched on giant screens, craning out of parking decks, and herding around televisions at bars across downtown. Each shot meant tension and release as it missed.

The ninth miss came on a floater by Irving with two minutes left and the scoreboard still locked at 89–89. He'd gotten a matchup with Curry and tried to exploit it, but his touch was off. Iguodala came out with the ball and tore off to the other end, trying to manufacture a scoring chance with speed. It was a smart play—the Cavs were sluggish—and it quickly turned into a two-on-one fast break with Iguodala speeding down the floor along with Curry and only Smith back for the Cavs.

No one running the floor or watching it unfold could have known this, but what was about to happen would end up becoming a signature moment. A play standing still on its own from the mess that came before it, frozen in time as one of the single most dominant defensive plays in league history by one of the league's single most dominant players forever more.

Iguodala picked up his dribble and tossed a chest pass ahead to Curry, who caught the pass and immediately fed it right back, bouncing the ball off the floor as he followed the fundamentals of executing a fast break. Iguodala caught it in stride on his way to the hoop. At this point, Smith was scrambling to defend both players and committing a foul wouldn't have been the worst decision. Because of the pass, Iguodala had an angle on him.

What Smith didn't see was James in a dead sprint to get back into the play. One of the fastest ever to play because of his long strides, James made up ground, but was still three or four feet behind as

Iguodala took to the air with the ball in his right hand. Smith stuck his hands straight up, not fouling, and Iguodala adjusted, moving around him to get a clear shot.

It was clear. And then it wasn't.

James came steaming into the lane, zooming past Curry with his eyes wide in a mix of determination and desperation. He flung both hands into the air, not knowing what the crafty Iguodala was going to do, which side of the basket he was going to go to. But Smith, in addition to slowing Iguodala slightly, shielded the approaching James from Iguodala's view and he never saw it coming.

It happened so fast that people in the arena couldn't even clearly see what took place. James pinned Iguodala's shot against the backboard. It went from a sure hoop, and a Warriors lead on their home floor, to nothing.

James had executed chasedown blocks dozens of times over the years, but nothing like this. It may have instantly become the single greatest play of his career. It combined all his talents—his speed, his size, his athleticism, his competitiveness, his intelligence—to size up the angles and close the distance.

"I would definitely rank it No. 1," James told *Business Insider* later that summer. "Just because of the magnitude of the game, what was going on at that point in the game and I had to run through a couple guys, and get around a couple guys to get to that position. You know, it was a big moment, not only for that particular moment in the game, but for Cleveland sports history. Now that you can kind of look back on it, a lot of people are saying that.

"For me, I think a lot of people will base a game-winning jump shot, or a dunk, or something that happened offensively [as their most memorable play]. For a staple play for my legacy to be a block, something defensively to help us win, that's the ultimate for me."

It would become known as "The Block."

By that point in the game, James already had registered a triple double, joining Jerry West and James Worthy as just the third player in league history with a triple double in Game 7 of the Finals. He was, as Lue implored him to be at halftime, much "better."

As significant as it felt in the moment, it was still a tied game. The

Block had perhaps saved the game, but it didn't win it. Both teams missed again, including Curry, who was unable to summon the magic he had all season, as he badly missed a three, shooting it so far right that it hit nothing but backboard. Lue called a timeout with 1:09 left, the teams now having missed 12 straight shots.

As Lue huddled with his coaches to ponder the play call, James sat on the bench with Irving standing alongside him. Smith sat next to James, cursing about the previous few plays. James tried to look around Irving to catch Lue's eye. As Lue walked to the huddle holding his clipboard, James pointed at Irving.

As great as James had been all series and all game, he and Lue agreed to set the play up for Irving to have the ball. Lue designed a play that would isolate Irving on Curry. Lue figured with the rhythm Irving showed in the second half, combined with the beating Curry had taken all series long, the Cavs' point guard would have a quickness advantage matched up against the two-time MVP and would be able to get by him on his way to the basket, where he'd either have a layup or the chance to draw a foul. Lue made a sub, putting Richard Jefferson in for Tristan Thompson. It took the best rebounder off the floor but would force the Warriors to guard Jefferson outside the paint, the idea being to open driving space for Irving.

Lue called for the Cavs to run "Horns," a favorite play of his old coach, Phil Jackson. Only the ball wasn't going to Michael Jordan or Kobe Bryant. It was going to Kyrie Irving.

"He wants to come out every night and destroy his opponent," Lue later explained. "We knew and he knew we had confidence in him to take that shot. I thought he was going to go to the basket. We had the matchup we wanted, but he took a three-point shot. But he's been making that shot his whole career."

"Horns" did its job. A pick set by Smith forced a switch of defenders and moved the bigger Klay Thompson off Irving and got Curry on him. As soon as Irving got Curry on him, he dribbled backwards a few steps toward the Oracle Arena logo at center court, putting the two on an island.

Curry backpedaled as Irving slowly approached the three-point line. Irving dribbled through his legs to his right, then through his legs to his left, then back through to his right. He was probing Curry. While dribbling the ball with his right hand, he executed a hesitation dribble to his right. It surprised Curry for a split second—typically when right-handed players go into a shot they cross the ball over from their left hand to their right to get it in shooting position. But Irving hopped right and immediately went up with the ball in his right hand. It was awkward but the kind of thing Irving practiced all the time, one of his little tricks to open space. It wasn't much, an extra foot or two, but it freed him up to launch a clean shot from deep on the right side, beyond the three-point line.

Curry raised an arm to contest, but Irving—near the spot on the court where he fractured his kneecap in overtime of Game 1 of the Finals a year before—faded away to create the shooting angle. James stood in the corner as the shot went up, contorting his body along with the path of the ball as it made its way toward the rim, trying to will it in.

It fell through the net. Finally the ice broke, and it put the Cavs up by three, 92–89, leaving only 53 seconds on the clock between Cleveland and an end to a fifty-two-year championship curse.

It became known as "The Shot."

Feeling the pressure, the Warriors designed a similar play for their star guard, Curry. Just like the Cavs did on their previous possession, the Warriors ran a high pick-and-roll between Curry and Green, hoping Cleveland would switch, and they did. Irving switched onto Green, leaving Love matched up one-on-one against Curry a few feet beyond the three-point arc.

Numerous times over the previous two seasons Love had been benched late in games because of his defensive issues. He often struggled covering his own man, much less one of the most elusive players in the league. It was thought with this exact weakness—that he could be attacked as the weak defensive link—he wouldn't even be on the floor at the end of games against the Warriors. Yet here he was, on Curry with a championship on the line.

Curry started looking for an opening for a three-pointer to tie the game. The 6-foot-10 Love shuffled his feet, beating the 6-foot-3 Curry to the spot he was dribbling toward and forcing Curry to cross the ball over and head back to his right. Love's momentum was taking him out of the play, but he quickly steadied himself and recovered and was able to get Curry back in front of him. Curry passed it to Green on the right wing to reset and Green tossed it right back to Curry, now some 40 feet from the basket. Love looked to see if he could switch back to defend Green, but no, he was out by himself to manage Curry.

For most players, the thought of pulling up from that far away from the basket with the game on the line would be absurd. But Curry isn't most players. He made virtually the same shot to beat Oklahoma City at the buzzer during the regular season.

So Curry pump-faked, and Love, thinking the Warriors superstar could very well shoot it from that deep, jumped off his feet. With Love off balance, Curry dribbled to his left and then crossed it over back quickly to his right. Love scrambled, his feet moving faster than any of his teammates had ever seen. He kept his eyes locked on Curry's, trying to keep up. After nearly 14 long seconds with Love on him, Curry finally launched a three-pointer. Love was in position and he reached up his arm, blocking Curry's vision.

Curry could've made the shot. One of the greatest shooters of all time with unmatched confidence, he could've made the shot in the dark. But Love made it tough. And the pressure made it tougher. And the shot missed off the rim with 30.7 seconds left, James zipping in to grab the rebound. The Cavs had the ball and, thanks to Love's work, they still had the lead. The championship was in sight.

It became known as "The Stop."

James, Irving, and Love. The trio who'd come together and stayed together to try to reach this moment. All the meetings, the social media, the injuries, the coaching battles, the controversies, the doubts. They were there together and each of them had delivered their own championship moment.

Irving rushed up the floor to try and get an easy basket to seal it, but the Warriors recovered, Iguodala blocking him at the rim. The ball was slapped right back at Irving as he was careening out of bounds, but he was able to save it without stepping on the baseline and lobbed it back out to a trailing Love beyond the three-point line with 22.4 seconds left.

The Warriors had a foul to give and used it to stop the clock. James inbounded the ball back to Irving, who again drove straight for the hoop, only this time found James with a perfect pass as he exploded into the lane. James leapt off the floor after receiving the pass, aiming to power dunk the ball in what probably would've been dubbed "The Dunk" had it been allowed to happen.

With no choice, Green met him in the air and fouled him hard. And clean. But it caused James to miss and tumble to the court, bracing his fall with his right wrist and elbow with 10.6 seconds left. In 2002, when James was seventeen, he broke his left wrist on a play similar to it, as he was undercut on a dunk. In 2010 he developed an issue with his right elbow, and for years since he'd worn a sleeve to help protect it.

James was awarded two free throws, but as he writhed on the ground in pain, clutching his right wrist—the one that controls his shooting hand—a doomsday scenario started to play out in the minds of the downtrodden Cleveland fan base once again. James slammed his left fist on the court in both frustration and pain. What if he couldn't shoot the free throws?

Cleveland called its last timeout as members of the medical staff—head trainer Steve Spiro and James's personal trainer Mike Mancias among them—rushed all the way down the floor from the Cavs bench to attend to James on the opposite baseline.

James was able to stay in the game after the timeout and made his way to the free throw line, still wincing in pain as he held his wrist in his left hand and rotated it. He shot his first free throw... and missed it. Nothing but the back of the rim. Another miss and the Warriors could get the rebound with two timeouts remaining and a chance to tie.

He stepped off the line, pulled up his jersey to wipe the sweat off his face, adjusted his arm sleeve, wiped the sweat off his hands onto the back of his shorts, and went back to receive the ball from the referee. The crowd hissed, trying to will another miss. This time he made it, rattling it in.

The Warriors called timeout, down 93–89 with 10.6 seconds left. James momentarily put both fists in the air, just as he did ever so briefly after Irving made three less than a minute earlier, before bringing them down and simply holding up the index finger on his right hand.

"One stop," James said. "One stop. One fucking stop. One fucking stop."

Lue took over the huddle. All series long, as it played out over the course of nearly three weeks, Lue used whatever practice, shootaround, and walk-through time the team had to drill end-of-game situations.

Only with each of the first six games of the series being decided by 10 or more points, the Cavs never had a chance to implement what Lue was teaching. It became a running gag within the team even, causing Irving and Iman Shumpert to razz their coach for spending so much time on something they never got a chance to use.

This was their chance, however. One defensive possession stood between Lue's team and the NBA title and it was playing out right in front of him and the rest of the Cavs bench.

It was merely a formality.

Curry missed a three—his fourth consecutive miss of the quarter to finish his night 6-for-19 from the field—with 3.4 seconds left. The Warriors got the offensive rebound with 2.2 seconds left, but there was no four-point line for him to try to tie the game.

The game was over. The Cavs were champs. The city of Cleveland was a winner. And LeBron James, at long last, had delivered on his promise of a title for his hometown.

James was back on the floor, hammering it again with his fist, this time in joy.

"Cleveland," he said with tears in his eyes, "this is for you."

EPILOGUE

When he was a kid, LeBron James's favorite sport was football, and there was a time when some who watched him play believed he could've become an All-Pro tight end with his size, quickness, and hands. It wasn't meant to be; James gave up football at age seventeen despite being an All-State wide receiver as a junior in high school. Yet here he was in an NFL locker room holding a championship trophy.

The Oakland Raiders locker room to be exact. That was where he was about two hours after winning his third NBA title and the third time accepting the Bill Russell Trophy from the man it was named for as Finals MVP. He'd come there with a bottle of Moët champagne in his hand and a cigar in his mouth, part of a stash of goods a member of the Cavs front office had secretly been sent to buy in case they needed them for a locker room party. More than $4,000 worth of ski goggles and cigars were sent by owner Dan Gilbert with orders not to breathe a word of it to general manager David Griffin, who would've seen it as a jinx.

James was in the locker room because that's where the NBA had set up a favorite annual tradition of postgame photos with the Larry O'Brien Trophy. Every member of the team got to take them for posterity. James wanted three. One with his wife, Savannah, sons LeBron Jr. and Bryce, and infant daughter Zhuri, who had been a special guest with James at his postgame interview session. He wanted one with his mother, Gloria. And one with his three closest friends: business manager Maverick Carter, agent Rich Paul, and right-hand-man Randy Mims.

As James waited his turn, Richard Jefferson came up to him. After fifteen years as a pro, Jefferson had just won his first NBA title and emotionally announced after the game that he'd be retiring. He was later talked out of it and signed a two-year deal to stay in Cleveland. James ended up re-upping too, signing a three-year, $100 million contract the following summer.

"I have tons of friends that have won championships. I've seen the videos from the portrait room. I've seen the pictures. It only made me wonder more if I'd ever get my chance," Jefferson said. "This is everything that I've always dreamed it would be. Imagine what it must have been like for LeBron? Making this all happen. The championship. The comeback. The joy. And doing it in the place he grew up?"

In the moment, Jefferson asked James, "Tell me, was that the most stressful game ever?"

"It was close," James said, recalling his 2013 Finals Game 6 victory with the Miami Heat in overtime after Ray Allen made a shot just before the buzzer to save the team's season.

Thinking of Miami, James was brought back to something else. Something that happened nearly two years earlier when he'd decided to leave the Heat and come to Cleveland to chase the dream he was living at that moment.

"When I decided to leave Miami—I'm not going to name any names, I can't do that—but there were some people that I trusted and built relationships with in those four years who told me I was making the biggest mistake of my career," James said. "And that hurt me. And I know it was an emotional time that they told me that, because I was leaving. They just told me it was the biggest mistake I was making in my career. And that right there was my motivation."

James hinted at a secret motivation for a long time but refused to reveal it. Even now he held back, though it was a serious hint he was referring to Heat president Pat Riley, the man who challenged him not to run out the first door when Miami lost in the 2014 Finals.

"I knew what I was doing," James said. "I knew what I was doing, and I mean, tonight is a product of it."

Just then Paul walked over to show James his phone. Kyrie Irving was giving his press conference and talking about seeing James's mastery in the deciding game.

"I watched Beethoven tonight," Paul said, reading Irving's words about James.

Irving had delivered too, his partnership with James succeeding under the greatest pressure. As James was weeping with joy and hugging family, Irving found his father, Drederick, and sister, Asia. As he hugged them he didn't quite feel a sense of joy at first.

"I was waiting for more questions about 'What about you shooting on this possession?' Or 'What about you doing this or that?' I was done," Irving said. "I was so defensive that I didn't celebrate right after we won. I just hugged my dad and my sister. My dad is looking at me like, 'What's wrong?' I'm telling him, 'I'm waiting for someone to come up and say something to me about what happened during the game.'"

Irving's defiance about his critics didn't last. Soon he was in the locker room and grabbing his phone. He FaceTimed with his hero, Kobe Bryant, who had been texting him and encouraging him during the postseason.

"All I was thinking in the back of my mind was Mamba mentality," Irving said, using Bryant's nickname to explain his thought process before the game-winning shot. "Just Mamba mentality. That's all I was thinking."

There was another piece of business for the Cavs once they all got into the locker room. Their championship puzzle. They flipped open the case, and as the team stood around screaming, Ty Lue had the honor of putting the sixteenth piece into place. The final golden niche was in the shape of the state of Ohio. Lue slammed it in with both hands.

The room quickly filled with smoke as the cigars started smoldering and the champagne started flowing. Security guards tried to stop the smoking—it was against the law to smoke in the building. The Warriors had left the Cleveland visitors' locker room smelling of champagne the year before; the Cavs would leave the Oakland visitors' locker room smelling of smoke.

It wasn't the first cigar of the week for Mike Mancias, James's trainer for the previous ten years. His wife had gone into labor with the couple's first child the day after Game 6. It lasted twenty-six hours before his son, Malcolm, was born. After they shared their moment with their son, Mancias's wife, Heather, said, "Go, go to Game 7." Mancias had missed the team charter but boarded another plane, one for Cavs employees, the morning of the game and made it to the arena in time to put James through his pregame stretching routine. It was his first Father's Day.

Gilbert and fellow owners Nate Forbes and Jeff Cohen were walking around with magnum-sized champagne bottles with each of their names and the team logo engraved on them. They had been a gift when James returned to the team, but the men agreed to save them until they could be used to celebrate a championship. Gilbert bought the team in 2005, and he'd spent more than $850 million in salaries and luxury taxes, built a $25 million practice facility, and fired five coaches and two general managers to get to this point. He'd earned a celebration.

But the postgame party in Oakland was nothing compared to what Gilbert had planned. After the Cavs won Game 6 to even the series, Mark Cashman, the team's equipment and travel manager, started planning what to do if they won. He secretly arranged for a pit stop and kept it quiet.

As the team began to pack up and head to the airport down the empty streets late on a joyless Sunday night in the East Bay, the flight crew on their plane filed a new plan with the destination being Las Vegas' McCarran Airport. Cashman had booked buses to meet them at the private jet terminal and take them to XS Nightclub inside the Wynn hotel complex.

They landed at 1 a.m. and a short time later walked into the club to see a giant screen congratulating them on their championship, a line of cocktail waitresses wearing James jerseys holding up a sign that read "We Believed," a custom cake shaped like the Larry O'Brien Trophy, and two giant tubs with twenty-five bottles of high-end champagne. A lot of time and effort had been put into a party that might never have happened. The Warriors, meanwhile, had to cancel their planned championship celebration for a third and final time.

Kevin Love arrived holding a WWE-style championship belt over his shoulder. Matthew Dellavedova was wearing the Tommy Bahama shirt from the Lil' Kev ad. James was wearing a shirt with "RWTW" splashed across the front. It stood for "Roll With The Winners."

After a few hours at the club, the team went to Allegro, an Italian restaurant off the casino, to have some pizza before going to Cleveland, where they'd be met at the airport by around 20,000 fans.

It was in this same hotel James had made his final decision to go home to Ohio two summers earlier, beginning a journey that was even more difficult than he could've imagined. He never could have foreseen the battles with David Blatt, the struggles to mesh with Irving, that he'd find a partner in J.R. Smith of all people, that veterans Richard Jefferson and Channing Frye would be inspirations, that a gritty little Aussie named Dellavedova would help along the way, that he'd lead the greatest comeback in Finals history with three consecutive hero performances sealed with the defining play of his career, a blocked shot of all things. Or that he'd be right back at the Wynn soaking in a championship. It didn't feel like full circle, it felt like the end of the adventure of his life.

"It's not even relief, it's just excitement," James said as he closed his eyes and tried to sum up his feelings in the moment.

"I'm coming home. I'm coming home with what I said I was going to do."

ACKNOWLEDGMENTS

This book essentially started inside Oracle Arena in Oakland, California, in the hours between the end of Game 7 of the 2016 NBA Finals and dawn. Fortified by beverages and peanut butter sandwiches swiped from the Cavs locker room as workers cleaned up empty champagne bottles, documenting the most fascinating story of our careers began.

It was a whirlwind project that wouldn't have been possible without help from the Cavs organization and especially players LeBron James, Kevin Love, Kyrie Irving, J.R. Smith, Channing Frye, Tristan Thompson, Iman Shumpert, Matthew Dellavedova, and Timofey Mozgov. A special thank you to Richard Jefferson for the introduction to this book.

In addition, Cavs coaches Tyronn Lue and David Blatt, owner Dan Gilbert, minority owners Nate Forbes and Jeff Cohen, general manager David Griffin, assistant general manager Trent Redden, vice president Tad Carper, equipment manager Mark Cashman, and media relations staff B.J. Evans, Jeff Schaefer, Cherome Owens, Sarah Jamieson, and Alyssa Dombrowski. The support of player representation agency Klutch Sports with agents Rich Paul, Mark Termini, and Andy Bountogianis was essential. Additional assistance from Adam Mendelsohn. Help from agencies Priority Sports, BDA Sports Management, Creative Artists Agency, Wasserman, Goodwin Sports Management, and 24/7 Sports Management was much appreciated.

This book wouldn't have been possible without the backing of ESPN and Chad Millman, Henry Abbott, and Matthew Wong, plus colleagues Malinda Adams, Marc Stein, and Ramona Shelburne. Thank you to colleagues Jason Lloyd, Joe Vardon, Chris Haynes, and Ethan Skolnick as well. Finally, Sean Desmond at Hachette, Daniel Greenberg at LGR Literary, and Mark Zimmerman at Headline Media Management.

Thank you for reading.

–BW, DM

INDEX

Wall, John, 150, 160–161

Walton, Luke, 163–164

Washington Wizards, 79, 104,
150, 160–161, 179, 180

Wechsler, Jeff, 123

Westbrook, Russell, 108, 153

Wiggins, Andrew, 16, 22,
24–25, 54–55,
60–62

William, Prince, 83–84

William Morris Endeavor, 8

Williams, Mo, 138, 148, 155

wink-wink deals, 58

X

XS Nightclub, 246–247

Y

Young, Thaddeus, 63

Z

Zeller, Tyler, 45

ABOUT THE AUTHORS

Brian Windhorst is a senior writer and a television and radio analyst for ESPN. He covered the NBA for the Akron (Ohio) *Beacon Journal* and *Cleveland Plain Dealer* from 2003 to 2010 before joining ESPN. A native of Akron, he and his wife, Maureen Fulton, live in the Midwest.

Dave McMenamin has been an NBA reporter for ESPN since 2009, working as a beat writer and television analyst primarily covering the Los Angeles Lakers and Cleveland Cavaliers. He began covering the league in 2005 for NBA.com. He played collegiately at the University of Limerick in Ireland and graduated from Syracuse University, where he was a student manager for the 2003 national championship team. A native of Philadelphia, he is an avid shoe collector.